Managing
Public Disputes

Susan L. Carpenter

W.J.D. Kennedy

Managing
Public Disputes

*A Practical Guide
to Handling Conflict
and Reaching Agreements*

Jossey-Bass Publishers • San Francisco

MANAGING PUBLIC DISPUTES
A Practical Guide to Handling Conflict and Reaching Agreements
by Susan L. Carpenter and W.J.D. Kennedy

Copyright © 1988 by: Jossey-Bass Inc., Publishers
350 Sansome Street
San Francisco, California 94104

Library of Congress Cataloging-in-Publication Data

Carpenter, Susan L., date.
Managing public disputes.

(Jossey-Bass management series) (Jossey-Bass public
administration series) (Jossey-Bass social and behavioral
science series)
Bibliography: p.
Includes index.
1. Conflict management. 2. Problem solving.
I. Kennedy, W. J. D. (date). II. Title.
III. Series. IV. Series: Jossey-Bass public administra-
tion series. V. Series: Jossey-Bass social and behav-
ioral science series.
HD42.C37   1988   658.4   87-46342
ISBN 978-0-7879-5742-1

A NOTE TO THE READER
This publication has been electronically reproduced from digital information.
Jossey-Bass is pleased to make use of this technology to keep works of enduring
value in print as long as there is a reasonable demand to do so. The content of
this book is identical to previous printings.

JACKET DESIGN BY WILLI BAUM

FIRST EDITION
HB Printing   10 9 8 7 6
Code 8804

A *joint publication in*

The Jossey-Bass Management Series

The Jossey-Bass
Public Administration Series

and

The Jossey-Bass
Social and Behavioral Science Series

Contents

Preface   xi

The Authors   xvii

**Part One: Public Controversies
and Conflict Management**   1

1. Understanding Public Disputes: The Spiral
   of Unmanaged Conflict   3

2. Dealing with Conflict Productively:
   Alternatives and Case Examples   18

3. Developing an Effective Program of Conflict
   Management: Ten Principles   52

**Part Two: A Step-By-Step Process
for Managing Public Disputes**   67

4. Analyzing the Conflict   71

5. Designing a Strategy and Setting Up the
   Conflict Management Program   92

6. Adopting Procedures, Educating Parties,
   and Developing Options   116

7. Reaching and Carrying Out Agreements   137

**Part Three: Ensuring the Success
of Conflict Management**   155

8. Guidelines for Making the Program Work   157

9. Paying Attention to Underlying Dynamics:
Values, Trust, Power   197

10. Handling the Human Side of the Process   224

11. Removing Roadblocks   258

References   279

Index   285

Preface

This is a book for decision makers who deal with public disputes. We wrote it for professionals in government, business, and citizens' groups who make decisions about public issues as a regular part of their daily working lives.

Most books about mediation and conflict management have been written for the mediator. But professional mediators intervene in only a few of the thousands of big and little public disputes that erupt in this country every year. We do not expect this situation to change, nor do we advocate that it should. We believe it will be far more productive for society as a whole if people responsible for handling public disputes will understand and apply sound conflict management practices themselves rather than rely exclusively on third-party professional assistance. This book is designed to help managers and others who are not mediation specialists to develop proficiency in the use of conflict management skills. Specifically, *Managing Public Disputes* will enable readers to determine how a mediation process should be structured, who should be involved, and how problems can be minimized. It will also help readers recognize when the assistance of a trained mediator is desirable.

As a dispute develops, the parties involved can choose to make things better or worse, but they usually are not aware that they have options. After years of watching controversies unfold, we are convinced that disputing parties move progressively and often unconsciously from disagreement into destructive combat because they know of no better way to work out their differences. Extended, escalating conflict is costly—in time as well as money. In this book, we present a problem-solving process based on our conviction that through their own actions people can reduce the costs of conflict.

In the past decade, we have intervened as professional third parties in scores of disputes over public issues. Our experiences range from county regulation of sand and gravel mining to national policy on radioactive waste disposal, from a controversy over preservation of a historic railroad trestle to expansion of an international airport. We have been mediators in a two-year-long statewide conflict over water development and in emerging controversies that required a third party only long enough to help the disputants find effective ways of negotiating their differences. These experiences have been the testing ground for the ideas offered in this book, ideas that, except where specified, can be applied by persons skilled in conflict management practices, without the assistance of a professional third party.

Although each dispute is unique, certain patterns of behavior and consequences can be discerned in conflict situations. The dynamics of conflict and resolution are thus generally predictable. We can identify guiding principles that have proved effective in enough varied situations to give us confidence that they are sound. In addition to our own experiences, we have sought out the lessons learned by other people who have dealt with public disputes. We have also drawn on the literature in the related fields of international dispute resolution, labor-management negotiation, and community and interpersonal mediation.

The purpose of this book is threefold. First, we want managers and other professionals to become more aware of the role a well-designed process plays in dispute management. Second, we present evidence that workable alternatives to litigation and other conventional adversarial procedures are available. Third, we provide practical suggestions for techniques that can be used to manage disputes. How these techniques are applied, by whom, in what order, and in what combination depend on the particular circumstances. Throughout the book, we emphasize the importance of analyzing each situation as a new and unique phenomenon and fashioning an approach that will fit the people who are involved and the issues they are facing. We hope that some of our readers will use the ideas presented here as mediators in other people's disputes. More likely, however, managers who find these concepts useful will apply them in their jobs to avoid unnecessary problems, limit the damage caused by conflict, and perform their management responsibilities more effectively.

Throughout the book, we use the word *manager* in the most general sense of the word to mean "one who conducts business"; we also use it interchangeably with such terms as *decision maker, professional,* and *official* and to denote a person who applies conflict management techniques in the solution of a problem. We assume, except where we say otherwise, that the person has the responsibility within an organization for solving a problem and is not a professional third party.

Overview of the Contents

The book is divided into three parts. Part One provides an overview of public controversies and conflict management. Chapter One focuses on the characteristics of conflict in the public arena and the destructive effects of unmanaged conflict. The chapter highlights the differences between public disputes and controversies, such as those between labor and management where stakeholders are easily identified and the power relationships are clear. We describe the common elements of public disputes, among which are the lack of formal guidelines for carrying on negotiations and the probability that the parties will possess widely differing levels of expertise. In tracing the effects of unmanaged conflict, Chapter One describes what happens when people become caught up in an expanding conflict, how they progressively commit resources and incur costs, and how they begin to turn away from the moderates in their group and accept the leadership of militants. Chapter Two looks at the ways people deal with conflict and offers seven case examples that illustrate alternative procedures. In this approach, the decision maker moves from being the advocate of a single rigid position to the role of cooperative negotiator, and the goal changes from winning a battle to solving a problem. The case examples demonstrate the successful use of conflict management techniques in widely differing situations ranging from single-day meetings to projects demanding many months of effort. Chapter Three provides ten principles to consider when conducting a program—the importance, for example, of treating every public dispute as a mixture of procedures, relationships, and substance even though it may appear to be a simple disagreement over a technical question. Other concepts include the importance of developing a strategy before taking action and following a pre-determined sequence of steps in implementing a plan.

Part Two presents a step-by-step process for managing public disputes. Chapter Four gives detailed advice on methods for collecting information, conducting interviews, and analyzing a conflict situation. Sample worksheets are provided. Chapter Five explains how to design a conflict management strategy and set up a program. The chapter sets forth eight separate tasks that should be considered in designing a management strategy, including such essentials as working out an accurate definition of the problem, establishing an acceptable program goal, determining who should participate, and selecting an appropriate meeting structure. Chapter Six explains the first three steps in conducting a program—adopting procedures, educating the parties, and developing options. Chapter Seven addresses the final steps of reaching and carrying out agreements.

Part Three is about factors affecting conflict management programs. Chapter Eight offers guidelines for making a program work, exploring in depth methods for dealing with procedural problems that arise when the public is involved in efforts to resolve a conflict, such as dealing with the news media, involving constituents, and informing the public about the progress of negotiations. A separate section is devoted to the use of third parties in part or all of a conflict management program. Chapter Nine explores the underlying dynamics of conflict including the influence on negotiations of values held by the parties, the importance of trust, and the significance of different kinds of power relationships. Chapter Ten suggests measures to take when special problems arise. The chapter explains techniques for handling reluctant participants, keeping people at the negotiating table, controlling efforts to gain revenge, and handling situations where intense emotions dominate discussions. Chapter

Eleven addresses two all-too-familiar predicaments in managing public disputes, the difficulty of getting people to agree on a common base of information for their negotiations and finding an effective strategy when discussions reach an impasse.

Acknowledgments

This book is an account of what we have learned in more than a decade of experience working with people caught up in public controversies. We express our profound appreciation to the public officials at all levels of government and the decision makers in private organizations who were willing to take the risk of trying something different.

Many friends and colleagues contributed to the writing of this book by helping us sharpen and refine our ideas. Our special gratitude goes to Peter Fogg for his unfailing support of this endeavor and his constructive criticism of the material. Pete's own substantial expertise in conflict management has been an important asset. Henry Lansford helped us enormously with his meticulous editing and his knowledge of content. Kathryn Loberg proved tenacious and skillful in redoing innumerable drafts and providing secretarial help. Members of the ACCORD Board of Directors have been a source of advice and a valuable reality check in our project work. Many of our conflict management projects have been cooperative ventures with professional colleagues. We have enjoyed the interaction and benefited greatly from them. We would especially like to thank Peter Adler, Lorenz Aggens, Gail Bingham, Heidi Burgess, Deanne Butterfield, Marion Cox, Robert Hernbrode, Stephen Hodapp, John Ehrmann, John Huyler, Lawrence MacDonnell, Christopher Moore, Alice Shorett, David Straus, Donald Straus, and Patricia Swift. Lawrence Susskind and his associates at the Program on Negotiation at the Harvard Law School generously provided the opportunity and support for reflection.

Over the years, we have received major financial support from philanthropic foundations and private companies. We are grateful to John Mitchell and William Douglas of the Boettcher

Foundation, James Wilson of the Rocky Mountain Energy Company, and Anne Murray and Robert Barrett of the William and Flora Hewlett Foundation for the resources to do our work and write about it.

February 1988   Susan L. Carpenter
                                                   Washington, D.C.

                                                   W.J.D. Kennedy
                                                   Boulder, Colorado

The Authors

Susan L. Carpenter is a consultant living in Washington, D.C. She received her bachelor's degree (1968) in anthropology from Lawrence University, her master's degree (1972) in international education from the University of Massachusetts, and her doctorate (1976) in future studies, also from the University of Massachusetts.

Carpenter was associate director of ACCORD Associates, a nonprofit conflict management organization in Boulder, Colorado, for ten years. She has worked as an impartial third party on local and national public disputes and has trained people to use conflict management skills. She has written numerous articles for professional journals and has spoken widely to national associations and conferences on the topic. Carpenter spent a semester as a visiting fellow at the Program on Negotiation at the Harvard Law School. She has served on national advisory boards for groups including the American Academy of Arts and Sciences' Program on the Processes of International Negotiation and the U.S. House of Representative's Committee on Science and Technology. She was a Peace Corps volunteer in Ethiopia, where she taught school for two years. Carpenter is a member of the Society of Professionals in Dispute Resolution.

W.J.D. Kennedy has been Executive Director of ACCORD Associates for thirteen years. He received his bachelor's degree (1946) in English literature from Harvard College. Kennedy has directed conflict management programs and served as an impartial third party in public disputes around the country. He has consulted with and managed meetings for private organizations and city, county, state, and federal government agencies. He has written numerous articles on conflict management for professional journals and has given presentations to a wide diversity of audiences on the subject, including the House Committee on Science and

Technology of the United States Congress. Kennedy has served
on state human rights commissions, the Secretary of the Interior's Coal Advisory Committee, the Planning Group for the
National Science Board's Regional Forum, and the Advisory
Committee to the Colorado Land Use Commission.

Managing
Public Disputes

Part One

Public Controversies
and Conflict Management

This section provides an overview of public controversies and conflict management. It explains why conventional approaches to coping with conflict often fail and presents workable alternatives. Chapter One sets the scene by describing the characteristics of public disputes, pointing out that they are often quite different from labor-management conflicts and family disputes. The dynamics of unmanaged conflict are explained using the concept of the expan___ spiral.

Chapter Two outl_____ ___ ___ ___ ___le commonly take when confronted with ___ ___ ___ ___ ___ ___s why familiar procedures often make ___ ___ ___ ___ ___er describes the components of an alt___ ___ ___ ___ ___lving problems. Seven case examples i___ ___ ___ ___ ___lict management in widely diverse situa___ ___ ___ ___e-day meetings to projects demanding m___ ___ ___ ___'hese cases are referred to frequently ___ ___ ___ ___illustrations of situations in which the p___ ___ ___have been applied and tested.

Chapter Three sets forth ten rules the authors have found to be essential in all successful conflict management programs—principles that seem logical and necessary in the abstract but that frequently are ignored when decisions are made under the stress of conflict.

1

1

Understanding Public Disputes: The Spiral of Unmanaged Conflict

Disputes over public issues come in all sizes and shapes. They occur between communities and their decision makers, between factions in government, between organizations, and between organizations and the public. Some conflicts erupt into bitter confrontation and rapidly grow worse. Others are chronic disagreements that flare up periodically, then die down and become dormant for a time. Many disputes are predictable; others catch us by surprise. Conflicts that are splashed across the morning newspaper or performed live on the evening news are so public and so political that they are hard to resolve by non-adversarial means, but for every confrontation that reaches national attention, there are thousands of smaller, less glamorous controversies that cost people time, money, and anxiety and that readily lend themselves to conflict management techniques.

Few people enjoy dealing with conflicts. Conflicts are unpleasant and stress provoking. They distract people from pursuing more productive endeavors, and they are expensive. But not all of them are destructive. Some conflicts may lead to a sharpening of critical issues and the creation of new systems and institutions beneficial to society. The open expression of disagreement is natural and necessary in a free society (Coser, 1956; Curle, 1971; Himes, 1980). Indeed, efforts to stifle dissent are the first sign that a democracy is in trouble. Conflict is inevitable, but sometimes resources are squandered in "putting up a good fight" rather than more wisely used in solving a problem. And often the costs are incurred incrementally, with escalating

3

damage to everyone not assessed until it is too late. The challenge to a manager is not to try to eliminate conflict but to handle disagreements as productively as possible.

Our focus is on public disputes: controversies that affect members of the public beyond the primary negotiators. Public disputes nearly always involve one or more levels of government —often as a party, and usually as a decision maker. Disputes may center on a proposed project, on the development or application of regulations, or on questions of local, state, or federal policy. Although techniques for managing public disputes are similar in some respects to other forms of conflict resolution, such as labor-management bargaining and family dispute mediation, public disputes tend to be more complex, and they demand attention to factors that are unimportant or nonexistent in disagreements in which only two parties are involved.

Throughout this book, we use anecdotes to highlight ideas. We also refer frequently to seven case examples that are described in Chapter Two. We chose these cases—which range from a negotiation of a few days between three parties to a multiyear, 30-party, decades-old dispute—to illustrate the wide diversity of situations in which conflict management procedures have been applied. Our experience convinces us that all managers —program directors, elected officials, and professional staff—can use these procedures effectively in their work. Success in conducting a conflict management plan will depend on a manager's awareness of the peculiarities of public disputes and on the ingenuity he or she uses to deal with them. The ideas presented in this book are intended first to help professionals design and organize an effective program and second to come to their aid when the inevitable hitches, setbacks, and surprises show up.

Characteristics of Public Disputes

Public disputes are decidedly different from most labor-management conflicts and family disputes, in which the adversaries are few and are easily identified. Although no dispute is exactly like another, public disputes do have common characteristics.

Complicated Network of Interests

Public disputes involve several (often many) parties. And the parties are groups or organizations, not individuals. Representatives at a negotiating table are therefore responsible not just to themselves but to others as well, and they are sometimes people of diverse and competing interests. A convener has the problem of deciding (with the concurrence of the parties) who should be represented in a negotiation. For example, in a comparatively simple negotiation of a railroad right-of-way and trestle, on what seemed to be a single issue, the representatives included elected officials from two counties, staff from each county, a regional supervisor, a local manager of a federal agency, a state manager, and both volunteer directors and professional staff from two citizen groups, who also spoke for several other groups that had agreed to pool their representation. If all interest groups had demanded separate representation, there could have been as many as twenty parties at the table, with several individuals from each party in many cases. One can expect a complicated network of interests when a controversy involves a public issue.

New Parties Emerge. No matter how carefully a program is designed to include all the interests, it is common for new parties to be identified as the process unfolds. Often, during deliberations, issues that had not been considered central to the discussion are identified and determined to be important. These new ideas suggest new participants. In one dispute over water management, it became clear after several months of negotiation that attention was shifting from agricultural use in the lowlands to water diversion at high elevations. It became necessary to add a representative of the ski industry, who would not have been interested in discussions about lowland water use but who did have a major economic stake in use of water in the mountains. In other situations a party that has a direct stake in the outcome will surface to the surprise of other participants and will demand a place at the table.

Varying Levels of Expertise. Public disputes often involve complicated financial questions, complex regulatory procedures, and detailed technical data. The understanding of technical information may vary dramatically among individuals involved in a negotiation. In a public meeting to review monitoring procedures for a nuclear facility, a scientist stood up, waved a 300-page document at the anxious citizens seated in the audience, and said, "This is my master's thesis. There is no way you can possibly understand all of the complex issues associated with radiation monitoring in this book." Although some of the citizens did have a working understanding of the subject, they knew that the scientist was correct. They resented his arrogance, but they also feared the imbalance of power implied by their lack of scientific knowledge.

Different Forms of Power. Power comes in a variety of forms, including that derived from financial resources, legal authority, knowledge and skills, numbers of people, access to decision makers, personal respect, and friendships. Government agencies gain power through administrative policies, regulations, and directives. They usually have substantial technical information as well. Private companies have financial resources to gather information, acquire technical expertise, and engage in political and public relations campaigns. Citizen groups, who often see themselves as powerless, exercise power through political pressure and through litigation. Experience in negotiating is also a form of power, as are knowledge, political leverage, and constructive working relationships. Money, of course, is power, and organizations involved as parties in a conflict may vary significantly in their ability to commit financial resources to solving a problem. Some have the money to assign staff members to do technical studies, develop strategies, and produce materials. Others rely entirely on volunteer assistance and may not have the resources to do as thorough a job as the paid staff of their adversaries.

Lack of Continuing Relationships. In many public disputes, the parties do not know each other and have no desire to continue relationships after the problem is settled, although some of the individuals representing negotiating organizations may have continuing relationships with each other. A public utilities commissioner, for example, knows the staff of the office of consumer counsel and the managers of regulated utilities, but the commissioner may not be familiar with a group of local citizens that is organized for the sole purpose of fighting the siting of a proposed power plant. This situation contrasts with labor-management and family disputes, where, even though strong differences are present, the parties may temper their actions because they know that they will see each other after the conflict is over. When people do not understand the history of the other organizations involved and their problems and special sensitivities, they are more likely to make incorrect assumptions about the motives of their adversaries and they may unintentionally issue provocative statements that make resolution more difficult.

Differing Decision-Making Procedures. The organizational structures of conflicting groups vary enormously, which means they use widely differing procedures for making decisions. Some groups are legally constituted as governmental units or as for-profit or nonprofit organizations. They have boards of directors who are responsible for the organizations' actions and they have clearly defined management structures. Other groups are loosely formed committees brought together for the sole purpose of advocating a position in a conflict. Leadership may be self-proclaimed and tenuous, and other organizational roles may be unclear. Corporations have established hierarchies for making decisions, and it is possible to determine who is responsible for making a decision and how that decision is to be made. Government organizations also have their hierarchies, but determining who will make the final decision may be less certain. On the other hand, some public interest advocacy groups rely heavily on consensus decision making, where the entire membership of an organization is consulted and must agree to any action that is taken.

Difficulties arise when decisions must be made quickly. Parties with a hierarchical decision structure are usually represented by responsible individuals who can make decisions and

commit their organizations. Representatives from loosely organized groups, however, require more time to consult with their
membership and achieve consensus, and their decisions may
not hold.

Unequal Accountability. Accountability varies among
groups depending on the type of organization. Corporations are
held accountable by law for their behavior. They are concerned
about their public image and have ongoing relationships with
governments and other organizations, which subject them to
additional accountability pressures. Citizen groups do not have
the same legal constraints. Their behavior and the reliability of
their commitments depend on the character of individual members and on public opinion.

Procedures Not Standardized

No Formal Guidelines. Unlike labor-management negotiation and international diplomacy, public disputes have few institutional mechanisms for resolving conflicts. Disagreements become long-lasting conflicts or are settled in one way or another
without standard procedures for convening the parties for face-
to-face discussions to resolve their differences. Government
seems the logical convener, but it is rarely seen as a disinterested
third party by business or the public. The influence of governments on the way conflict is handled is complicated by uncertainty as to which level of government or which agency within
one level has responsibility for solving the problem. In fact, a
common difficulty in managing public disputes is sorting out
jurisdictional issues (President's Commission, 1980).

Enforcement of agreements is also done on a case-by-case
basis. A court may agree to oversee a settlement, a governor
may accept the responsibility for monitoring an agreement, an
organization acceptable to all parties may be asked to supervise
implementation or a committee may be established for such a
purpose. But many efforts to resolve public disputes break
down at the end, in the enforcement of the agreements.

Influence of Government Rules and Regulations. A complex system of federal, state, and local rules and regulations influences efforts to deal with public problems. Mandated public hearings, ex-parti rules preventing discussion between parties and regulators, obligatory public comment periods, and other regulations governing the way decisions are made exist to protect the public interest. Unfortunately, they can also constrain discussion and restrict a search for new options, and, quite often, it is not so much the laws as their interpretation and administration that determine whether government is a help or a hindrance. These government regulations vary from case to case (Fisher, 1969; Fox, 1981).

Broad Range of Issues

Public disputes usually involve a wide range of complex issues. A controversy over toxic waste storage, for example, raises health and economic issues as well as the technical questions of how to construct and maintain facilities. The issue of public confidence in a waste storage company's management may be more important than the skills of the engineers. Separate issues of future monitoring for safety, maintenance responsibility, transportation, values of adjacent property, quality of life, and other social and economic effects nearly always dominate the selection of a technical solution.

New Issues Emerge. Public disputes are complicated to begin with, and as negotiators explore the concerns associated with a specific issue, new topics for discussion often arise. Negotiators must be prepared to address new issues as they come up and to give them attention equal to the problems they originally expected to address.

The Importance of Technical Information. Another characteristic of public disputes is the importance of technical information in understanding the nature of a problem and in finding alternatives to a conflict. Each side brings its own set of facts and figures into the discussion, and all sides must agree on a common data base before solutions can be developed. Parties rarely have equal access to all relevant information or equal ability to understand or use the figures. In some cases, necessary information is not available to any of the parties because it has not been analyzed in ways that address the specific questions being raised.

Strongly Held Values. Nearly all public controversies entail divergent beliefs about what is right and what is wrong, what is just and what is unjust. Many policy decisions are essentially choices among competing values, and some of the most heated of all public controversies result when someone's fundamental beliefs about what is important are threatened. Values may remain unstated, but they come out in such statements as, "People are more important than birds" and "All you care about is making a fast buck."

Accusations of greed or elitism do not get to the bottom of the problem. Often what appears to be an intractable confrontation between competing economic interests or a clash between developers and preservationists has its roots in the differing experiences and worldviews between the young and the middle-aged, between urban and rural, between those who have lived through a depression and those who have not. Neither side can understand the other.

In this time of rapidly changing values, bitter and sometimes violent clashes occur between those who try to force their ideas on others and those whose sacred beliefs are threatened. But not all differences over values must come down to the nonnegotiable pro-abortion/right-to-life kind of warfare. Conflicts happen not because the values are different but because one side demands that the other side give in.

What are the consequences of having many parties in a dispute? How important are long-standing animosities? What is the significance of the technical content of conflict? These and other similar questions are essential elements in an approach to resolving a public dispute. The danger is that factors such as these may be so far outside a decision maker's normal experience, so unfamiliar as elements to be considered in drawing up a management plan, that they will be underestimated or ignored, and the result may be failure of the entire program. Public disputes are different from most other conflicts in their complexity and unpredictability. These characteristics are important to remember in designing a conflict management program.

The Spiral of Unmanaged Conflict

Conflict is dynamic. Unmanaged conflicts seldom stay constant for long. Simple solutions that might have worked in the beginning may be ineffective and even cause more damage if they are attempted when the conflict is fully developed. For example, restoring communication between warring factions will simply make matters worse if the wrong people do the talking or if the parties no longer trust each other.

The following sequence is typical of public disputes: One or more parties choose not to acknowledge that a problem exists. Other groups are forced to escalate their activities to gain recognition for their concerns. Eventually everyone engages in an adversarial battle, throwing more time and money into "winning" than into solving the problem. The following description outlines the evolution of an unmanaged conflict. Figure 1 depicts the changes in activities, issues, and psychological perceptions that occur as a conflict escalates.

The Problem Emerges. An organization, private or public, announces that it is contemplating changing conditions for community residents—tear down a historical building, build a new development, or widen a road, for example. At this point there is curiosity or mild concern. A step up the spiral occurs when citizens try to obtain more information and receive an unsatisfactory response. Inquiries come at a time when plans are incomplete, and officials wish the citizens would go away until they know what is going to happen themselves. But citizens are worried now.

Figure 1. Spiral of Unmanaged Conflict.

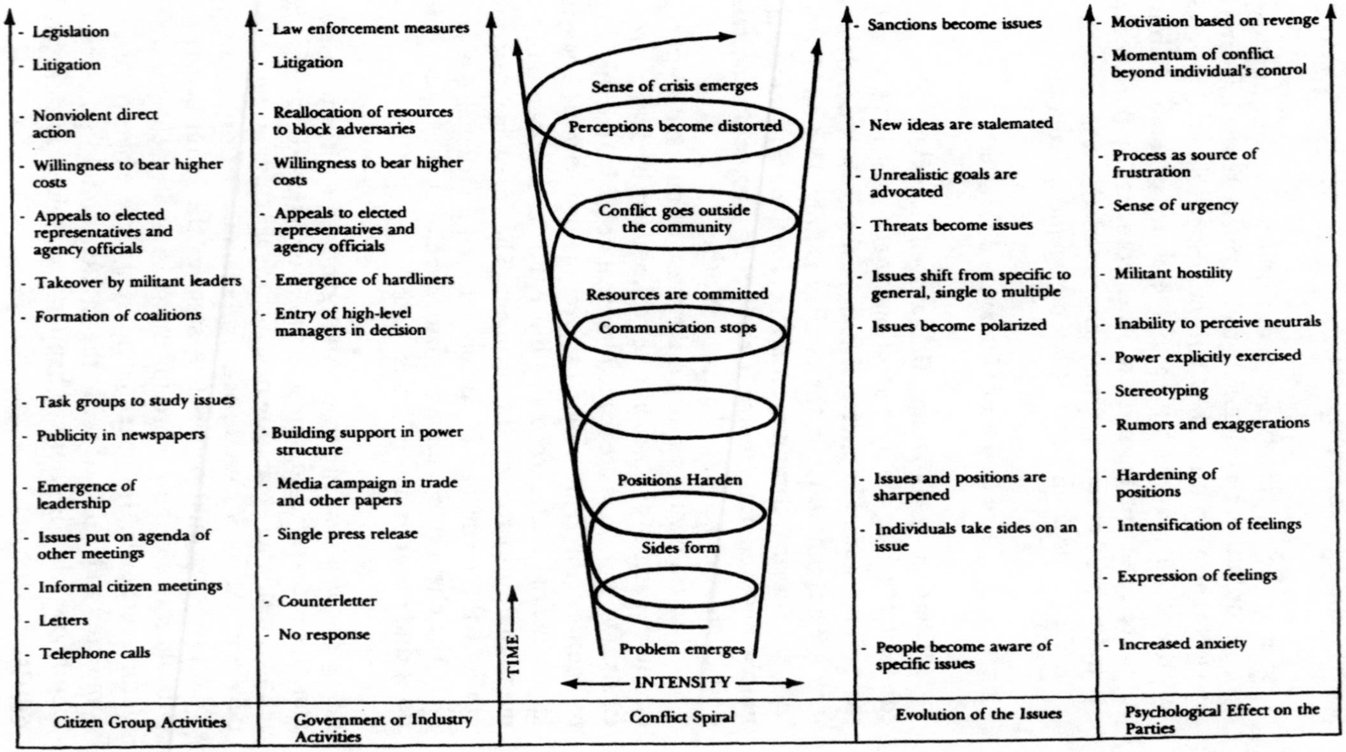

Citizen Group Activities
- Legislation
- Litigation
- Nonviolent direct action
- Willingness to bear higher costs
- Appeals to elected representatives and agency officials
- Takeover by militant leaders
- Formation of coalitions
- Task groups to study issues
- Publicity in newspapers
- Emergence of leadership
- Issues put on agenda of other meetings
- Informal citizen meetings
- Letters
- Telephone calls

Government or Industry Activities
- Law enforcement measures
- Litigation
- Reallocation of resources to block adversaries
- Willingness to bear higher costs
- Appeals to elected representatives and agency officials
- Emergence of hardliners
- Entry of high-level managers in decision
- Building support in power structure
- Media campaign in trade and other papers
- Single press release
- Counterletter
- No response

Conflict Spiral (INTENSITY / TIME)
- Sense of crisis emerges
- Perceptions become distorted
- Conflict goes outside the community
- Resources are committed
- Communication stops
- Positions Harden
- Sides form
- Problem emerges

Evolution of the Issues
- Sanctions become issues
- New ideas are stalemated
- Unrealistic goals are advocated
- Threats become issues
- Issues shift from specific to general, single to multiple
- Issues become polarized
- Issues and positions are sharpened
- Individuals take sides on an issue
- People become aware of specific issues

Psychological Effect on the Parties
- Motivation based on revenge
- Momentum of conflict beyond individual's control
- Process as source of frustration
- Sense of urgency
- Militant hostility
- Inability to perceive neutrals
- Power explicitly exercised
- Stereotyping
- Rumors and exaggerations
- Hardening of positions
- Intensification of feelings
- Expression of feelings
- Increased anxiety

Sides Form. Reluctance to discuss plans is seen as deliberate stonewalling. Caution is interpreted as deceit. People who until now have not thought they had a stake in the issue begin to move toward one side or the other. More people form definite opinions and feel the need to get together with others who have similar views. They meet and support positions similar to theirs. They choose sides. As groups, they write letters to officials and try to persuade the news media that their position is the only correct one. Reporters find the differences between the parties to be fertile ground for news stories. The conflict expands as more people learn about it in the press.

Positions Harden. People talk more with others of similar views and less with people with whom they disagree, even in circumstances that are not related to the dispute. Positions harden, and people become rigid in their definitions of the problem and their opponents.

Communication Stops. Information is exchanged haphazardly between the parties. Misunderstandings are common, and communication takes on an increasingly adversarial tone. The timing and methods used by officials to involve the public may be out of phase with what is happening in the developing conflict. Public hearings can be too late and too adversarial to have a positive influence.

In the early stages of conflict, people talked with each other and exchanged opinions. But somewhere along the way public discussions turned to public debate. People are frustrated by the situation and angry at each other. They become intolerant of other points of view and lose interest in talking about perspectives other than their own. Listening to counterpoints is unpleasant because they have invested heavily in one side of the argument and this is no time for second thoughts. As a result, conversation between the parties stops, and information is used as a weapon to promote a position or win a point. Information that would lead to a solution no longer flows between the parties.

Resources Are Committed. Until now, most citizens have been dismayed by the growing controversy. Outspoken leaders have been seen as troublemakers. From this point on, moderates will be given less attention and militants will become more influential. As positions become more narrow and more rigid, they also become clearer. Bothersome questions of fairness, the shades of right and wrong, are less of a problem. Individuals gain a sense of personal power in being a part of the group. They are ready to commit resources and to incur costs, aware that serious demands will be made on their personal time and on financial resources.

Conflict Goes Outside the Community. People begin to look outside the community for support and power. They appeal to state or national political figures and ask for help from national organizations. What was once a community problem expands into a new, much wider arena of conflict.

In forming coalitions with outsiders, the local groups acquire additional financial resources and expert knowledge about the ways to carry on a fight, but their goals are absorbed into broader programs of the national organization.

Outsiders are less reluctant to attack local individuals personally. They see the residents who disagree with them solely as adversaries and not as people they will have to greet in church or at the next PTA meeting. Lawyers or other professional "hired guns" come between the parties and prevent personal negotiation. Moderates lose control to new, more militant leaders. Relationships between the parties become openly hostile. Threats are exchanged. People do not like to be threatened, so the threats become issues themselves.

Perceptions Become Distorted. Parties lose objectivity in their perceptions of the character and motives of their adversaries. Shades of gray disappear and only black and white remain. Whatever "our" side does is honest, and whatever "their" side does is malevolent.

Neutrals are seen as part of the enemy because they are not on "our" side. Throughout the growth of the conflict spiral, people narrow their focus and become less capable of generating new strategies for solving the original problem.

Sense of Crisis Emerges. The community is divided into factions. Normally residents are accustomed to altercations between officials and irate citizen groups and they expect the town to work out its disagreements. But now, it seems, there is little hope of resolving the original dispute. Long-established confidence in the community's ability to handle its problems wavers and gives way to a sense of crisis. Newspapers highlight arguments between community leaders and ignore positive efforts toward resolution.

The initiating organization realizes that its project is seriously threatened. It feels embattled, grows tense and rigid, and says things it wishes it hadn't. The news media pick up and report the rhetoric.

The parties are now willing to bear higher costs, costs that would have seemed unreasonable earlier. Their goal becomes progressively to win at any cost. They try intimidation and destructive use of power, thus adding to the issues and to the heat of the conflict. Clashes over peripheral questions and personal vendettas assume their own momentum. In the angry, tense atmosphere, the parties commit themselves to destructive retaliatory actions that in calmer times would have been rejected as beneath their consideration.

Outcomes Vary. The next step may be litigation. Uncertainty as to which side will gain the most is then replaced by uncertainty about when the trial will be held, which lawyer will prevail, and how close the judge will come to solving the problem. All chance for direct negotiations between the parties is gone. Costs continue to mount.

Or the government may make the final decision. Government agencies prefer to cooperate with the parties, but they may be forced by circumstances to assume the role of regulator. Flexibility in the choice of options and the manner in which regulations are administered is lost as an agency becomes the enforcer.

Violence is another possibility. Vindictiveness and desire for revenge are sometimes present in public conflicts, but they rarely lead to personal injury or vandalism. Occasionally they do when all other methods have failed. Violent confrontation has occurred in disputes over high-voltage power lines, over the killing of whales and baby seals, and in other situations in which the effects of an action seemed irrevocable and catastrophic (Nagler, 1982).

The concept of the spiral emphasizes several important points. Unmanaged conflicts tend to become more serious because the people involved in them are anxious, fearful, and suspicious of the other side. They progressively raise the stakes without knowing fully what the consequences will be. They do not notice that their perceptions of their adversaries and themselves are changing and that they are progressively incurring risks and costs that would have seemed intolerable earlier in the struggle. Complex public disputes can become sinks for resources that the parties never meant to commit.

Many conflicts start with a resolvable problem and grow beyond hope of resolution because they are not dealt with early. It is sometimes said that the conflict manager should let a situation "ripen" or polarize before attempting to handle it. This suggestion seems tantamount to telling a doctor that a bad cold should be allowed to develop into pneumonia before he or she prescribes treatment. On the contrary, the great value of taking a hard look at where the dispute is on the spiral is that one can then choose an interim strategy that will slow down or stop expansion of the conflict. The purpose of conflict management activities, such as establishing communication, defining issues, and facilitating effective meetings, is to interrupt the spiral of conflict.

The cost of pursuing destructive conflict includes damaged reputations, fractured personal relationships, and community disruption, as well as the more easily recognizable financial expenses of legal fees, delayed project costs, revenue losses, and personal time. Resources are spent in carrying on the fight rather than solving the problem, and the damage to the community may be irretrievable. (For other perspectives on ripeness, see Lax and Sebenius, 1986; McCarthy, 1984.)

Our society tends to accept confrontation as inevitable. Conflicts unfold as somehow preordained. If no action is taken to change the dynamics, concern and curiosity change into fear and anger and then into conflict behavior—choosing sides and calling each other names. The lesson of the conflict spiral is not that its progress is inevitable but that it is predictable when nothing is done to manage the conflict. (For more about the dynamics of unmanaged conflict, see Boulding, 1962; Deutsch, 1974; Kriesberg, 1973.)

2

Dealing with Conflict
Productively:
Alternatives
and Case Examples

Considering how common conflicts are in their daily routine, it is surprising how limited the range of methods is that professionals use to deal with conflict. Some managers handle disagreement by taking a firm position about a preferred solution and then attempting to force it on others—who may, as a consequence, become adversaries fighting for their own positions. Or they elect to ignore a dispute, hoping that it will disappear. In general, people who make management decisions pay insufficient attention to the process they use to make them. As a result, they sometimes waste human and financial resources by following practices that are familiar, and therefore comfortable, but that are often ineffective.

Conventional Approaches to Managing Conflict

Managers commonly have considerable discretion within their organizational constraints as to how to respond to conflict; however, as was pointed out earlier, managers often choose less effective methods because they are unfamiliar with more productive options. All too often, they follow one or more of the conventional approaches to handling conflict: avoiding the issue, leaping into battle, finding a quick fix, and falling into the Solomon trap.

Avoiding the Issue

Conflict is unpleasant. No one likes to deal with angry letters, irate telephone calls, and hostile people. For a time it seems easier to ignore a conflict than to deal with its unpleasant ramifications, especially when there is so much else that needs to be done in managing a project.

For some managers, confessing that a conflict exists is the equivalent of admitting failure. "Our district, have problems? No, everything is just fine. We had a little problem with a few citizens in a community down the road, but we fixed it," says the official and proceeds to deny that any problem exists. It often appears easier to avoid an issue, pretend that everything is all right, and keep it from superiors in the hope that it will go away. Unfortunately, conflicts rarely disappear. They can become dormant but then resurface in a more complicated and virulent form, making them even more difficult to manage (Carpenter and Kennedy, 1981).

Leaping into Battle

When individuals realize that they are mixed up in a disagreement, their first reaction is likely to be "I don't really need this" and the second "How dare they do that to me! I'll show them!" People resent being placed in the middle of a conflict, but in our society they are so used to having and being adversaries that they instinctively assume that someone has set out to oppose them. Rather than calling the other party and asking for more information, they decide that they must protect themselves, and they begin at once to draw up a plan to defend their interests. If the dispute becomes a public issue, the plan will almost certainly contain such aggressive activities as holding public meetings, appealing to the news media, mounting letter-writing campaigns, lobbying politicians, staging public demonstrations, and, eventually, initiating litigation (President's Commission, 1980).

People jump into taking an adversarial approach for a

variety of reasons. For one thing, parties who have a history of unsatisfactory relationships are less likely to trust each other when a new conflict arises. Someone who has observed the adversarial tactics of another party in the past will be highly suspicious of any offers to "sit down and be reasonable on this one." Characteristically, people in a dispute mirror the behavior of their opponents. If one side has launched an adversarial campaign, the other side will respond in kind. If this group begins to use nasty rhetoric, that group will think of words even more unpleasant. The first side, not wanting to be outdone, chooses to become even tougher. Strategies for dealing with each other continue in the upward-expanding spiral of conflict described in Chapter One.

Parties in dispute are especially likely to choose adversarial behavior when the stakes are high—when an important principle or interest is threatened and their adversaries are not paying enough attention to their concerns. They may feel that they must demonstrate how important the issue is by taking a tough visible stand. Compromise or willingness to talk with the other side may be interpreted as a softening of their resolve, both by their adversaries and by their constituents.

Some conflict situations catch people by surprise. When a proposal or decision is announced publicly, some of the affected parties may have no idea that an issue is even being considered, much less that a decision is about to be made. They are offended that they have not been consulted, so taking no time to consider the merits of the proposal, they conjure up the worst possible implications. They are angered as much by the process that was used in making the decision as by the decision itself.

People in trouble become hostile and combative when they feel they have no other alternative. "I wish there was something else we could do, but I don't know what it would be. I guess we're stuck with fighting this out." They sense that another approach could better serve their long-term interests, but they have no idea what that alternative might be or how it can be initiated.

Finally, parties choose an adversarial approach because it is a familiar tactic for dealing with disagreement. "Why not let the lawyers take care of it? That is the way we've always done it." Having a lawyer represent one's cause is an acceptable, if not economical, convention in public and private organizations. Whether the fight is waged in the courtroom, through administrative proceedings such as testimony in public hearings, or in the legislative arena, the steps are clearly prescribed by custom or law.

Unfortunately, the outcome of an adversarial strategy is not as predictable for the parties as the logical procedural steps they follow to get to it. The most persuasive of arguments does not necessarily result in a judge's favorable ruling. A well-prepared and technically elegant presentation at a public hearing does not guarantee that the right issues will be addressed or that satisfactory decisions will be made. In adversarial proceedings, parties focus on winning and risk loss of everything if they fail. Even if they "win," the victory may not solve the core problems, because legal decisions are made on points of law and not on technical or social criteria. Animosities harbored by the losing side often increase, making the next confrontation with the same parties even more difficult to handle. The victory may in fact be a long time in coming, because opposing parties can block implementation of a legal decision for years by using the appeal process (Berger, 1977; Bok, 1983).

In situations in which the facts can be reasonably determined and the parties are known, the legal system can work well. But public conflicts involve a range of perceptions about what the issues are, complex technical conflicts outside the legal arena, and parties who may never be fully identified. What is legally correct may not be what is best for the parties, because courts cannot review all of the social and technical factors and their consequences. Often, intense, prolonged investigation is required to establish what is actually in the broad public interest, with the final determination made by the parties themselves. Yet the agents of the parties negotiate on points of law, and the people most affected are removed from direct contact with each other.

When parties choose to enter the legal system, it becomes more difficult for them to exchange information and adjust their positions. As a result, satisfactory solutions may be overlooked, and resources that could otherwise be devoted to finding creative solutions are poured into carrying on a fight.

Finding a Quick Fix

A third response to conflict is the quick fix—producing a solution immediately. Public controversies bring instant visibility to the organization creating a problem or responsible for solving it. Public pressure mounts to "do something," and the manager "takes care of" the problem by declaring a solution. Unfortunately, the cry to do something too often gets translated into doing *anything*. The solution appears before the facts are clearly understood—before the parties understand the range of issues and without their having thought through the options.

Much to a manager's frustration, rather than finding a public relieved because action has been taken, he or she is faced with a new round of criticism, this time focused on the solution itself (see Figure 2). The conflict grows.

At this point the official decides either to stick with the proposed solution and commit resources to "selling" it to the public (who seldom are interested in buying) or to concede defeat, withdraw the proposal, and retreat to develop another solution using the same flawed process.

The Solomon Trap

The Solomon trap is a fourth response to conflict. It has four phases (see Figure 3). The person responsible for making a decision about a controversial program conscientiously seeks to identify all affected parties and, through a variety of mechanisms, asks them for their views. A series of well-publicized public meetings is held, key individuals are identified and asked for interviews, and written comments are solicited. The responsible organization contributes research on the history of the issue and offers its own comments—consistent, of course, with the organization's mission and current priorities.

During the second phase of this strategy, the official sifts

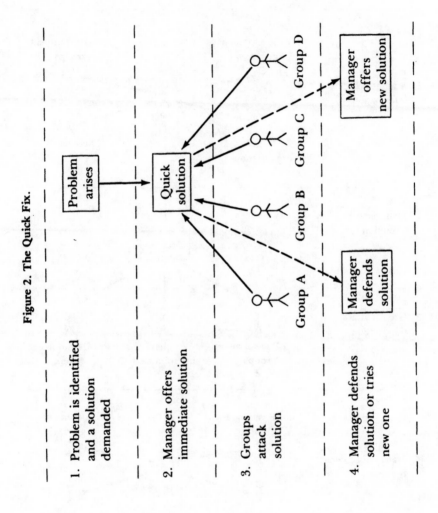

Figure 2. The Quick Fix.

1. Problem is identified and a solution demanded

Problem arises

2. Manager offers immediate solution

Quick solution

3. Groups attack solution

Group A   Group B   Group C   Group D

4. Manager defends solution or tries new one

Manager defends solution

Manager offers new solution

Figure 3. The Solomon Trap.

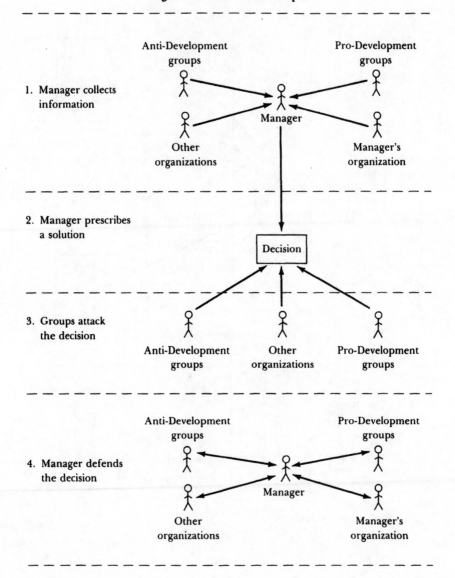

through all the comments that have been received, weighs the trade-offs, gives due consideration to questions of fairness, and crafts a solution that comes closest to addressing everyone's interests and that is in harmony with the agency's goals and priorities.

The third phase begins when the official announces the decision to the parties, who are dismayed to discover that their key issues have not been addressed exactly as they wanted them to be. During phase one, each group had carefully educated the manager about solutions it thought should be included in the decision. "He seemed so sympathetic to our concerns when we talked to him. What happened?" Parties' disappointments turn into feelings of betrayal. "The agency must not have been listening to us or they would have understood how important our suggestions were." The entire decision is considered unacceptable, and they prepare to oppose it. They lash out at the official, attacking the decision as irrational and irresponsible. He or she is partly consoled by the thought, "Well that's what I'm paid to do—make tough decisions and then catch the flak. After all you can't please everyone."

The final phase of this strategy involves the decision maker spending an inordinate amount of time defending the virtues of the proposal to each of the concerned parties. The time spent explaining the rationale delays implementation of the proposal, and it becomes more unlikely that it will ever be implemented. By this point, the parties may become so frustrated and angry with the decision that they will not support it no matter what accommodations are made, and the only satisfactory action is to throw the decision out and begin from scratch to develop a new one. The decision offered to the parties may have been a reasonable solution, but because they did not understand the process, the parties now demand active involvement in the decision making.

The point of discussing these four strategies is not to say that they should never be used but rather to suggest that parties should understand the risks that accompany each approach. In some situations, it may be entirely appropriate to avoid initiating an alternative conflict management activity. Information critical to a discussion may be unavailable, parties may need additional time to organize their constituents, or the issue may not be negotiable. Parties also may choose an adversarial strategy when an important legal precedent must be established and compromise of any sort is inappropriate. Too often, though, chances for an effective solution are lost when managers choose an inappropriate course. They should have a broad repertoire of tools for dealing with conflict and should know when to use each one. (For additional reading about responses to conflict, see Blake and Mouton, 1984; Thomas, 1976.)

Alternative Approaches for Managing Conflict

The natural course for a manager to take in selecting a conflict resolution strategy is to use familiar procedures. Since we live in what is often called an adversarial society, the strategy chosen is quite likely to be a competitive one because that is the way we customarily address our problems. As previously noted, traditional adversarial strategies are entirely appropriate in some circumstances, but they may also pit adversaries against each other in a costly and destructive battle in which no one comes out a clear winner. Alternative conflict management procedures have been used successfully in public disputes at every level of complexity, from neighborhood quarrels to debates over national policy (Bradley, 1985; Carlson, 1985; Harter, 1982; Huelsberg and Lincoln, 1985; Lake, 1987; Levitt and Kirlin, 1985; Meeks, 1985; and Richman, White, and Wilkinson, 1986). These approaches share several characteristics.

The Decision Maker Is a Facilitator. No longer the political strategist figuring out how to keep ahead of other parties, and no longer acting as the sole decision maker, the manager brings parties together to help determine the best solution. The emphasis is on cooperation. Resources are committed to identifying a decision that diverse interests can live with, rather than forcing a unilateral position on the competing groups. Instead of trying to restrict participation, a common tactic, the professional manager gains *more* control over the situation by ensuring that all the necessary parties are there at the table, recognizing that parties in a dispute often engage in adversarial behavior because no other approach is available to protect their interests.

In both the quick fix and the Solomon trap the manager is the focal point for making a decision and then finds himself or herself subject to attack from all sides. An alternative approach finds the decision maker bringing all parties together to exchange information and develop solutions to the problem (see Figure 4).

The Focus Is on Solving a Problem. Parties are encouraged to view the conflict as a problem to be solved rather than a battle to be won. "How can we solve the problem?" is the question that is asked, not "Who has the right position?" The manager lays out the consequences of continuing to fight and offers another approach—to sit down and find a way to deal with the problem that respects the interests of all of the parties. The final decision of whether to participate is up to them, and if the benefits of working out their differences through a negotiated process do not make sense to them, they should not engage in alternative conflict management activities.

Parties Meet Face to Face to Work Out Differences. The people who are affected by a decision are identified and brought into the process. They do not deal through agents such as lawyers. They sit down with other parties, some of whom are their adversaries, to solve a problem. They define the problem together, educate each other about the issues, and develop and assess reasonable solutions. This practice is in sharp contrast to the dynamics of a public hearing or to lobbying efforts with decision makers, in which parties compete with each other to set forth their views most aggressively.

Parties Help Shape the Process. At the beginning of a program, parties are asked to help in developing a process they think would work best to solve their problem. As the discussions evolve, they continue to offer suggestions about the management of the process and to suggest and support needed

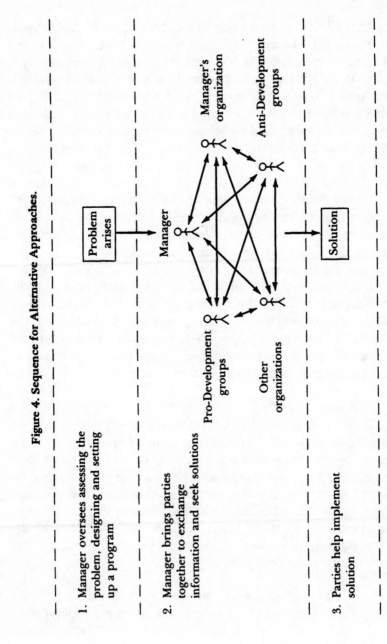

Figure 4. Sequence for Alternative Approaches.

1. Manager oversees assessing the problem, designing and setting up a program

2. Manager brings parties together to exchange information and seek solutions

3. Parties help implement solution

Problem arises

Manager

Manager's organization

Anti-Development groups

Pro-Development groups

Other organizations

Solution

changes. When external factors create special demands on the participants, they share in making decisions to deal with these factors.

Decisions Are Made by Consensus. The goal of consensus decision making is to reach a decision that all parties can accept. The parties reach agreement by gathering information, discussing and analyzing it, and convincing each other of its merits. They combine or synthesize proposals or develop totally new solutions. Not everyone will like the solution equally well or have an equal commitment to it, but the group recognizes that it has reached the best decision for all parties involved. They do not vote, because decisions made by voting create winners and losers, and disgruntled losers can cause problems later on by challenging the decision. If that challenge fails, they may attempt to sabotage the decision's implementation.

Case Examples

The following case examples serve several functions. First, they provide a context for the ideas presented in succeeding chapters. Second, they illustrate the wide variety of circumstances in which conflict management approaches are useful—from three parties concerned about the use of a local parcel of land to thirty parties locked in conflict over complex statewide plans and policies. In some situations the parties in a conflict were just beginning to move toward serious confrontation, while in others the parties were at the top of the conflict spiral. Finally, the case studies reflect how varied conflict management procedures can be, even though the same guiding principles and framework were used in all of them. (For additional case examples, see Bingham, 1984; Talbot, 1983; Wondolleck, 1986.)

For each case study, we explain the context, describe the activities the parties used to prepare for a program, and recount the sequence of steps used to reach agreements, with the conviction that the procedures are sound and can be recommended for use by anyone who has a similar problem to solve.

The Town and the Park

*Poor communication and distrust characterized a
conflict over the purchase and management of a
parcel of land. In an informal two-day session the
three central parties identified common goals and
developed recommendations for a cooperative community program.*

The park service proposed that the boundaries of a national park be extended to add 800 acres of land to the park.
This proposal precipitated a gradually escalating disagreement
over land use that involved the park service, a nonprofit conservation group, and the citizens of a small town adjacent to the
park.

Part of the land had been acquired by the conservation
group, which intended to convey title to the park service. However, title to some parcels of the land was questionable, which
prevented the park service from accepting the gift. The park service began a federal condemnation action to clear title to the
parcels in question.

Eight years after the controversy had begun, the town
asked the park service to discontinue condemnation proceedings and abandon its plan for park expansion. The people were
greatly concerned about the effect that more tourists would
have on the community. They were also anxious to continue
their established uses of the area for hunting, fishing, and traditional cultural activities, and they were concerned that the
land's inclusion in a national park would preclude these activities.

The residents discovered that the government had filed
"adverse possession" actions for the land parcels in question. If
these actions were successful, they would eliminate the claims
that some 120 people had on various pieces of land. The local
people felt that the conservation group was involved in this
process in some nefarious manner, since it had been issuing
contradictory statements about its intentions. From then on,
suspicions increased dramatically and positions hardened. The

citizens of the town saw both the conservation group and the park service as the adversaries.

An officer of a philanthropic foundation was concerned about the worsening situation in the town and thought that someone outside the dispute should be brought in to help the parties sort out their differences. The first step for the outside facilitators was to collect background information about the situation—books about the area, the town newsletter—and to talk with foundation officers who were familiar with the meetings and negotiations that had occurred over the preceding months. The community emerged from this investigation as proud of its culture, geographically isolated, and deeply spiritual—all of which meant that an outsider would have difficulty building trust.

The next task for the outsiders was to meet with local residents and listen to their concerns. Conversations with community leaders were lively, cordial, and candid, but a lot of anger and frustration lurked just below the surface. It was clear that the land in question had high spiritual value and was also a base for the way of life that the community wanted to retain.

Representatives from the park service and the conservation group and a score of residents gathered on the porch of a local person's house. The parties arrived without an agenda and with no clear goal for the discussion. The outsiders had been asked to come at the last minute in the hope that they could prevent a destructive clash between the three parties, but they also had no specific role. After introductions, everyone agreed that the first item of business should be a discussion of what the group wanted to accomplish during the first day. The visitors were asked to guide the discussion. Tension gradually relaxed as the participants found that instead of having to carry on a fight, they were talking among themselves about a positive and non-controversial procedural question.

Next, the facilitators suggested that each person say what he or she needed to have considered in a plan to solve the problems the groups had been fighting about. Ideas were recorded on wall sheets as each person spoke, so that everyone knew that the suggestions were being heard. The participants spoke cautiously. They had become accustomed to thinking about the other parties as enemies, and they expected to be subjected to hostile challenges. But out of an atmosphere of suspicion and anxiety came a list of remarkably compatible interests. The items on the list reflected the backgrounds and perspectives of the individual speakers, who each had a special element of concern, but instead of clashing, the items fit together. The parties were astounded to find that some of the principal points were nearly identical. For example, all three parties wanted to protect the life-style and traditions of the community, and all three wanted to protect the land in question from ecological harm. They realized that none of their major points seemed impossible to achieve.

When all the interests had been recorded, each person, in turn, talked about the barriers to meeting their needs. Again, the comments reflected the individual concerns of the speakers, but there did not seem to be any irresolvable collisions between the suggestions.

The afternoon was devoted to solutions. A total of twenty-seven specific recommendations went up on the paper sheets. Discussion focused on several main themes:

1. Organize a land trust to hold and manage the land in the interests of all the parties.
2. Establish an office in the town to train local people to manage the area.
3. Postpone legal proceedings.
4. Establish a formal body in which representatives of the three principal interests could continue negotiations.

The next day, the group reconvened without representatives of the park service and the conservation group, who had left the previous evening. Before the meeting, the worksheets of the previous day had been reviewed and summarized into "Where do we go from here" sheets, which were now put up on the meeting rooms to help guide the discussion. When asked what they thought about the meeting, the people of the town said that the community had acquired a sense of equal power for the first time, and after all the years of fighting, a foundation had been laid on which the parties could build together.

As a result of the meeting and of negotiations that followed over the next several months without the assistance of a third party, the conservation group and the community worked together to establish a community program. A nonprofit corporation was set up to act as a local planning commission, and two local people were hired to conduct studies on what should be done with the land. The park service deferred its decisions until the studies were completed.

The Village

The village council, its staff, and a development company each needed help in understanding its own problems and in "team building" before they could successfully negotiate with each other.

The village was a new town, built about twenty years before as a tourist center catering to hikers, picnickers, and skiers visiting the surrounding wooded hills and rugged mountains. Although its sole reason for existence was its appeal as a tourist attraction, a substantial part of the center of town consisted of undeveloped land and a hodgepodge of garages, parking lots, and vacant lots. Most of the land and many of the buildings were owned by one large company that was unable to agree with the town government on proposals for development. As a consequence, the managers of stores and hotels did not enjoy the flow of business they thought they should have. They put pressure on elected officials to find an answer. For its part, the company was afraid that if its plans to develop the land were delayed much longer, it would lose its investors. Clashes between the company and the village became frequent, rancorous, and highly public.

Fearing that decisions about the land would be delayed indefinitely, a company executive and the mayor asked for third-party help in setting up negotiations between the company and the village. The first step for the outsiders was to interview several dozen village residents, asking general questions about the community and its future. The interviews disclosed the influence of past arguments on present decisions and how intense personal animosities were blocking negotiations even though both parties wanted to resolve the problem. The most conspicuous obstacles to negotiation were the deep enmities among members of the village staff and between the village staff and the elected council—not, as might be expected, between the council and the company (although they were bad enough). People within the village government made such vitriolic comments about each other that it seemed unlikely that the village government in its present condition could negotiate effectively with the company. The company was also having internal management problems, which, although not as severe as those of the village, could have limited the company's ability to discuss options and carry out commitments.

It was clear that productive negotiation would be impossible until both sides put their houses in order. A strategy was worked out to deal with management problems in town government and, separately, to help the company improve its internal communication. Over a period of two months, an outside consultant met with the village staff and council members, individually and in general working sessions. The staff members listed the characteristics of an effective town staff, described their concerns about their own performance, and talked about recommendations for improving their relationships and cooperating with one another. The council worked through a similar program, defining how an effective council should function and comparing their own experiences on the village council with their ideal model.

Two weeks later, the staff and council went through separate training sessions in meeting management, principles of conflict management, and techniques for resolving disputes. The staff went back to develop solutions to the problems identified earlier, reaching consensus on specific procedures for accomplishing their goals.

These discussions and training programs were designed to prepare the staff for a meeting with the council. The staff decided to be forthright about problems and solutions but to avoid any personal accusations, since the council had the power to hire and fire. Meetings between the council and staff took place on two days, a week apart. The meetings were devoted to discussions about mutual concerns and suggestions for improving the way they dealt with each other. The conversations were generally amicable, but at times individuals needed reminding that the purpose of the meetings was to solve problems, not to attack each other.

Meetings with the company were also designed to build a negotiating team. Substantial changes in market conditions and in the company's financial structure were creating a great deal of anxiety among the employees. Poor exchange of information within the company was making people even more nervous. Over the course of several meetings, the company managers listed the qualities of effective working relationships and procedures for carrying them out. Then they defined the traps they could fall into and specific procedures for making a cooperative plan work.

After the training of all groups was completed, the village staff felt confident enough to submit to the council and the company a proposal for a step-by-step joint planning process, beginning with establishing ground rules and defining the steps for negotiation. The proposal called for setting up a timetable, reaching agreement on the issues to be discussed, and establishing goals. At least four of the seven council members would attend every meeting. Representatives of all the major civic and business organizations would be at the table. Public involvement was to be assured by having the meetings open and also by soliciting public comments through questionnaires and newsletters.

After several more months of discussion between the council and the staff and between the council and the company, a meeting was held in which each council member in turn expressed a personal commitment to the entire concept and the company representatives confirmed their enthusiasm for the program. In a break with tradition, the parties agreed to make their decisions by consensus rather than by majority rule.

The Airport Scoping Meetings

Government officials decided to apply conflict management techniques in a series of highly emotional public meetings over a proposed new airport runway. Participants working in small groups were encouraged by facilitators to speak candidly and be specific about their concerns.

The airport was one of the nation's busiest. Rapidly increasing traffic was straining its capacity, causing delays during peak hours that cost the airlines millions of dollars each year. To address the immediate need for increased airfield capacity, the city proposed constructing an additional runway to reduce delays and congestion until a new facility was established. Three alternatives were considered, and an east-west runway to be located on federal land adjacent to the existing airport was recommended. The responsible federal agency was asked to prepare a draft and final environmental impact statement (EIS) for the airport expansion.

The federal agency was required by law to conduct "scoping" meetings as a prerequisite for preparing a draft impact statement. The requirement states that "there shall be an early and open process for determining the scope of issues to be addressed, and for identifying the significant issues related to the proposed actions." Agency responses to the dictates of the law regarding public hearings are not always the most creative part of their programs. However, these particular officials were determined to go beyond the narrow requirements of the law and involve the public in an effective exchange of information, even though they knew they would be working in an atmosphere of high emotion and hostility. Their goal was to conduct productive meetings by soliciting relevant issues from the participants and by minimizing unnecessary conflict and acrimony.

Since it wanted to obtain the broadest possible participation by residents, the agency aggressively sought methods to get people to the meetings. Five places were selected for the scoping meetings, spread over three counties. The agency mailed invitations to about 2,000 people, whose names were taken from lists collected from business and civic organizations. Announcements were sent to television and radio stations and to city and community newspapers. Personal telephone calls were made to selected individuals in each of the concerned communities, urging them to encourage others to attend the meetings. Careful consideration was given to preparing the agenda and thinking through the details of the meetings. Because people would work in small groups, school cafeterias and classrooms were secured along with auditorium seating.

Meeting facilitators and group recorders were hired to guide the discussions. They were provided with a list of important subjects, gleaned from interviews and articles, that could be expected to form the core of the discussions. The facilitators could then watch for these subjects and be sure they were pursued for additional information and clarification.

Each of the five meetings proceeded in the same way. Upon arrival, participants were given written materials describing the airport expansion proposals and explaining some of the alternatives. Each person was given a name badge with a letter identification (A, B, C, and so on) that identified the person's working group.

The agency manager welcomed the group, explained the purpose of "scoping" meetings, and set an important ground rule: "Representatives of the agency are here to listen and understand the issues you put forth but not to debate their merits." He then proceeded with a brief explanation of the EIS process and the specific proposal for a new east-west runway. Participants could ask questions to clarify information, but they were not permitted to make speeches or challenge the validity of the alternatives.

Next the facilitators identified themselves and explained how the rest of the meeting would work. Participants moved to their assigned working groups. Each group contained twenty to thirty people, who ranged from consultants who wanted a piece of the airport action to elderly people living in small residences on fixed and inadequate incomes who feared they might be displaced by new airport construction. Each group was managed by a facilitator who asked participants for their comments and who supervised a recorder whose task was to capture concerns on wall sheets posted in front of the group. Federal agency personnel were available to answer questions but not to debate the issues.

The facilitators' job was to draw out as much information as possible about people's concerns. This was a difficult task because many people had come to make speeches objecting to the proposed alternative as well as to express their anger over the proposed location of the new airport.

Another problem was that a large portion of some of the groups was made up of low-income elderly people who were resentful and frightened but unwilling to speak. The facilitators had to press gently but firmly to extract these people's concerns.

About 325 people attended the five meetings. The working groups produced a great many separate issues and specific concerns, which were grouped into eleven topic areas: land use, socioeconomic impacts, toxic material and disposal sites, air quality, geologic conditions, biotic communities, water quality, noise, safety, alternatives, and "other." The concerns identified by the public were used by the agency to determine which issues should be addressed in the EIS. While intense feelings about the new airport were expressed in all of the sessions, the facilitator-recorder system of meeting management worked well in gathering detailed information from concerned people in a highly emotional atmosphere and in much less time than more traditional public meetings would have required.

Oil and Gas Exploration in Wilderness Study Areas

Representatives of two oil and gas trade associations and four environmental organizations worked through their differences to produce a jointly signed letter recommending notification procedures for proposed oil and gas exploration.

Federal law required the government bureau to study lands with potential wilderness value and make recommendations about them. These areas, called Wilderness Study Areas, were essentially closed to oil and gas exploration and extraction until the bureau changed its policy as the result of a federal court decision. The bureau announced that new exploration and production could take place on preexisting leases within study areas. Responsibility for issuing permits for oil and gas exploration was shared by the bureau and another federal agency. Staff from both agencies were required to visit each proposed lease site and determine drilling procedures.

During one of these visits, a representative from an environmental group appeared and insisted on being included in the trip. The government agencies were caught between the oil and gas companies' concern about disclosure of proprietary information and the environmentalists' determination to have public review of the permitting process. The principal issue became how and when the public would be notified of a proposed exploration.

Even though the parties agreed on the importance of protecting wilderness areas, they had moved into highly adversarial positions on the procedural issues and were threatening litigation. Federal agency managers were beginning to receive criticism from their superiors in Washington, D.C. The job of the intervener was to reduce the accusatory rhetoric and bring representatives together in a search for solutions to the problem.

Over a period of three months, interviews were conducted with people who seemed to be central figures in the controversy—federal agency managers, oil and gas company executives, and environmental leaders. They answered questions about who should be included in negotiations, what the consequences might be of recent federal policy changes, and what issues they thought must be addressed in a negotiation. They were also asked whether they would consider participating in negotiations. Because the dispute was already thoroughly public and the primary parties had announced their positions, most respondents were angry at their adversaries and unenthusiastic about talking with them. However, through the influence of some key individuals who feared the consequences of an escalating conflict, they gave lukewarm agreement to participate.

People on both sides and in the federal agencies doubted that anything would come of the efforts. They thought that the discussions had become too polarized, and they had little hope that the longtime adversaries would negotiate in good faith.

The interviews produced three separate sets of concerns. Environmentalists were interested in protecting wild areas and increasing acreage designated as wilderness. They especially wanted prior notification about the proposed issuance of drilling permits so that they would know where and when drilling was expected and could participate in the review of applications.

Industry concerns focused on the need for prompt approval of drilling permits and rights of way because delays were costly and sometimes forced oil companies to withdraw altogether. Companies also wanted to protect information about plans for exploration that would be useful to competitors.

The federal agencies in the middle wanted to clarify the question of access to information and to reach agreement on permit procedures with both industry and environmental groups to avoid unnecessary legal proceedings and political problems.

At the first meeting representatives of all parties presented lists of concerns they had prepared before the meeting. The meeting was facilitated, and the discussions were recorded on newsprint. To their surprise, the representatives reached several important procedural agreements, including who should participate—four environmental groups, two industry groups, and two federal agencies—and what information was needed from the agencies. They agreed to meet for sixty days and then assess their progress. These agreements were cleared with their boards of directors and superiors.

The next four meetings were held over a period of two months. The strategy was to proceed step by step and see how far they could get. To the many doubting bystanders inside and outside the participating organizations, each successful meeting had to be an anomaly, yet the negotiators proceeded from agreeing on procedures to listing issues and reviewing current federal rules. From there, they moved into determining what additional information was needed and who could provide it. They then worked out a range of alternative solutions for the harder issues and discussed their advantages and disadvantages. At the final meeting, they reached agreement on notification procedures and the general content of a joint letter to the state director of the bureau, a development that amazed nearly everyone, including the negotiators. After several more drafts the letter was signed by all parties and sent to the director.

The Old Railroad

> *Two county governments, a federal agency, and four citizen groups with different interests developed a cooperative action plan to address a problem before it erupted into a more serious conflict.*

In the latter part of the nineteenth century, a railroad was pushed across a wild and rugged mountain pass to connect frontier communities and haul ore from the area's mines. The project was something of an engineering tour de force, requiring the construction of tunnels through hard rock and enormous wooden trestles over deep chasms. Eventually the railroad company completed a tunnel that replaced the route across the pass, and the rails and cross ties were removed. Although it was passable to vehicles only in the summer months, the old railroad bed gradually became a popular destination for a wide variety of recreational users. It was listed in the National Register of Historic Places. The road was maintained through an informal cooperative agreement between the counties at each end of the route and a federal land management agency, an arrangement that worked well for many years—until a partial collapse of one of the tunnels and weakening of the timbers holding up a trestle forced the federal agency to close the road for safety reasons.

Although the action was generally accepted as necessary, it frustrated a great many people. The trip over the road had become a major tourist attraction for residents of the nearby metropolitan area and a source of revenue for local retail merchants. It was a destination for railroad enthusiasts, photographers, and amateur historians, and it was a fine starting point for a hike into the adjacent wilderness area.

Everybody wanted to solve the problem and to protect the historical and natural values of the area, but money was a serious problem—repairs to the tunnel and trestle would be expensive, and budgets were getting tighter. There were jurisdictional concerns among the government entities, and officials worried about liability insurance, public pressure, and broader land management policies. Railroad buffs wanted to repair the tunnel and replace portions of the trestle. Wilderness advocates wanted to be sure that whatever was done to the road would not threaten the wild areas nearby. The situation had not become seriously adversarial, but several attempts to get the parties together had failed, and concern was growing that a solution had to be found quickly, before available money disappeared and temporary closures became permanent. People were beginning to develop divergent positions about what ought to be done. Newspaper reports of verbal exchanges between the groups were taking on a sharp edge. The conflict spiral was expanding.

A commissioner of one of the counties and the district manager of the federal agency agreed to ask for help in setting up a negotiation and running the first few meetings. They thought, and the other parties agreed, that they needed assistance in making a positive start.

After making a preliminary review of the situation, the facilitators concluded that the controversy was ready to go one of two ways: either expand rapidly into a full-fledged public dispute, or turn toward a cooperative effort to set goals and find the necessary money. The challenge was to channel strong convictions and a lot of technical knowledge into a constructive program. The facilitators proposed a strategy and checked it out with the three governments and four citizen groups that represented a range of interests from historic preservation to wilderness protection.

Their suggestions included the use of consensus to reach agreements, ground rules covering the role of the news media and observers, and the distribution of background materials before the first meeting to describe the history of the railroad, its present condition, and the sequence of events leading up to the present situation. The parties themselves collaborated in the preparation of the materials and in their distribution.

The facilitators began the first meeting by reminding the participants that they all cared a lot about the problem but that blaming each other would not produce any answers. The facilitators acknowledged the substantial body of knowledge possessed by the participants and organized the sessions to demonstrate that everyone could work together despite earlier acrimonious conversations. The meeting focused on joint identification of all the obstacles that had blocked progress before and an assessment of possible options. The first meeting produced a list of technical and administrative issues, some of which would need substantial research before they could be addressed. The parties assigned themselves tasks that they agreed to complete before the next meeting—tasks that required the parties to maintain communication to share information before they met again.

At the second meeting (two weeks later), the task groups reported on their findings. Despite the extraordinarily short preparation time, the participants worked out an action program that included financial commitments by all parties and a chronological plan of administrative decisions. A coordinator, one of the representatives, was designated to make sure that the assignments were carried out.

Big Game Damage to Agriculture

A long history of animosity, inept political intervention, and widely differing values preceded an eight-month negotiation by fourteen participants. Two mediators facilitated the negotiation sessions and helped solve other problems when they arose. The program was convened by the state Division of Wildlife.

The progressive loss of wildlife habitat to farms, subdivisions, and shopping centers forces wild animals onto private lands when natural winter food stocks run out. Traditionally, farmers and ranchers have tolerated wildlife damage to crops, haystacks, and orchards as a part of the cost of doing business. But the costs of wildlife depredation are mounting rapidly at a time of severe economic crisis for agriculture. The problem is especially acute in western states, but eastern states and some European and African countries also experience variations of the same competition between animals and human development.

Although damage prevention and compensation were subjects of debate and legislative action for many years in one particular western state, the expense had increased so significantly that the Division of Wildlife and groups who paid hunting license fees that financed the program became seriously concerned about the eventual economic consequences. Agricultural groups, on the other hand, felt that the program was not sufficiently responsive to their needs. Facing a major public confrontation that would eventually be fought out in the legislature, the Division of Wildlife asked for help in designing and managing a negotiation process in which all the major parties would try to develop recommendations for statutory changes that would improve the program.

The battle over game damage compensation had been fought so long and so publicly that there was no question about who the primary parties were. The mediators visited as many of them as possible under the limitations of the project budget and talked with others by telephone. Each conversation explained the purpose of the project, asked whether the person would participate if invited, and sought suggestions for other people to be interviewed. The familiar dilemma of keeping the negotiating group to a manageable size and still having the necessary people at the table was gradually resolved by selecting representatives of the main interests whom others would accept to speak for them. An unusual characteristic of this project was that most of the participants followed work schedules determined by the time of year and the weather. They could be expected to miss meetings because events like hunting seasons and lambing time took precedence over everything else. Thus, two individuals from each major interest group were invited, rather than one, to ensure continuity from one meeting to the next.

In addition to the primary parties—cattlemen, sheep producers, fruit growers, the Division of Wildlife, wheat farmers, hunting outfitters, and hunters—two additional groups were invited: an urban environmental organization and an association of sportsmen who were trying to develop new methods of working with the Division of Wildlife.

Before the first meeting of the game damage working group, each representative received a letter inviting him or her to serve and explaining the project, a draft agenda, and a proposed set of ground rules. At the first meeting, the participants approved the ground rules and adopted the principle of making decisions by consensus. Things were proceeding smoothly until the Division of Wildlife suggested that the group focus on five issues of particular concern to the Division, a suggestion that produced instant reaction and strongly hostile comments from some of the participants who already expected the Division to try to control the agenda.

It was clear that the parties would have great difficulty in negotiating solutions until the tension between them was reduced, and it was also evident that there were significant differences of opinion on what the purpose of the negotiation ought to be. The group turned to working out a formal statement of intent for the project before discussing any substantive issues. In negotiating the wording of the statement, they found that they could cooperate even though views ranged widely on what the purpose ought to be. The discussion was constructive, candid about disagreements, but reasonable. The parties found that they did not have to attack each other to make a point.

Next, the group worked out a list of eleven categories of agricultural products for which game damage could occur. They then discussed the specific types of damage and methods for controlling each of the categories. A great deal of work was done by the participants in small task groups between meetings. At the close of each session, responsibilities for acquiring necessary information or continuing discussion over specific issues were assigned to individuals, who reported to the group at the next meeting.

Several months after the negotiations began, one of the

representatives mentioned that his organization resented the wording of the press releases that the Division issued each year to announce game damage payments, because they always implied that his group was the beneficiary of overly generous payments. This chance comment, which revealed the reason for unexplained hostility between the representative and the Division, became an opportunity for the Division to demonstrate its intention to be receptive to the concerns of the parties at the table. The Division acknowledged the concern in writing and issued instructions to Division personnel that they must be careful to word their press releases more fairly. The action was a breakthrough in the negotiations because it gave clear evidence of a desire to change established relationships.

The meetings were facilitated in a relatively informal way, with discussions controlled only when it seemed that the parties might be leading up to an infraction of the ground rules or when people strayed into personal reminiscences. A special problem was that some of the parties had had a bad experience with an earlier negotiation on a similar topic in which the chairman had altered the meeting records to fit what he wished had happened. Detailed minutes clearly marked "Draft" were therefore sent out to the participants, and corrections were aggressively sought as the first order of business in each meeting.

The group examined each major topic in terms of its origins, its statutory base, and the consequences to interested parties of possible modifications to the statutes and regulatory procedures. By the close of the first phase of the project, the group had reached general agreement on twenty-three specific statutory recommendations.

The Water Roundtable

The complexity and importance of the issues, the large number and variety of participants, and the length of time required for the negotiations made the water roundtable an exceptionally large mediated negotiation. While the size of the mediating team varied from time to time, it averaged four full-

*time members. The roundtable was an unequaled
chance for the mediators and the parties to try out
procedures for dealing with constantly emerging
problems. The deliberations covered highly technical data, economic trade-offs, and life-style issues.*

The city is in a mountain region of the western United
States, where water is scarce. While more than 80 percent of the
state's population lives east of the mountains, almost 70 percent
of the state's native water supply lies on the western slope. The
city and other adjacent communities rely for their water on a
massive and complicated system of diversion structures, storage
reservoirs, and tunnels under the mountains. The projects have
been the source of conflict and litigation for decades. Most of
the disputes have arisen out of the efforts of agricultural organizations, business groups, and local governments to protect their
interests, but many of the recent conflicts have centered on objections to the adverse environmental effects of the development projects (Carpenter and Kennedy, forthcoming). This is
the story of one set of conflicts.

As its metropolitan area grew, the city turned to large
structural solutions to its increasing need for water. Its plans,
and the attention of its adversaries, focused on proposals to
construct a large dam and storage lake for water diverted from
the western side of the state. With the city apparently headed
for construction of this project, the stage seemed set for the cul-
minating clash between the competing parties, one that would
be fought out in the courts over many years at a cost of millions
of dollars. To many of the state's leaders, the risks were too
great. Some better way of making decisions about water management had to be found. They called in a team of mediators.

In a preliminary review of the situation, which included
discussions with a dozen people, the mediators concluded that
the negotiation should focus not just on the dam project but on
the broader question of how the city should obtain its water
supply. The next three months were spent assessing the situation and developing a strategy to prepare for negotiation.

After interviews with over forty knowledgeable people

across the state, a negotiation strategy was designed that included the following steps: (1) establish ground rules; (2) identify the interests of the parties; (3) review and agree on basic supply and demand data; (4) develop agreements in principle; (5) work out preferred alternatives; and (6) determine the best package of specific methods to meet the city's water needs. The water roundtable would hold plenary session about once a month in meetings convened by the governor. In addition to general sessions, task groups and other small groups would work in specific areas to develop ideas and assess information for subsequent plenary consideration. The general strategy developed in the preparation phase was the essential framework for the ensuing negotiation. Although changes were made when necessary to accommodate new events, the strategy worked well as the basic structure.

A central consideration in establishing the roundtable was determining who should participate. The parties themselves were involved in the selection process in order to assure that the group was compatible. The issue of fair representation was overcome in large part by establishing the concept that decisions would be made only by consensus and not by majority rule. Finally, thirty individuals were invited to participate, representing urban and suburban water groups, business people from the eastern and western sections of the state, agriculture, western local governments, and western water interests.

In the first few meetings, the participants reached procedural agreements on ground rules for behavior and the use of substitutes, and they decided that the meetings should be closed to the news media (see Exhibit 6, "Sample Set of Ground Rules," in Chapter Six). After intense discussion, they also reached consensus on two substantive topics: the geographical area to be examined, and the time period to be considered. They agreed that the area should be the region directly affected by the activities of the city water department, and the time should be the period up to the year 2010.

The next step was to divide the roundtable membership into four balanced working groups for the purpose of developing lists of interests that the roundtable should address. The composition of each group reflected the diversity of the round-table membership. The four lists of interests were consolidated into one, which the parties used as a reference in devising proposals to meet the city's water needs.

Roundtable representatives, faced continually with the need to keep in touch with their constituencies, used a variety of approaches to maintain needed contact. For example, the environmental community established an organization known as the Environmental Alliance, which comprised seventeen environmental organizations in the city area. The alliance met regularly between plenary sessions to discuss the previous meeting and to develop strategies for future meetings.

To ensure general public involvement in the roundtable process, meetings were held at several locations in the state. Recognizing the long-standing tensions between eastern and western area interests, the first public meeting was held in a major city in the western part of the state. Periodic mailings summarizing the issues under consideration were sent to a list of 400 people. Later in the process, roundtable members made presentations about the negotiations to public and private organizations.

Three task groups of roundtable members were established to review the major options: water development, including system management; water use efficiency (conservation); and groundwater development. The roundtable also established a continuing committee charged with the responsibility of developing a common data base. The task groups and the continuing committee met regularly, collecting, synthesizing, and discussing data, and preparing reports for the plenary sessions.

Six months after the roundtable began, the four task groups produced substantial written reports, addressing a wide range of issues central to the negotiation process. In these reports, roundtable members expressed agreement on several fundamental assumptions, including expected population growth to the year 2010, system water supply, and the water savings that would result from conservation measures. Although some outside technical assistance was used, roundtable members were primarily responsible for producing these reports.

The roundtable was designed to enable the parties to reach a sequence of agreements throughout the negotiation rather than waiting for one final agreement. In reaching agreements in principle, the parties defined the general areas in which agreement had already been reached. Several key issues were addressed. Some, such as an agreement not to attempt to use water supply as a means to control population growth, were solutions to long-standing controversies. The agreements in principle gave the parties a framework within which they could work as they produced specific proposals. At this point, the roundtable established a technical scoping committee to address legal, institutional, financial, and technical questions emerging from the discussions of the task groups. In addition to roundtable members, other participants with necessary technical skills were included on this committee.

When environmentalists reiterated their opposition to the proposed storage project, they were challenged to present an alternative plan, and they accepted. Other roundtable members offered to contribute money to hire a consultant to assist the environmentalists in the production of a computer-based water supply model to facilitate the development of their proposal. Western area representatives also proposed to work out a plan.

Since roundtable participants from the western area had no single organization to represent them, the governor established a Western Water Advisory Council, whose members represented western water organizations, environmentalists, and elected county officials to assist in the development of a plan. The city water developers, the Environmental Alliance, and the Western Water Advisory Council each produced a comprehensive proposal for addressing the city's water needs. Roundtable members reviewed and discussed each plan.

Almost a year and a half after its beginning, the roundtable established a deadline for reaching specific agreements. At a final two-day meeting, components of the three proposals submitted earlier were considered. After intensive discussions and negotiations lasting through the first day and into the night, roundtable members reached substantial agreement on a package that called for the simultaneous investigation of the dam and an alternate water exchange plan, mitigation of impact from any projects that might be built, and additional storage on the western side of the mountains. It also specified the development of a statewide water conservation program and assured participation by environmental representatives in the preparation of a systemwide environmental impact statement.

The draft agreement represented a consensus of views among roundtable members with highly diverse interests regarding a general approach for meeting the water needs of the city through the year 2010. It was a general blueprint, which then had to be implemented. The primary mechanism for implementation was the use of more specialized committees appointed by the governor.

The federal agency responsible for preparing an environmental impact statement established a coordinating committee made up of roundtable members to assure more direct involvement of the roundtable in the development of the statement. In the process, engineers of the Environmental Alliance discovered serious methodological errors in the study, a discovery that saved the agency and the community enormous expense because it was made early enough for the errors to be corrected.

After the agreement was reached, state and local institutions responsible for water management took over management of the process. For more than two years after the agreement, roundtable committees continued to work together and with the federal agency.

3

Developing
an Effective Program
of Conflict Management:
Ten Principles

Over the years, as we have worked with complex disputes, certain basic themes have surfaced repeatedly in response to one difficult situation after another. This chapter presents ten principles that we have found helpful in dealing with public conflicts. The principles may seem obvious and simplistic, but we are amazed at how often they are overlooked by capable people in the midst of conflict. Managers handle disputes every day, but like other human beings, they tend to get caught up in the escalating spiral of conflict. They become personally involved in the emotional transactions that naturally occur, and they become less capable of using common sense. These ten principles can help the manager focus on productive strategies for resolving differences.

Principle 1. Conflicts Are a Mix of Procedures, Relationships, and Substance

It is natural for people involved in a dispute to assume that they can reach a resolution by finding a technical solution to the substantive problem at issue. But equal attention must be given to human relationships and the procedures people use to work out their disagreements. Efforts to solve complicated problems by technical criteria alone cause more conflicts than they resolve. Technical people are usually most comfortable working in their fields of special competence, and they are often uneasy when faced with "people problems." Nobody likes to be confronted with distrust and even hatred (if the conflict has gone on long enough), especially when defending a position that is based on solid facts. Yet human feelings are just as real as scientific data, and emotions condition the way people handle information. Decisions are made and battles fought not by numbers and computers but by complicated and unpredictable human beings.

Human relationships were far down the list of priorities demanding the attention of company management planning to open a new Wyoming coal mine. They had enough problems with engineering difficulties and financial matters, and besides, the nearby town would welcome a new business and new jobs in the area. Which was true. The town did need new jobs, but the residents had no information about the dimensions of the project and the size of the work force. They feared the effects of explosive growth in their community, and they resented not being told what was in store for them.

When the company heard that some residents opposed the project, it decided to send its public relations team from company headquarters in Houston to solve the problem. The company representatives sat down with some of the business leaders in town who had made speeches supporting construction of the new mine. Over a congenial lunch, they decided that the town would appreciate a gift of new lights for the softball field. The community experts flew home to Houston confident that they had successfully laid public opposition to rest. Two days later, the weekly edition of the local newspaper carried an irate editorial and letters to the editor that were even angrier than before the visit.

By avoiding the people who were concerned about the mine and failing to investigate the reasons why they were upset, the public relations team had confirmed people's worst fears about the procedures the company would use in dealing with the community. Residents who had been indifferent to the controversy before the visit were given something simple and tangible to worry about. Even some supporters of the new mine became concerned that the company was unwilling to work with the community to solve problems its activities would cause.

Throughout this book, we emphasize the importance of following in sequence the steps of a conflict management plan, carefully assessing human factors as well as technical issues, bringing the parties into the plan early, and designing a strategy for the particular circumstances. If people are consulted as the plan develops and asked for suggestions to make it work better, they will be much more likely to trust the plan when it is applied.

As the process unfolds, a manager must also be sensitive to changes. Additional time may be needed for parties to educate each other or to work with their constituency groups. The person in charge must continue to check with parties to see whether they feel the process is fair and whether there are ways it might be improved. The manager should always ask, What is the most productive way to proceed?

At the same time that a manager is evaluating and refining the process, he or she must also attend to relationships among parties, asking such questions as: Are they able to work together? How can they gain a better understanding of each other? What changes are necessary to make interactions more productive? Should ground rules be adopted to guide how parties talk to one another?

Principle 2. To Find a Good Solution, You Have to Understand the Problem

Instead of acting on assumptions and the stereotypes that commonly creep into controversial situations, an intervener should begin by untangling the muddle of emotions, perceptions, needs, and cross-purposes that surround the issues. The mining company in the previous example failed to look beneath the surface and find out what people in the community were really concerned about. As a result, the company did the one thing that would most infuriate everyone except the softball team and its business boosters. Ten years later this incident is still a favorite story throughout the entire state to illustrate industry's lack of knowledge about small communities.

In another situation, a planner could not understand why local residents objected so strenuously to the construction of a new office building in a commercial park adjacent to their neighborhood. Citizens had not complained about any of the other buildings that had been added to the park, and the developer thought he had been particularly sensitive to neighborhood concerns.

The citizens appeared in droves at city council meetings and inundated planning staff members with calls to register their opposition. The planning department suggested that the neighborhood association invite the developer and the planning staff to one of its meetings to review the proposal together. The planner thought he could resolve the conflict if the community had a chance to see how attractive the building was going to be. The developer prepared a series of slides to illustrate the new facility and focused his presentation on all the extra services he was prepared to perform.

Soon after the meeting began, the planner realized that the office building was not the real problem. Rather, the citizens were concerned about the dramatic increase in traffic on their residential streets created by the commercial park in general. Citizens' efforts to persuade the city to install stop signs and redirect traffic away from residential streets had been ignored. The only recourse left seemed to be to challenge the construction of the next office building to come up for review. The conflict was over how to handle the traffic, not whether a building should be constructed.

Time invested in understanding a situation pays off in increased productivity when the parties meet to resolve their differences. Up-front preparation enables the parties to reach an agreement more efficiently and avoid traps caused by not understanding the substance of the problem or the sensitive dynamics of the controversy.

A manager assembles this information through visits with individuals directly affected by the dispute and with others who are less involved but who are well informed about the situation. By a combination of listening, cautious probing, and cross-checking with other sources, he or she attempts to understand what the parties are trying to accomplish and why. A manager defines the problem and identifies the affected parties, the important issues, the past and current dynamics among parties, and what the parties need from an agreement.

Principle 3. Take Time to Plan a Strategy and Follow It Through

The bigger, nastier, and more public the controversy, the greater the pressure on a manager to resolve it quickly. But, especially in complicated high-pressure situations, it is essential to stop, think, and work out a strategy. Moving to a solution without a sound plan can delay progress and jeopardize success. A quick-fix approach is likely to produce a "Band-Aid solution" that will cover the wound temporarily but not heal it (see "Finding a Quick Fix," Chapter Two). The last thing managers who are up to their ears in problems want to hear is a suggestion that they take extra time to plan before conducting a program, but developing logical steps toward a solution will produce better results and save time in the long run.

Even in less urgent circumstances, people in an argument may fail to work out a sequence of steps to get them to their goal. Investors and planners in a large western city convened a group of leading citizens interested in developing the last large tract of available land in their downtown area. They intended to reach agreements on the type of development that should occur, but they found themselves talking about narrow issues, such as the types of roads that would be needed, before they had any idea of how the land would be used. The discussions floundered because no one proposed a process for moving the participants toward general agreements on an overall approach and *then* to specific components.

Although the precise form of a conflict management plan will be determined by the particular situation, a strategy should pay careful attention to the following management components:

- Finding a common definition of the problem.
- Determining mutually satisfactory procedures for carrying out a negotiation.

- Identifying the issues and interests of each of the parties.
- Developing a range of options for solving the problem.
- Agreeing on a solution.
- Deciding exactly how agreements will be implemented.

Principle 4. Progress Demands Positive Working Relationships

Although accurate and consistent data are needed to understand complex public issues, data alone will not resolve them. Information is of little value unless people are able to use it to solve a problem. Parties in a dispute must be willing to exchange information, make agreements, and keep their word. But people who are caught up in the dynamics of conflict reach a point where they stop talking with each other. This happens both because it becomes distasteful to talk with adversaries and because communication with the other side may be viewed with suspicion by one's own associates. Of course, when the flow of information between the parties ceases, it becomes difficult for them to clarify perceptions and transmit or receive new data needed to solve a problem. The parties cannot discuss alternatives or make adjustments. Instead, they generate information that promotes their own positions and convey it, often with irritating inaccuracies, through outside parties or the news media. When a conflict has become seriously polarized, even useful and accurate information is received with distrust and falls on deaf ears.

The destructive consequences of hostile relationships were evident when a state department of health was attempting to resolve a community water quality problem. People in the community, alarmed that their drinking water might not be safe, thought they were not getting adequate help from the state. As time went on, their alarm turned to fear. The rhetoric turned nasty, and the department of health knew it had to do something to improve its relations with the community. It assigned a young lawyer to explain the procedures the department was following to solve the problem. He assured the community that everything was under control. Unfortunately, the lawyer's patronizing style only increased the citizens' anger.

They began to attack the lawyer and the agency, accusing them of incompetence. Finally, the lawyer was replaced by someone who was more sensitive to the concerns of the community. When the residents felt they were working with someone they could trust, they agreed to sit down with the state's technical staff and work out solutions to the problem.

The words people use have a strong influence on their relationships. Adversaries cannot break off from fighting while they are exchanging verbal blows. People in conflicts readily agree that verbal attacks prevent progress and increase hostilities, but once they start trading insults it is hard to stop. Yet the rhetoric must cease before negotiations can begin. Sooner or later the parties must start to trust each other if commitments are to be made and solutions found.

Other sections of the book address methods for creating and preserving working relationships (see Chapters Eight and Ten for specific recommendations). The point here is that while technical information is important, equal attention must be given to human relationships.

Principle 5. Negotiation Begins with a Constructive Definition of the Problem

The parties must agree on what the problem is before they start resolving it. The preliminary review of the dispute will almost certainly turn up some disagreements about issues and causes. Often, reaching an agreement on the central issue that should be addressed is the first problem and the first success of a negotiation.

It is important to avoid using a problem statement that can be answered with a "yes" or a "no." The people in the village (see Chapter Two) first asked, "Shall we build a new hotel?" Some said "yes," some said "no," and the battle was joined. They began to make progress when they backed off and posed the problem as "What is the best use of the vacant land?" and "How do we provide accommodations for visitors?" They got down to business when they decided that they clearly needed a hotel in town and that what they really wanted to talk about was what the hotel should look like.

Whenever possible, an issue should be defined as a mutual problem to be solved, perhaps as a description that synthesizes several definitions, or conversely, as a potentially solvable part of a broader set of issues.

Another case illustrates the importance of thinking through the definition. At issue was a federal ban on the use of Compound 1080, a poison used to kill coyotes. Compound 1080 was banned by the federal government because it also killed eagles and other wildlife. After the ban was imposed, woolgrowers, who already had many serious economic problems, complained that they were losing more lambs. The contending parties had to decide whether the problem was (a) whether or not to use 1080, (b) how to kill coyotes, or (c) how to save lambs. Each issue required a particular mix of parties at the negotiating table and a different set of technical resources. It was necessary to select one of the three issues as the explicit focus of the discussions to prevent the entire effort from breaking down into irrelevant quarrels over divergent goals.

Principle 6. Parties Should Help Design the Process and Solution

A government or industry manager has final responsibility for finding a solution. But the way he or she approaches the decision may well determine whether the solution can be carried out. Asking for opinions and then issuing a directive misses the opportunity to place some of the responsibility for reaching a satisfactory conclusion on the shoulders of the contending parties. And if a manager does not share information with the parties, they are unlikely to understand fully what the alternatives may be. As a consequence, they may oppose even the most reasonable solution proposed by the manager.

It is tempting for a program manager to try to "sell" his or her solution. People who work closely with a problem as part of their daily responsibilities are likely to see a sensible way to solve it. They are frequently surprised by the diversity and intensity of opposition aroused by what they thought were clearly the right decisions. Sometimes after they have done everything right—consulted with all the people involved and developed a plan that meets the wishes of the parties—everyone attacks them

anyway. The unfortunate manager can only puzzle over the un-
fairness of it all: "I just can't understand why they don't like
my proposal. I listened carefully to all the sides and came out
with what I think is the best solution possible."

One federal land manager told us about a dispute over
livestock grazing rights on public lands. For more than a decade,
ranchers had fought over the control of a tract of land. The land
manager had spent several years trying to persuade the parties
to adopt a "reasonable" solution—his solution—and was totally
frustrated that neither side would accept it. Instead, the parties
continued to pursue an exhausting, unproductive quarrel. The
irony is that if the manager had brought them together and
asked them to work out a proposal for what should be done,
they probably would have come up with an answer similar to
his. But they were not brought into the decision process until
too late. Someone else had decided what the issues were and
how they should be addressed. The parties had no personal
stake in the method of making the decision, which made it easy
for them to stand aside, arms folded, and criticize *the manager's*
approach. It often happens that people are so put off by being
told what the decision is going to be, rather than being involved
in making the decision, that they reject it regardless of its merits
(see "The Solomon Trap" in Chapter Two).

Principle 7. Lasting Solutions Are Based on Interests, Not Positions

Traditionally, each side in a negotiation takes a position
knowing that it will not get all that it asks for. The positions become realities in themselves separate from the original issues.
The positions, not the problem, determine the direction of the
bargaining, especially if they have been stated publicly. The
negotiators sit around a table and bargain away chips one by
one. The side that has the greatest staying power gives away the
fewest chips and wins, at least for the moment. Each side progressively gives up things that it had previously insisted it must
keep. But positions are a poor foundation on which to build a
successful resolution of differences, composed as they are of

anxieties, resentments, desires, public pronouncements, face-saving, and playing to constituents. Positions limit the range of opportunities for solutions.

For years, a land management agency wanted to place a new ranger station in a remote section of its management area. People in a small community nearby strongly resisted the plan and were able to block it politically. Agency personnel could not understand why the local citizens were so opposed to a proposal intended to protect land that was important to the community. The agency manager happened to meet informally with a town leader over another matter and asked casually why the community had objected so adamantly to the construction of the ranger station. The answer was a shock: "Because you would put in an outsider as a ranger." "You mean that if we agreed to staff the station with a local person, you would accept a station?" the manager asked. "Sure" was the quick response. Shortly thereafter, the manager promised to appoint a local person, and the community dropped its opposition. In this case the dispute had come down to the question of which position would win and which would lose, and for a long time both sides lost.

An alternative way to find solutions is to persuade the parties to disengage for a moment and do something that will be unfamiliar and even uncomfortable at first: talk with each other about their interests—what they need in an agreement for it to be acceptable. Focusing on interests forces contending parties to back off from their stated positions and perform a straight-forward task—talking about themselves. When they talk about themselves, they lose their adversarial tone, and their opponents begin to understand why they have the positions they have. People in a dispute may have one position but many interests, some more important than others. The stand they take is often determined by a combination of motives rather than a single clear objective.

Most interests are reasonable and can be described. The realization that the other side's needs are not as outrageous as its apparent position can awaken hope that there may be a way to solve the problem. When the list is laid out for the group to review, and the adversaries hear what is said and consider the list, they often discover that in contrast to their stated positions, their interests are different but not mutually exclusive. This happens with surprising frequency, even in hot disputes. Efforts to solve the problem can be built on the realization that interests are not necessarily in conflict.

Issues surrounding national air quality regulations had become intensely polarized and the positions on every component entrenched when a federal commission convened a nationally representative group of business leaders, environmental advocates, and state and local regulators to explore alternative air quality procedures that all groups could live with. Early in the program, parties' positions were acknowledged, and participants were asked to be open to alternatives that might also satisfy their group's interests. At the workshop, participants met first in their respective interest groups. They were asked to list what they needed from a good regulation and then, in a separate discussion, what they thought each of the other two groups needed. The lists were posted for all workshop participants to see. Each group came remarkably close to describing the needs of the other two groups. While each group's interests were different, their interests were not mutually exclusive.

The process of listing interests is likely to be successful because it is uncomplicated and because talking about what they really need makes sense to people caught up in a conflict. In listing interests, the parties should be free to express their thoughts without challenge or criticism.

Principle 8. The Process Must Be Flexible

In any complex conflict situation, several management plans will appear to be feasible. A person conducting a program should be careful not to commit too early to an exact design. Time requirements, the cast of characters, perceptions of the issues, and many other elements may change as the separate components of the problem are analyzed and more clearly defined. During the first few months of the water roundtable (see Chapter Two), several participants vociferously insisted that the entire effort should take no more than six months. Others, looking at a history of four decades of conflict, thought it would require at least two years. The consensus was that they should wait and see. As the dimensions of the problems emerged, it became clear to everyone that much more time than six months would be required to collect and analyze data, negotiate agreements, and carry them out.

In another situation parties agreed to try to resolve a long-standing municipal zoning controversy. They outlined the six issues that they felt needed to be covered and proposed an order in which the issues would be addressed. Halfway through the discussions a participant suggested that another issue be added to the list, and the parties nodded in agreement. It seemed to make sense to them. However, the city planner convening the session was worried that the parties were establishing a bad precedent. He told participants that it was too late to add items to the agenda because it would throw off their already tight schedule. Participants sat politely through the remainder of the meeting. When, after the meeting, they were not able to persuade the planner to change his mind, they boycotted the next negotiation session. The planner then had two choices: to add the issue to the agenda or to abandon the negotiation effort. He chose the former and the parties were able to work out an agreement.

Flexibility does not imply haphazard management. A process manager always operates with a carefully thought out plan, but a plan that evolves with the discussions of the issues and with changes in relationships among the parties. The group may decide, for example, that additional parties should be represented, that technical or legal expertise is required, that a system of subcommittees can best handle certain issues, or that additional research is necessary to resolve data discrepancies. A process plan is a preliminary blueprint that gives initial direction but is continuously modified as more appropriate or specific methods are identified. Flexibility allows smooth adjustment to changing circumstances.

Principle 9. Think Through What Might Go Wrong

To most people, planning a meeting means deciding what they want to accomplish and laying out procedures for getting there. They tend to devote much less attention to what might go wrong. Something almost certainly will go wrong, because negotiation is a dynamic process. People change their minds and their behavior. They may unexpectedly become more conciliatory, and a topic that enraged them last week will no longer seem important. Or an approach that was acceptable a month ago may become controversial. Something that someone said between meetings can be so offensive that one of the parties threatens to leave the table.

Anticipating exactly who will produce a surprise and what it will be is difficult, but it is possible and highly advisable to explore, alone or with colleagues, the range of problems that might arise and how to handle them. Each approach will have its advantages and disadvantages. It is best to discuss possibilities in advance and agree on guidelines for acceptable and unacceptable responses. An advance decision about how far one is willing to go to accommodate a sudden change in direction will prevent long uncomfortable silences while the manager tries to figure out what to do next.

When problems do occur, the manager will be prepared to make suggestions to move the process along. Before a meeting he or she might have the following discussion with a colleague: "I hope Joe won't bring up that old argument again, but if he does, we can't let it discourage everyone else. If it comes up, we will call a break and talk to Joe about it." "I think that Alice is a lot madder than she is letting on. I bet she will go after the state people in the meeting. We had better remind everybody about the ground rules and that we intend to enforce them as soon as we open the meeting."

On the other hand, it may be time to apply a part of the strategy that forces the parties to take responsibility for their progress. It may be the moment when a meeting manager turns to the group and says, "All right, how do you want to handle this?" This kind of strategy call is much easier to make if it is an option that has been identified in advance.

Principle 10. Do No Harm

Primum non nocere—"first do no harm"—is a guiding principle of the medical profession. It should also be a precept of conflict management, which exists to help people solve problems, not create new ones. We address a portion of this topic in the section "Personal Risk" (Chapter Ten), but the issue is broader than just the need to protect individuals from harm. Ill-conceived conflict management programs can raise controversies into higher levels of destructiveness, damaging the interests of many people and making resolution much more difficult.

Some years ago, a federal agency was faced with the dilemma of determining which parcels of federal land within one state should be designated as wilderness areas. The notion of using a consensus process appealed to the agency because it offered the prospect of bringing together conflicting parties who would sit down and determine the best designation for each parcel of land. That was the hope. The reality was that the agency allowed itself only twelve weeks to achieve its mission. Within that period the agency expected to identify all the parties; then, with the parties, determine what constituted consensus; and finally reach consensus on each of over 200 areas.

At the end of the twelve-week project, the agency not only did not have its consensus, but it had created a group of angry citizens who were more frustrated after having participated in the process than they had been before it began. They did not have enough time to perform any of the essential steps: identify critical issues, establish criteria for determining designations, and systematically review each of the areas to determine which designation it should receive. Instead, parties became angry, suspicious, and hostile toward one another and toward the sponsoring agency. Consensus building acquired a bad name in the state. More than five years later people who were involved in that program still said that they would have nothing to do with any type of a "consensus process" because it did them more harm than good.

Conflict management programs must be carefully structured so that adequate time is allowed to organize the program properly, identify the key parties, and develop an appropriate process. Unless sufficient attention is given to a constructive process, important working relationships may be damaged and trust among the parties destroyed. If the job cannot be done properly, it should not be attempted.

Part Two

A Step-By-Step
Process for Managing
Public Disputes

 The following four chapters present a step-by-step process for managers and others who are faced with public conflict in their jobs or who are asked by others to help them resolve their differences. The process is divided into three phases of conflict management: preparing a plan, conducting a program, and carrying out agreements (see Exhibit 1). Chapters Four and

Exhibit 1. A Process for Managing Public Disputes.

Preparing a Plan
- Analyze the conflict
- Design a strategy
- Set up a program

Conducting a Program
- Adopt procedures
- Educate parties
- Develop options
- Reach agreements

Carrying Out Agreements
- Establish a monitoring system
- Work out details
- Renegotiate sections
- Handle violations

Five describe activities associated with preparing a plan; Chapter Six and the first half of Chapter Seven address steps for conducting a program; and the remainder of Chapter Seven discusses carrying out agreements.

While we recommend strongly that anyone embarking on some form of conflict management program consider carefully the suggestions in these four chapters, we also recognize that it is sometimes difficult or even impossible for a manager in the middle of a dispute to carry out every component as suggested. Externally imposed deadlines, for example, will influence the amount of time that can be spent preparing for a program, and, if a manager's organization is viewed as the cause of a problem, it will be difficult for someone on the staff to conduct interviews. The suggested process is intended to be used as a set of guidelines for people who have the responsibility for managing public disputes. It can be used as the basis for a staff discussion about strategy or referred to as a personal tick list. Whether managers and their professional staffs prepare and conduct the programs themselves or elect to bring in outside assistance for all or part of the work, they must understand the components of an effective program. We urge that every step be considered and followed as far as possible.

Preparing a Plan

In the complexity and uncertainty of public disputes, the more attention given at the beginning to preparing a conflict management program, the better the chances of a successful outcome. The preparation stage involves all the activities that occur prior to bringing parties together for face-to-face discussions. Preparation is divided into three components: analyzing the conflict, designing a strategy, and setting up a program. Managers analyze conflict to gather information and draw conclusions about a problem, then design a resolution strategy to fit a particular issue. Finally, they initiate activities necessary to set up a program.

Conducting a Program

Conflicting parties sometimes assume that if they can just sit down and talk about their problem, they will come up with a solution. And if the parties are few and the issue simple, they may be successful. It is more likely, however, that parties who do not establish and follow a logical progression of steps will focus prematurely on solutions without understanding the problem or what other people need in a solution. Enormous amounts of time will be consumed justifying solutions that do not address the interests of the other side. The potential for agreement may be lost entirely. Four sequential steps offer a constructive process: adopting procedures, educating parties, developing options, and reaching agreements.

Carrying Out Agreements

Too often parties get lost in the relief of reaching an agreement and fail to specify how agreements will be implemented. Despite the best of intentions, commitments are often not kept because no one is sure how to fulfill them. People feel let down and begin accusing each other of bad faith. Relationships among parties deteriorate, and another round of conflict begins. Parties must establish procedures for carrying out their agreements that include ways to monitor, adjust, and enforce them.

4

Analyzing the Conflict

Public disputes are rarely as simple as they first appear. Under the pressure of conflict and the need to find a solution, people in conflict tend to focus immediately on what seems to be the substance of the controversy and try to deal with it, without realizing that woven into any dispute are a mix of personal agendas, tensions between organizations, good and bad relationships between individuals, and a history of previous encounters that color current activities. A thorough understanding of the situation leads to a management strategy designed for the specific components of a dispute and, in turn, to lasting solutions.

Conflict analysis involves three steps: preliminary review, collecting information, and assessing information. Whether conducted by a manager's staff or a third party, conflict analysis should take into account the considerations outlined in this chapter.

Making a Preliminary Review

"We need some help with a problem we have here in the county. This thing could get nasty if we let it go on much longer, and we want to get the people together and see if we can solve it now. Can you give us a hand?"

"What's going on?"

This imaginary telephone conversation between a county commissioner and the manager of a state agency is the way it begins. The commissioner calls the manager because he or she has demonstrated a willingness to provide help in handling controversial situations in the past or, perhaps, because the manager's agency has administrative responsibility for some aspect

71

of the problem. At any rate, the manager embarks on what we call a preliminary review. The discussion could continue as follows:

"We have been arguing with the Forest Service for months about an old abandoned railroad station. It sits on Forest Service land near a trail between two lakes. The trail is used a lot in the summer and the Forest Service is concerned about people making a mess of the area and possibly getting hurt climbing around on the building. We understand their problems, and we agree that something has to be done. But, as county commissioners, we are under a lot of pressure from two directions. Railroad buffs and historic preservation people want us to protect the building and control access to the land. On the other hand, the tourist shop and grocery store owners, who are there because of the lakes, say the building is too far gone and ought to be torn down. Everybody, including the Forest Service, likes the old building and would be sorry to have it go, but we can't agree on what has to be done."

"How do the different groups feel about each other?"

"Well, nobody is really mad yet, but they are getting anxious because the Forest Service has a budget problem coming up and they may not have the money to do anything after October."

"What about the railroad buffs?"

"Well, a national railroad club is having a tour here next fall and the station is one of the star attractions. Several years ago, a railroad artist painted a picture of the station and a lot of people have seen it on calendars."

"Do you think we could get people together to talk about what should be done?"

"Yes, I think folks would be willing to do that."

When someone calls to talk about a problem, a conversation such as this is likely to unfold. The manager gathers pieces of information about the situation and puts them together into a preliminary understanding of who is involved, what they are concerned about, and the parties' interest in resolving their differences. Questions are asked without conveying any opinion about the people or the issues, in light of the fact that, no matter how congenial a relationship may be with the person at the other end of the telephone line, he or she may be dead wrong about the problem. The parties, for example, may turn out to be a lot madder at each other than the county commissioner thinks they are. It is extremely important not to leap to conclusions after one or two conversations and to be cautious about next steps. Talking to the wrong people first—those who everybody knows are at the extreme end of the range of opinion—and asking questions that give the impression of being biased may set into motion a system of suspicion and hostility that will destroy personal credibility and any hope that conflict management techniques will help the parties solve their problem (Curle, 1971).

Additional information is obtained from written documents—newspaper and magazine articles and government reports—and from discussions with people who are familiar with the situation. It is preferable to talk first with people who are knowledgeable about the problem but are not directly involved as central players. Being less involved in the dynamics of the dispute, they are likely to give a more objective overview of the situation. Also, at this early stage, before a "license to operate" has been obtained, it is risky to talk to primary parties, who may see an outsider as meddling in their affairs—unless, of course, the caller has a direct responsibility for solving the problem. If a manager happens to know some of the individuals personally, he or she can chat informally with them about their perceptions of what is happening, but even with a personal relationship, it is a good idea to be careful about what is said.

After talking with a few people, a manager may decide that more information is needed or that the request for help is simply someone's nervous reaction to a temporary difficulty and that the problem will be solved without assistance. It can also become clear that one person's hope for resolution through the use of conflict management techniques is unrealistic under the circumstances. The parties may have decided that they must go to court to set a legal precedent, and they may be correct in doing so. Or one party may be so determined to defeat another that they could not possibly negotiate with each other. Sometimes the conditions in which negotiations would have to take place would put the parties at risk. For example, there may not be enough time to carry out a program, and the parties would simply confront each other publicly with no opportunity to work out their differences. Or, as happens quite often, the parties would begin negotiation just before elections in which some of the key individuals might be replaced, making any agreements reached in negotiations impossible to implement.

If a preliminary review reveals that parties are not interested in any form of conflict resolution, the expense of a full-scale analysis has been saved (Wondolleck, 1986). If people are interested in solving the problem, a preliminary review helps a manager structure a more thorough analysis with a basic sense of the conflict and who the players are. In further interviews, the manager will appear knowledgeable (but not an expert) about the problem, rather than uninformed.

Collecting Information

The first step in a formal analysis is to collect detailed information about the dispute. Often people assume that if they understand the substantive issues they will be able to find a reasonable solution to their problem, but conflicts are a mixture of people, procedures, and substance. If one group distrusts another or thinks the process being proposed is unfair, a substantive agreement will be difficult to reach no matter how reasonable a proposed solution might be. Information must be collected about all elements of conflict—people, procedures, and substance—if a satisfactory resolution is to be found. In the game damage case described in Chapter Two, the woolgrowers were interviewed about their perspective on the issue. Most of them were of Greek extraction, and one said jokingly, "What we need up there is a Greek game warden." In a pleasant way, he was saying that any resolution of the dispute over damage payments would have to include a change in the way agency field representatives dealt with the public. In later discussions, agency management acknowledged the importance of improving this part of the game damage program.

Determining What Information Is Needed

Before beginning to collect information, the manager must review what he or she already knows about the conflict. Is it clear who the primary parties are and what additional parties might have a stake in the outcome? Have the spokespeople for each group been identified? What is the history and what are the current dynamics of the controversy? What issues are central to each of the major parties? How does each side see the problem? What additional information is needed to understand the situation? The manager cannot assume that information acquired a month ago is still current. He or she must check out facts and pursue areas where information is lacking, keeping in mind that conflict situations are dynamic and that people's perceptions of the problem and of each other are apt to change rapidly under stress.

Identifying Sources of Information

Information about a conflict is gathered from three sources: direct observation, secondary sources, and personal interviews. A combination of all three is used to assess a major conflict.

Direct Observation. Observing how individuals conduct themselves and hearing how they talk about the issues and the other parties is extremely useful but may be difficult if there is a great deal of tension and suspicion. It is often valuable to attend meetings of the interested groups, who will usually invite an outsider if the purpose of the visit is made clear. Sometimes it is possible to attend open meetings where the parties run through their customary methods of dealing with each other, a valuable experience because it gives one a clear view of the special little twists that people put on their comments and the reactions they get from their targets. Very often, parties who want to have a dispute resolved will welcome a manager's initiative as a sign that someone is interested in their side of the issue. When-

ever possible, it is desirable for a manager to attend meetings
held by several different sides, not just one. It is essential not to
comment at a meeting about the substance of the dispute or
show support for one point of view.

Secondary Sources. Secondary sources include minutes of
meetings, private or public reports, tape-recorded or videotaped
events, research conducted on the issues, newspaper and magazine articles, and other written, oral, or visual materials that
provide information about a conflict. Secondary sources should
be read, if possible, before conducting personal interviews. They
offer useful background information about the chronology of
the dispute and the dynamics between parties.

Personal Interviews. Of the three sources of information
about conflict, personal interviews provide the richest detail
about a situation. If people being interviewed trust the interviewer, they are likely to give more varied perspectives and a
greater sense of the subtleties of the issue than can be obtained
through direct observation or from secondary sources. Personal
interviews are a means for cross-checking other people's perspectives and for sorting out differences.

Interviews also offer an opportunity to introduce and discuss the possibility of using an alternative method for resolving
a controversy:

"We're considering bringing the sides together to talk
about their differences. Do you think your group would be interested in participating?"

"Yes, but we would have to be assured that the other side
won't attack us."

"If we established a ground rule to that effect, would
that help?"

"Yes, I think so."

Interviews provide the opportunity to establish rapport
with each person interviewed. The credibility built during the
initial interviews will be important if the manager plans to work
with the parties later on.

Conducting Interviews

Selecting People to Be Interviewed. The manager must be selective about the individuals to be interviewed, since it is unlikely that there will be time to interview everyone who is involved in a public conflict. One should begin by identifying the categories of parties, such as government agencies, business concerns, and citizen interest groups. The next step is to list specific organizations involved in the conflict that fall under each category. The final task is to identify at least one person from each of the major organizations. If different points of view in an organization become evident, more than one person should be chosen for interviewing.

A manager should also identify opinion makers in the community—people to whom others go for advice. Even though they are not directly involved in the controversy, they can provide a valuable overview of what is happening, and they can suggest others who should be interviewed. A sense of how the community operates can be essential in designing an effective conflict management strategy, but this information is not always easy to obtain. A community relations manager for a federal agency found this out when she tried to resolve a growing dispute between her agency and a small community. Her predecessor in the job had several personality imperfections, one of which was that he usually said indiscreet things to the wrong people. As a result, he had managed to alienate the community. The new manager was baffled by her inability to organize a working session with residents to discuss methods for improving communication between the community and her agency. The mayor and the village council seemed to think it was a good idea and said they would participate, but she could never quite reach a point where they would set a date. She asked people in state government who she knew had been working on other programs in the village how she could find out what she was doing wrong. Their advice was to talk to a retired state senator who lived in the area and knew everybody in town. She called him and set up an appointment. Sitting in his kitchen, she received a short course on how the system really operated. He told her that the mayor and the council had long since backed away from the issue she was concerned about and had turned over complete control to four very outspoken people who had formed their own committee. He said, "Nothing will move until you go and talk with them and they give you their approval."

The purpose of deliberately selecting a wide range of people to interview is to get a sound cross section of opinions from different perspectives. People from dissimilar groups will describe the issues and causes differently, and it is not unusual for individuals within the same organization to hold varied opinions of the problem as well. The manager must be careful to avoid the interviewer's trap of believing likable people and disregarding the opinions of less-appealing people.

Choosing an Appropriate Person to Conduct the Interviews. A professional staff member can conduct interviews if the agency or individual is not seen as the cause of the problem. If either is viewed as substantially involved, however, the manager will probably have to find a person or organization that has no stake in the problem to conduct the interviews.

Age, sex, race, professional status, and previous relationships with an interviewee can influence how much information the interview will produce. The more comfortable a person feels with the person gathering information, the more useful the responses will be. Interviewers should think about their dress, speech, and manners and their effect on the person being interviewed. What one chooses to wear to visit a rancher at his home will probably be different from what one wears to interview the president of a large metropolitan bank. In one case a staff person from a federal agency on the East Coast was sent to interview residents of a small rural western town. He arrived in brand new cowboy boots and hat, flannel shirt, and blue jeans. He looked awkward, foolish, and totally out of place. The reactions of local people varied from amusement to offense at the naive stereotyping. While the best rule is to be oneself, there are no clear rules about when to adjust that principle to fit the realities of the situation. The interviewer should dress in what would normally be worn in a given situation. If the interview setting is informal, the preferred attire is casual clothes. On the other hand, Saul Alinsky's caution in *Rules for Radicals* is worth thinking about: "If I were organizing in an orthodox Jewish community I would not walk in there eating a ham sandwich" (Alinsky, 1971).

The interviewer must preserve absolute impartiality on the substantive issues of the dispute. When people ask for an opinion about the problem, the interviewer must be cautious about answering, because any indication of bias will jeopardize his or her ability to manage a dispute resolution program.

The interviewer should also be a good listener and avoid temptation to say too much just to keep the conversation going. If a person is reluctant to talk, the interviewer should relax and let the other person pick a comfortable pace. It is important not to push too hard for information. After all, the interviewer is there by the courtesy of the person being interviewed.

Finally, the interviewer must be capable of keeping confidences. Once the trust of the interviewee is gained, the interviewer may suddenly be startled to find that he or she is being handed more privileged information than bargained for, information that could damage the speaker's job or position in a group if it were ever revealed.

Selecting the Sequence of Interviews. The advantages of talking first with people not directly involved in the dispute are that the interviewer will probably get a more objective view of the situation and that the information given will help avoid talking with the wrong people or asking the wrong questions. It is important not to spend too much time with any one party early in the interview schedule, or the interviewer runs the risk of being identified with that side of the argument. After meeting with people outside the dispute, the interviewer should begin talking with members of the conflicting parties.

Deciding What Questions to Ask. Since conversations seldom go exactly as planned, the interviewer must think through in advance which questions are important to cover in an interview. General categories include:

- What is your view of the situation?
- What issues are important to you (your group)?
- What other individuals or groups are involved?
- Who else should I be talking to (on all sides)?
- How do you think this problem can be resolved?

After asking these open-ended questions, the interviewer should consider questions that help refine or clarify a response or that summarize what has been said. For example, after listening to the answer to the question, "What is your view of the situation?" the interviewer might say, "So your view of this problem is _____?" giving the person a chance to confirm or clarify the summary. After the question "How do you think this problem can be solved?" an interviewer might pursue more detailed questions about a conflict management program.

Establishing a Format for the Interview. The opening few minutes of an interview are spent establishing the credibility of the interviewer and explaining the purpose of the visit. The interviewer describes his or her background and role in the program and explains how the interview fits into a larger effort. The opening should be kept brief unless the respondent asks more questions about the interviewer's credentials.

The bulk of the interview will focus on questions regarding the nature of the conflict. The interviewer asks people to clarify and elaborate when appropriate, and summarizes their comments to them to be sure that what they have said has been correctly understood.

As the time approaches for the conversation to end, the interviewer should check with the person to see whether he or she has anything to add to what has already been said. The person should be thanked for his or her help and time. Following is an example of how such an interview might sound:

Interviewer: I appreciate you taking the time to see me today. As I explained on the telephone, the planning department is concerned about the problem between the residents of Shadywood and the Sheridan developers. I have been asked to talk with individuals who are concerned about the proposal so I can understand the issues and see if there might be a way to deal with the differences. Can you tell me what you think about the current proposal to develop the downtown river area?

Resident: We don't like this plan. As you probably know, our neighborhood association has been concerned about development along the river for the past five years. We've made it very clear that we don't want to see any development next to the river.

Interviewer: So you're opposed to any development that might go in along the river downtown?

Resident: Yes, we see that stretch of land as the only place left in the downtown area where we can preserve some open space. Everything else looks like it is going to be developed.

Interviewer: Preserving land along the river downtown for open space is important. What other objections do you have to the proposed project?

Resident: Well, the traffic on the roads in that area is terrible today. Imagine what it would be like if they put in that large development. It would take us an extra fifteen minutes to get out of the downtown area every night.

Interviewer: So traffic is another issue. Do you have others?

Resident: That developer gives me problems. He can't be trusted. His figures are way off and he says one thing one day and another thing the next. He probably wouldn't follow his plans if they ever got approved.

Interviewer: Can you give me an example of what he has done?

Resident: Yes, we invited him to come to our neighborhood association meeting and he refused. He's always so arrogant when we try to get information from him.

Interviewer: If we arranged a meeting for people concerned about the development, including the developer, would you be willing to come?

Resident: I guess so. I can tell him why we're opposed to the plan, but I bet he won't come.

Interviewer: You've been most helpful. Before I go are there any other people you think I ought to see?

The resident named several people who had been actively opposing the project. The interviewer thanked the resident for her help and asked whether it would be possible to call again if the planning department needed more information.

Listening for Useful Points. An interviewer asks open-ended questions to help the speaker talk about the problem—questions that cover general topics related to the conflict. At the same time, an interviewer listens for information that will provide additional insights into the parties, the dynamics of the dispute, and the substantive issues.

For example, an elected official may be keen on getting a solution to the problem because she is about to announce her candidacy for higher office and would like to use resolution of this conflict as an example of how well she manages problems. If the dispute is not resolved quickly, it could reflect poorly on her administration.

The interviewer should listen for information about main interest groups currently involved in the controversy and other groups that may become involved later. The interviewer should also determine the roles individuals play within their own organization and the influence they have inside and outside their group. It is important to identify how parties plan to use power and to note any information about values, attitudes, and motives that might influence the discussions. Also of interest will be how each group functions, how information is conveyed internally, and how decisions are made. The interviewer needs to listen for key issues and interests of each side and topics of secondary importance. (For a list of what to look for in an analysis, see Marcus and Emrich, 1981; Wehr, 1982.)

Recording the Information

A manager should decide in advance how ⸱⸱ information that will be gained in an interview. The two ⸱⸱ common methods are written notes and tape recording. Writing during an interview requires that the interviewer split his or her attention between the person being interviewed and taking notes. Some guidelines for taking written notes are:

- Be conscious of the comfort level of the person being interviewed. If the person is tense, take few notes.
- Explain to the person that the notes are strictly for personal use and that they will not be seen by anyone else (if that is true).
- Use key words, abbreviations, and other forms of shorthand to help minimize writing. After completing an interview, talk into a tape recorder as soon as possible and fill in details that were not captured in the interview.
- Maintain eye contact with the person as much as possible. Do not get lost in note taking.
- Take a few minutes before the end of the interview to read the notes and verify their accuracy.
- In the more complex controversies, consider bringing two people to the interview, one to take notes and the other to ask questions. The tasks can be alternated during the interview.

Tape recording is an efficient system for gathering information but may have the disadvantage of inhibiting the person being interviewed. The interviewer should ask the person for permission to use a tape recorder and should explain how the tape will be used and who will have access to it. The person should be told that the tape can be turned off at any point, particularly if a sensitive topic is covered. After each interview, the interviewer would be wise to capture the information gained in one interview before going into the next, so that major and subtle points are not lost, especially if they were not recorded during the conversation.

Completing an interview information sheet (see Exhibit 2) after each interview helps standardize information and makes analysis much easier.

Exhibit 2. Interview Information Sheet.

Person (name, affiliation, title, role):

View of problem:

Issues (what they are, how important they are):

Interests:

Perception of other parties:

Comment about resolving conflict:

Special concerns:

Other comments:

Other Considerations

In-Person Versus Telephone Interviews. Interviews conducted in person are more effective than telephone interviews, for several reasons. It is easier to build personal understanding when meeting face to face, and the more confident a person feels about the interviewer, the more information he or she is likely to provide. Interviews conducted in person also provide an opportunity to observe the surroundings, such as photographs and other items that give clues to the person's interests and values, and to observe facial expressions and body movements.

A telephone interview is better than nothing, but the conversation should be thought through beforehand. The interviewer should expect the person at the other end of the telephone line to be wary, especially if he or she does not know the interviewer. One should not be surprised if the conversation begins with a hostile tone. At the end of the conversation, the interviewer should spend some time reviewing what has been said so that the other person understands that he or she has been heard.

Timing. A time should be chosen that is convenient for the person being interviewed. The interviewer needs to be explicit about how much time the interview will take and should not exceed that amount of time without asking permission. One might say, for example, "I have taken forty-five minutes of your time. Thank you so much for your help." The interviewee will either make a move to close the discussion or will offer to continue the interview.

Location. The interview location should be a place that is convenient and comfortable for the interviewee and where a conversation is least likely to be interrupted or overheard. The interviewer should consider asking the person to select a place to meet.

Assessing the Information

An efficient way of organizing the collected material into a consistent pattern is to use three tools: the conflict analysis chart, the conflict dynamics continuum, and the conflict analysis summary. They form a systematic method of reviewing and evaluating a great deal of heterogeneous information.

Organizing the Information

Information about the controversy may be in the form of handwritten notes, printed materials, typed memos, or recorded tapes. If several people are involved in gathering information, they should share information with each other as they go along.

Filling out a conflict analysis chart (see Exhibit 3) will help organize the information. Here are guidelines for using the chart:

1. Begin by listing a party, then fill out all the remaining columns with information about it, its issues and interests, how important each issue is to the party (of high, medium, or low importance), what its sources of power are, what if any positions it has taken, what options it supports, and whether the party is interested in resolving the dispute.

2. In the "Other Comments" column, note other pieces of information important to the conflict that came out in interviews or from other sources. For example, a city council may be reluctant to negotiate an issue until elections are held, or some people may hold deep resentment toward others because of the way they were treated in the past. Refer to "Listening for Useful Points" earlier in this chapter for additional topics to include.

3. When the columns are filled in for one party, begin with another and work across the columns again.

The completed chart provides a detailed list of the parties, their issues, and their interests. The information will suggest how to proceed with a conflict management effort. At this point it is useful to write out a timeline, noting significant events such as major decisions that affect the controversy, future decision deadlines, critical meetings or events, and interventions made by other parties.

Next, a conflict dynamics continuum can be used to identify the dynamics in a conflict. One should read through the four choices under each category in Exhibit 4 and mark with an "x" the place on the line that comes closest to characterizing the overall dynamics of the dispute. A comment line is provided at the bottom of each category for remarks about special situations or conditions that are exceptions to the rating. For example, if nine of the ten parties are interested in working out solutions to a problem and one party is not, the factor may receive a 2 rating ("Want to find a solution that protects interests of

Exhibit 3. Conflict Analysis Chart.

Parties	Issues	Interests	Importance of issues (high, medium, low)	Sources of power/ influence	Positions/ Options	Interested in working with other parties	Other comments

Exhibit 4. Conflict Dynamics Continuum.

A.   Attitudes Toward Resolving the Conflict

```
1                    2                    3                    4
```

4.   Want to win at any cost. Have absolutely no interest in collaboration.
3.   Want to pursue an adversarial course to maximize individual gains.
2.   Want to find a solution that protects interests of parties.
1.   Want to terminate the dispute no matter what the cost.
Comments:

B.   Attitude Toward Solutions

```
1                    2                    3                    4
```

4.   Positions are entrenched. No apparent room for movement.
3.   Parties advocate own solution but are open to discussing others.
2.   A number of solutions have been identified and discussed. Parties are not wedded to specific positions.
1.   No positions have been proposed publicly or privately.
Comments:

C.   History of the Relationships

```
1                    2                    3                    4
```

4.   Hostile relationships. Bitter clashes in the past.
3.   Competitive interests pursued through intermediaries or agents. Adversarial, but not hostile relationship.
2.   Routine business, professional, or social contact with no adversarial activity.
1.   No previous contact.
Comments:

D.   Current Feelings About Each Other

```
1                    2                    3                    4
```

4.   Openly hostile toward each other. Vengeful. Desire to win at any cost.
3.   Divisions clear, sides formed. Suspicions carried over to other aspects of relationships. Reluctance to talk with people of opposing views.

Exhibit 4. Conflict Dynamics Continuum, Cont'd.

---

2. Mild distrust of each other. Each questions motives of others.
1. Respect among groups. No apparent reason for them to be suspicious.

Comments:

E. Role of Values

1	2	3	4

4. Values differences the focal point for the conflict.
3. Values differences important in the debate, but not the central issue.
2. Values differences exist, but not central to the controversy.
1. Parties' values similar.

Comments:

F. Investment in the Issue

1	2	3	4

4. Devoting most or all time to the issue. Diverting resources away from other projects. Taking career risks.
3. Committing personal and financial resources and time away from other work, incurring travel, communication, and material expenses.
2. Incurring minimal out-of-pocket expenses in gathering information, going to meetings, and engaging in research and discussion.
1. No costs incurred.

Comments:

G. Tactics Being Used to Deal with the Problem

1	2	3	4

4. Looking outside for support. Hiring professional agents (lawyers, public relations experts). Shutting off communication with other side. Attacking adversaries personally.
3. Writing letter to officials, stating public positions, committing resources, forming organizations.
2. Attending meetings, talking to officials and superiors, expressing opinions to news media, beginning to form sides.
1. Seeking information. Talking with friends and associates. Expressing concern.

Comments:

parties") on the "Attitudes Toward Resolving the Conflict" scale. One should note on the comment line which party is not interested and what effect this attitude will have.

The comparison of dynamics will give a picture of how polarized the conflict is and where the most serious problems lie. When the dynamics of a conflict have reached the fourth level in one area, it is likely they have also done so in other areas. The more categories that register a number 4 rating, the more difficult the conflict will be to resolve and the more time and care must be devoted to establishing relationships, building trust, and creating positive interaction among the parties.

Verifying the Information

After completing the charts, one should check for inconsistencies and gaps in the information. Contradictory information can happen because a person was misunderstood or, more likely, because people have different perceptions of the situation. Sometimes additional information is needed about a party or an issue before conclusions can be drawn. One may need to go back to people interviewed earlier to check out contradictions, or interview new people to gather additional information.

Interpreting the Information

The information is now organized into a pattern for interpretation of what has been learned about the people, the procedures they have used, and the issues in dispute. At this point one should identify areas of common interest and where conflicting views lie, how issues can be grouped, and how agreements can be put together. One should note special sensitivities people have about each other and about the issues. Finally, one should determine whether conflict management techniques will work. Are the parties interested in resolving the conflict? If they are, what form of management effort would make sense to them (Filley, 1975)?

One can use the questions in the conflict analysis summary (Exhibit 5) to help interpret the information contained in the conflict analysis chart and the conflict dynamics continuum.

Exhibit 5. Conflict Analysis Summary.

Parties
1. Who are the main parties and their key spokespeople?
2. Who are the secondary parties and their spokespeople?
3. Are the parties well defined?
4. Do the parties want to work toward a solution?
5. Are the parties capable of working with each other?

Substance of the Problem
6. What description best characterizes the conflict?
   a. Conflict focuses on different interests.
   b. Conflict focuses on strongly held values.
   c. Conflict focuses on perceived differences that do not really exist.
7. What is the most constructive way to define the problem?
8. What are the central issues?
9. What are the secondary issues?
10. Are the issues negotiable?
11. What are the key interests of each party?
12. What interests do parties have in common?
13. What positions have been taken?
14. What other options for resolution exist?

Procedures
15. What do parties think about using some form of conflict management? What suggestions do they have?
16. Does a consensus process serve the parties' interests?
17. What constraints might affect the structure of a conflict management process (timing, legal activities, resources)?
18. What other obstacles must a process overcome?
19. Which parties are experienced in using alternative dispute resolution procedures?
20. What are the chances for success?

A properly conducted conflict analysis lays the foundation for developing a conflict management plan. Time spent on analysis in the beginning will produce a better program. Keeping in mind that all conflict situations are dynamic, the manager should update the analysis throughout a conflict resolution program as new information is introduced and as people and their relationships change. Specific strategies for managing conflict will be discussed in the next chapter.

5

Designing a Strategy and Setting Up the Conflict Management Program

Analysis of the conflict will suggest whether or not using conflict management procedures is an appropriate way to handle a problem. If the parties are interested in discussing their differences and there is room for negotiation on the issue, the manager or other responsible person proceeds to complete the remaining two steps in the preparation phase: designing a strategy and setting up a program (see Exhibit 1, p. 67).

Although we list discrete tasks associated with each of the two steps, in practice these steps are conducted together as one unit. For example, activities associated with setting up a program frequently begin before all design tasks are completed, and, for political reasons, key individuals will be invited to participate in a project before the issue of appropriate roles is settled.

Designing a Strategy

Every conflict is different in some essential respects from all other conflicts. No simple process template fits neatly over all problems. Conflict management programs must be tailored to the particular characteristics of an issue and the parties who are involved. Approaches that work well for some people will be unattractive to others. An approach used in a rural area will frequently make no sense whatever in an urban area. In this chapter we offer a series of tasks to consider when designing a strategy and some ways to go about them:

1. Defining a problem.
2. Identifying external constraints.
3. Establishing a conflict management goal.
4. Selecting a meeting structure.
5. Identifying process steps.
6. Determining who should participate.
7. Defining other roles.
8. Considering other process issues.

Defining a Problem

In Chapter Three we emphasized the need to define the principal issues in terms that all parties can accept, remembering to avoid definitions that can be answered with a "yes" or "no" —questions like, "Should the city build a new airport?"—which accelerate conflict by forcing parties to choose sides. A more constructive approach is to begin a problem statement with a "how" or a "what": "How should the city deal with its current and future volume of air traffic?" A "how" or "what" question leads to developing a range of alternative solutions.

Working with the parties to define the problem begins in the analysis stage, when during an interview a question is asked such as, "How would you describe the problem?" If the person offers an either/or proposition, such as "Riverside needs another shopping mall," the interviewer could suggest an alternative, such as "What would you think about discussing the question of the future growth of the Riverside area?" Phrasing a suggestion in the form of an open-ended question encourages the other person to consider a broader range of solutions to the problem. When representatives of the three parties in the town and park dispute (Chapter Two) arrived at the meeting, they were prepared to do battle over the question "Should the park be expanded by 800 acres?" They had already expended substantial resources because of the implications of the answers to that question. Each had developed a vested interest in winning the fight, if for no other reason than to save face. But, as they talked about what they needed from a solution, they found to their amazement that they agreed more than they disagreed. They found that they should be devoting their energy and ingenuity to answering the question "How do we protect the ecological value of the land and preserve the character of the town?"

Parties often raise questions about the timing, the scope of the issues, or the geographic area that should be included in the discussions. For example, questions that might be asked about a growth controversy include: "How far in the future should we look, five years or twenty-five?" "Why do we have to limit this to commercial zoning? I'm concerned about the number of housing developments that are going in up there." "Why limit this to the Riverside area? I think that we should be looking at the whole county." The manager should test their suggestions, without attribution, with other parties who are likely to offer other perspectives on why a definition should be used or why a proposed change should be supported or opposed. After listening to what people are saying, the manager can make adjustments in the problem definition accordingly.

The problem itself often appears to be so obvious that spending time defining it seems a waste of effort. However, the precise definition has a strong influence on the development of the conflict management strategy. In some situations, the parties may readily agree on what the dispute is all about, but in others, they may disagree sharply on why they are arguing, and a substantial amount of time will be required to work out a satisfactory agreement on the definition. In the water roundtable case, the parties made a pivotal decision when they agreed that their efforts should address not the question, "Should the dam be built?" but rather "What is the best way of providing water to the city?" The latter opened up the debate to possibilities for solutions. They then spent weeks deciding what year (2010 or 2030) they should use as a reference point for their discussions.

Identifying External Constraints

External constraints on the parties must be considered in outlining a process. Does an organization have deadlines that will influence the pace of the discussions? Do other organizations need to have an agreement by a particular time? Are there active legal proceedings that affect the program? Are the appropriate people available to participate, or are they tied up in other matters? In one conflict over the future use of agricultural land in a county, discussions were suspended for several weeks in the spring because fruit growers had to work from dawn to dusk irrigating their fields and had no time to meet. Constraints of every kind should be identified and kept in mind as the plan develops.

Establishing a Conflict Management Goal

The next step is to determine a conflict management goal. Reaching an agreement may be the most obvious goal, but an analysis of the case may suggest others that are more appropriate. Conflict management goals include exchanging information, identifying issues and interests, developing acceptable options, and developing recommendations, as well as reaching agreements.

Exchanging Information. In the absence of information, people manufacture their own "facts." Disputes worsen when people do not have an opportunity to talk with one another about a problem. If an analysis suggests that parties do not have major substantive differences but do have serious misperceptions of each others' activities, a program designed to bring parties together to exchange information may be all that is required. On the other hand, the exchange of information can also be a component of a larger negotiation process (Carpenter and Kennedy, 1977).

In one case, a community became outraged when a company proposed to develop a mine near a populated narrow canyon road. The community translated the projected daily tonnage to be taken from the mine into the number of trucks required to haul the product. Before any details could be explained, the residents had begun writing angry letters to the editor of the local paper about the anticipated truck traffic. What the community did not know was that company plans called for building a railroad spur in the next canyon, where rail cars from the mine could link with existing train traffic, and there would be little truck traffic on the road. In this case a goal of negotiating agreements on project size, dust control, and safety signals would have been inappropriate. Instead, the residents needed an opportunity to hear directly from company representatives about their plans and decide how the project would affect them.

Identifying Issues and Interests. A group responsible for making a controversial decision can organize meetings to gather information about the issues, to find out what the issues really are, and to determine which issues are most important to the parties and why they are important. The group may not want to initiate more extensive discussions until the nature of the problem is clear. Gathering information about issues and interests may reveal insights into how the problem can be resolved, or it may suggest the need for additional conflict management activities. The scoping meetings for the airport case (see Chapter Two) were held for this purpose.

Developing Acceptable Options. When authority for making decision resides with one organization, it can invite parties on different sides of a controversy to sit down and develop options that will satisfy their respective interests. These options are conveyed back to the decision-making organization for its consideration. Simply identifying acceptable options may take less time than a full-fledged effort to develop recommendations or reach agreements, because, among other reasons, parties do not have to narrow options down to one and do not have to worry about final approval of their constituents.

Developing Recommendations. A more ambitious goal is to bring opposing sides together to develop joint recommendations. Here, a decision maker creates a structure for parties to educate each other about their views of the problem and to develop an acceptable solution. Parties focus on ways to solve the problem rather than on strategies to attack the initiating organization's proposal. The manager retains the right to make a final decision, but if the sides can agree on a recommendation, the decision maker gives it first priority. Government agencies have found this approach to be valuable in reaching decisions about controversial issues. In the game damage case, the "manager" with final responsibility was the state commission overseeing the activities of the Division of Wildlife. The members of the commission asked the parties to work out recommendations for changes in current statutes, which they, in turn, would take to the state legislature.

Reaching Agreements. The goal of reaching an agreement is addressed by an even more comprehensive program in which representatives of the parties come together to discuss a problem, educate each other, develop possible solutions, and agree on ways to resolve their differences. The purpose may be to negotiate agreement on a single solution to one problem or, as in the water roundtable, produce a series of answers to many interlocking issues. The process of following a sequence of management steps is essential to success, whether the problem is simple or highly complex.

Selecting a Meeting Structure

The meeting structure should support the conflict management goal. The four structures described here offer different ways to involve the parties and to set up a process. Large-scale disputes usually require more than one meeting structure.

Public Meetings. Meetings that are open to the public are useful for gathering information, for identifying issues and interests, and for soliciting suggestions for alternatives. They are not effective for developing recommendations or reaching formal agreements, because there is no opportunity to develop ideas and adjust positions.

Public meetings can be organized as an open-discussion, town meeting arrangement in which participants talk with each other and ask questions of other speakers, or they can be set up with a more formal structure, such as a public hearing, where only the people conducting the meeting are permitted to ask questions. The latter style of meeting tends to become a ritualistic series of short, pungent statements without adjustment in competing positions.

Public meetings may be used in conjunction with negotiation sessions when public response and acceptance of a proposed course of action are desired. The public can be involved early in the identification and review of issues, and it can participate later by commenting on solutions proposed by negotiators. Negotiators in the water roundtable held public meetings early in the program to solicit comments about the issues from as many different perspectives as they could reach. Later, after they had done a great deal of research and had come to some conclusions about the options, they held more meetings to explain their findings and solicit comment about them.

Task Groups and Advisory Committees. An official appoints a task group or advisory committee when he or she has the power to make a decision but wants to share the understanding and the ownership of it with affected parties. Task groups are usually used to address technical or political issues, and members are appointed because of their technical or political expertise. They may or may not represent a constituency. If the task group is made up of well-known and respected members of the community, citizens are far more likely to accept their findings than the conclusions of, say, a city planning department.

Problem-Solving Workshops. Problem-solving workshops are effective when the parties want to find a solution and are able to work reasonably well together. A major advantage of this kind of approach is that more people can participate and contribute their knowledge than in formal negotiations. Problem-solving meetings are designed to accommodate from twenty-five to two hundred or more people. The critical difference between an open problem-solving meeting and a public meeting is that people come to work out a solution, not simply to convey information. Their efforts are directed toward specific goals by a chairperson or facilitator using a resolution plan. The meeting is open, but it is clear to everyone present that all significant interests are represented, and the organizer makes sure that they are all there.

The meetings held to address the problems of the town and the park dispute were open to residents, and twenty or so participated in the discussion. They contributed substantially to the negotiation, helping with special knowledge about places and events. The setting, a porch of a house looking out over an ocean bay, contributed to the informal atmosphere, especially when a school of fish arrived in the bay and some of the participants left abruptly to grab nets and boats, but the most important element was the desire of everyone there to find an answer to a serious problem. The meeting itself proceeded through a logical sequence of conflict management steps.

Formal Negotiation Sessions. Formal negotiation sessions are effective when parties can be identified, the issues are definable, and parties want to resolve their differences. The parties must be willing to sit down and talk. Constituency groups delegate the responsibility of conducting discussions to their designated representative.

A formal negotiation session can be organized in one of three ways: open to the public, including observers and news media representatives who do not participate in the discussion; closed to all but designated observers; and closed to anyone who is not a negotiator.

Sessions open to the public are subject to the posturing that sometimes happens during discussions before an audience. Furthermore, it may be difficult to adjust publicly stated positions in order to explore new options when the press reports every shift in strategy. Negotiators may be reluctant to float "trial balloons" with the public spotlight picking up any hint of weakness.

Meetings closed to all but designated observers are more likely to produce hard decisions quickly. However, excluding the press always produces problems for a convener, and attention to informing the public becomes even more important. Conveners can expect a critical press and a suspicious public. Observers are selected for their knowledge of specific subjects or to report to important outsiders. Governors and congressmen, for example, frequently send staff members to listen to discussions of major policy decisions. Because observers have a less formal status than representatives, they tend to feel less bound by the ground rules. They should be explicitly advised of meeting rules and cautioned that they are responsible for observing them.

Negotiations that are completely closed to outsiders are unlikely in public disputes, because officials are extremely wary of being accused of making secret decisions in "smoke-filled rooms." This option has the additional drawback of excluding the useful advice of technicians and knowledgeable local citizens, thus obstructing access of participants to important information. Closed meetings without observers invite challenge by news media representatives, who readily become outraged at being denied access to discussions they want to hear.

Identifying Process Steps

The four general steps of a conflict management process are:

1. Adopt procedures.
2. Educate the parties.
3. Generate options.
4. Reach agreements.

The next stage in designing a strategy is to determine how many of these process steps are appropriate for conducting a conflict management plan. If the goal of the program is to exchange information or identify issues and interests, only the first and second steps will be needed. If the goal is to develop options, the first three steps should be followed. If working out recommendations or reaching agreements is the goal, all four steps must be covered. (Many authors have organized the activity of reaching agreements into procedural steps, including Filley, 1975; Fisher and Ury, 1981; Karass, 1970; Moore, 1986; Zartman and Berman, 1982.)

The amount of time that must be devoted to each step will depend on the conflict. When parties are less familiar with the issues, for example, more time should be devoted to education. For purposes of designing a strategy, it is only necessary to decide which steps to use and their general nature. The methods used to accomplish each step will be developed in cooperation with the parties after they have been convened. Specific techniques for each step are described in Chapter Six.

Adopting Procedures. The conflict analysis will disclose whether the parties have worked together in the past and how successful their efforts have been. But whether or not tensions are high, parties should always understand the process being proposed. And the less familiar the parties are with negotiation procedures, the more important it is to explain in detail how a program will be structured.

It is also important to review the analysis for information about parties' views of each other's ability to engage in productive discussions. Individuals almost always see themselves as reasonable but may raise doubts about another group's ability to act in good faith. If the relationships among parties are characterized by hostility and suspicion, ground rules that describe how parties will treat one another will be essential. Ground rules can also lay out procedures the groups will follow and define what issues will and will not be addressed. In designing a program, it is only necessary to identify whether ground rules are needed and what problems they are intended to remedy, not the rules themselves. Chapter Six describes in greater detail the types and uses of ground rules.

Educating Parties. The second step in the process is to determine how much education the parties must acquire to understand the context of the problem, the issues, and individual parties' interests. The education phase can be the most time-consuming of the four, especially when a great deal more information is needed, when some groups have far less understanding than others of the overall issues, and when the parties' perceptions of the problem differ dramatically. It is important, therefore, to be realistic about how much time will be necessary to educate the negotiators, and for them in turn to educate their constituents. If a dispute involves disagreements over data, an additional component—reviewing and agreeing on relevant data—must be added to the educational activities.

Generating Options. Have workable options been identified? How strongly are groups identified with specific positions? Do positions seem intractable, or is there room for adjustments? If a number of acceptable options exist, attention in this step can focus on crafting combinations of terms into comprehensive proposals. If no options have been developed or if parties' positions have become entrenched, more time will be required to devise options agreeable to all sides.

The step of developing options should be kept separate from the next step, reaching agreements. Otherwise people begin negotiating specifics before a full range of options have been identified and explored.

Reaching Agreements. The final step, reaching agreements, is introduced after the three preceding steps have been covered. Parties jointly establish criteria by which to assess their options, produce draft agreements, check back with their constituents, and agree on a final document. Adequate attention devoted to the three previous steps will increase the ability of parties to reach agreements.

Determining Who Should Participate

Who should participate can be determined by asking four questions:

- What form of participation makes sense?
- What general categories of participants should be present?
- How many participants should represent each category?
- What specific individuals can best represent each category?

Forms of Participation. Should participation be representative or open to all interested individuals? Representative participation is essential for a formal negotiation. It is appropriate for a task group and, in some cases, for workshops. In this form of participation, each interest group is represented by one or more individuals who speak on its behalf. Participants in representative negotiation usually become more committed to supporting the process and more willing to continue than people who are not representatives. Open participation is used for public meetings and workshops where formal agreements are not required.

Categories of Participants. The next step is to determine the categories of interests that must be represented. Major categories can also have subsets of interests that must be represented separately. For example, when a company proposed to build a scrap metal processing plant in the outskirts of a city, among interested parties were civic associations who welcomed the prospect of new business and an expanded tax base, business people who owned office buildings nearby and detested the idea of a "heavy industry" anywhere in the area, city government air quality and noise pollution regulators, residents of neighborhoods near the proposed site who opposed the project, city residents who favored the thought of a local facility clearing the city of derelict cars and converting them into neat packages of steel, and citizen groups who wanted to protect open space in the city. The problem for the conveners of the negotiation was how to cluster various interests into categories that could be effectively represented by single individuals. They had to look carefully at general categories such as "business" and "citizen groups" and choose the discrete points of view within them.

Number of Participants. A good working size for a group is eight to twelve people. Larger groups are desirable when diversity of knowledge and opinions is important. Because the issues are complex and the parties are numerous, larger groups take more time to reach agreements, and scheduling meetings becomes a problem. The more people involved, the more staff time required to coordinate a program. Thirty people can negotiate successfully, but a full-time support person will be necessary to coordinate their work.

How should each category be represented? If each organization wants separate representation but the group would then be too large, the manager should consider limiting representation to one person from each category, with an additional person designated as an alternate. It is not necessary to have an equal number of people in each category. Within one negotiation, some groups can have three representatives, others two, and others one. The essential point to tell participants is that because decisions are made by consensus, a group with one representative can block agreement as easily as a group with three. The manager should discuss representation with the parties, give suggestions for numbers of participants, and see how they feel about them. The parties should be told that the suggestions are flexible. To avoid being accused of favoritism toward one side, the manager will need to explain the criteria being used. The manager can work with all sides to develop the categories and to determine the number of individuals who will represent each party.

Identifying Individuals. The next question a manager must ask is which individuals can best represent each interest category? The manager should look for people who are knowledgeable about the substance of the issue, are respected members of their interest groups, and are able to get along with individuals from other parties. People who are technically competent but who tend to become abrasive or confrontational do not serve their own party's best interests in a negotiation, because hostile behavior offends other participants and makes them less willing to listen to legitimate concerns or agree to reasonable solutions.

Potential representatives can be identified in several ways. During interviews, people will mention individuals who should be considered as representatives. "You will have to get the president of the neighborhood association involved if this project is going to get anywhere. She knows everyone and is certainly familiar with the issues." Or, "You should really get the Pacific

Coast staff person involved because he has been working on these issues for years." People will suggest individuals to represent their group. Normally, there will be obvious choices for some positions and uncertainty about others.

The manager should draft a list of categories and the number of representatives desired in each category. He or she can attach the obvious names to positions and leave blank the positions that do not have a candidate, and discuss the list with key people of each party. Each group should have an opportunity to comment on the list of names already suggested and should be asked to contribute to the undesignated categories. If someone objects to a name, the choice can be discussed with other parties in an effort to determine whether to retain the nominee or seek another person.

An alternative is to suggest several names for one position and ask parties for their preference. The parties should be reminded that the choice should be someone who is knowledgeable, who represents an interest group, and who can get along with other people. If there are two positions to fill from six similar groups, the six groups should be asked to get together and choose the two people who can most capably represent their constituencies.

Again, the important principle is that parties are involved in the selection. They may be asked to nominate and select members from their own organizations, or they may be asked to comment on the entire list of proposed participants.

Defining Other Roles

A conflict management strategy should define as clearly as possible the roles that everyone associated with a negotiation is expected to play. In addition to participants, the selection of whom we have already discussed, there are other functions that must be given careful consideration. They include the roles of initiator, convener, sponsor, chairperson, facilitator, recorder, technical resource expert, logistical support person, and observer. In many cases, the same individual will perform several of these functions. Furthermore, not all of these roles are required or even desirable in all disputes. It is important, however, to think about the separate activities of a conflict management program, to determine what roles are appropriate, and to decide who should fill them. (For discussions of roles, see Forester, 1986; Lax and Sebenius, 1986.) We also call attention to a separate role, that of mediator, that would not be performed by a person involved in the dispute but that ought to be considered in the design of a strategy.

Initiator. Sometimes the first suggestion that the dispute be negotiated comes from one of the parties. In other cases, the process is initiated by a person outside the dispute. If the parties distrust each other, and they usually do in a conflict, a proposal to talk coming from an adversary is likely to be greeted with, "Why are they proposing this now? There must be something going on that we don't understand." A change in direction by a party in a dispute will be viewed with suspicion unless the reasons for the new approach are clear and unequivocal. It may be necessary to have a respected person or agency first broach the idea of negotiation to the parties. The individual's or organization's concern can come from a general interest in the welfare of the community or a desire for a fair resolution to a problem.

Convener. Parties are more likely to participate in a program if they are invited by a recognized, influential figure. The convener, one who formally brings the parties together, should possess stature in a community or be an official who has standing in an organization. An elected official—a governor, mayor, or county commissioner—may convene a meeting and then take no further part except to review the results of the process. Or a convener can play a more active role by serving as chairman or facilitator of the sessions.

Sponsor. A diverse group of sponsors representing competing interests, such as a chamber of commerce, a neighborhood association, and the League of Woman Voters, can help in establishing credibility for the process and in encouraging more skeptical parties to participate.

Chairperson. The chairperson of the sessions should be a respected individual who has the trust and confidence of all the participants. He or she opens and closes meetings, helps the group follow its agenda, and takes primary responsibility for seeing that the process runs smoothly. If the chairperson wants to engage more actively in the discussions, it may be necessary to bring in a facilitator to run the process. The chairperson is then free to contribute to the substance of the talks.

Facilitator. A facilitator's job is to help the group have a productive meeting. A facilitator is an impartial process guide who is responsible for managing the discussion so that parties can focus their attention on substantive issues and achieving their goals. He or she establishes an agenda, suggests and enforces ground rules, keeps a discussion on track, and offers process suggestions to help a group accomplish its goals. A skilled facilitator can use his or her knowledge of management process to get the most out of a group, often more successfully than a chairperson who relies on the authority of the chair.

Recorder. A recorder summarizes the main points that are discussed and lists all decisions made, usually on newsprint on the wall of the meeting room. Often a support staff person is acceptable to the group to serve this function, since it is highly visible and easy to supervise and therefore unlikely to raise suspicions of bias. For complex negotiations a person assigned to keep written minutes of the discussions is also desirable.

Technical Resource Expert. Technical specialists attend sessions and serve at the pleasure of the participants, answering technical or legal questions when asked. Usually, they are not formal participants.

Logistical Support Person. Complex negotiations involving many parties over an extended period of time require extensive logistical support. A logistical support person schedules and makes arrangements for meetings and compiles and sends regular mailings to the participants. If a facilitator or mediator is used in the negotiation, he or she will usually supervise these tasks.

Observers. Observers generally have an interest in and are knowledgeable about the conflict. They often are important in carrying out agreements. Observers can be representatives from the offices of elected officials, they can be staff members from participants' offices, or they may represent organizations that are not directly involved in the discussion but that have an interest in the issue. Observers attend sessions and participate only when called on by participants or the chairperson.

Mediator. In some disputes, the parties will decide that they need the help of a third party to analyze the conflict, to design a strategy, or, occasionally, to manage the entire negotiation. We explore the use of a third party in Chapter Eight.

Considering Other Process Issues

Additional topics to consider include timing, location, funding strategies, and news media strategy.

Timing. People should know what they are getting themselves into. A manager should be prepared to answer questions about how long the entire process is likely to take, how many meetings are planned, how many hours each meeting will require, and when the meetings will be held. These questions can be answered by reviewing the outline of process components, the number of parties involved, and the scope and complexity of the issues and then determining a reasonable schedule to handle them. Of course, no promise can be made that everything will follow a predictable and orderly sequence, because it probably will not. The manager should be prepared to adjust the program. Adequate time should be allowed for preparation between meetings and for parties to touch base with their constituents.

The amount of time required will depend on several other factors. If the group is small and all participants live near each other, they may be able to meet more often, but a frequency of once or twice a month is normally maximum. Whatever speed they decide on, the parties will probably spend more time together in more intensive sessions as they get closer to reaching agreements. A lot happens toward the end.

Meetings that last anywhere from a half day to a full day generally work best. Parties have enough time to make progress but are not away from their other responsibilities so long that the job of being a negotiator becomes a serious imposition.

Location. The question of where meetings will be held is an important one, symbolically and logistically. The answer can set the atmosphere for subsequent discussions and can have a strong influence on the productivity of a negotiation. For example, an offer by one party to go to another's office is generally viewed as a gesture of good faith, but insistence that a meeting be held in one's own place is often interpreted as an open play for power. The location decision can be a first sign of cooperation or a first contest of wills.

Parties can take turns hosting sessions or can agree to seek a neutral space. Each decision has its advantages and disadvantages. Rotating the location of sessions among the parties gives them an opportunity to see each other's home ground. The host has the advantage of having direct access to his or her own information but the disadvantage of being exposed to unexpected office interruptions. Neutral space, on the other hand, prevents either side from having an advantage, and since office interruptions are minimized, negotiators are more likely to concentrate on the meeting. The disadvantages of a neutral place include not having direct access to information or resource people, and the possible expense of renting the space.

The location should be equally convenient for everyone. There are enough tensions associated with a conflict management meeting without additional pressures being imposed by the choice of site. An alternative is to choose a retreat setting, where parties go off for an extended period of time—two or more days—to discuss the issues and explore options.

Wherever the meetings are held, the meeting room must

be comfortable—with good ventilation, adequate lighting, and reasonably comfortable chairs—and large enough to accommodate all participants. The meeting room arrangement can be used to set the tone of the discussions. A more formal setting with assigned seats around a table reinforces the importance of the effort, while a casual setting promotes informal interaction and opportunities to improve relationships. Most negotiating sessions are conducted around a U-shaped table. We do not know of any situation that is enhanced by a raised podium.

Funding Strategies. It is important to determine how much funding will be needed to support the process and where it will come from. From the process outline, one can estimate how much time will be required for meetings, what types of meetings will be held, and what staff and overhead support is desirable. Consideration must also be given to any additional resources that will be needed to cover research and technical assistance suggested by the parties, field trips to visit sites, production of reports, public workshops held in conjunction with private negotiating sessions, and travel costs for parties who incur major expenses. A pool of money to cover these needs should be established if at all possible.

Funding comes in different forms, including payments from parties, grants from third-party donors, and in-kind contributions of conference room space, refreshments, photocopying, and postage. Parties can share the responsibility of hosting sessions. A team of participants or members from one organization can also volunteer to conduct research requested by the group. Parties may agree to contribute equal amounts of money to support the process, or they may negotiate contributions according to each group's ability to pay. Funding from a third party is also a possibility. Private foundations and local, state, and federal government agencies are sometimes interested in funding part or all of a conflict management program if the issue falls within their scope of interest and if they believe that a solution is in the community's interest. In any case, who controls the funds and how they will be dispensed should be explicit, and donations should have no strings attached that are intended to influence the direction of the negotiations.

News Media Strategy. The group will need to decide whether any or all of the sessions will be open to the news media. As noted earlier, the news media's presence affects the dynamics of the sessions, because people are reluctant to experiment with new ideas if they know that their thoughts may be reported by the press. Although individuals may posture for the benefit of their constituents, the media can also exert a positive effect by keeping a public figure from behaving in an outrageous manner. Like the other issues discussed in this section, parties must share in the decision about the news media (see Chapter Eight).

Flexibility. Few conflicts remain static. As new information is acquired and people's attitudes change, adjustments will be necessary. The manager should work with the parties to refine procedures, offering suggestions and asking them for their advice on how to proceed.

Setting Up a Program

Setting up a program is sensitive work. How the program is described, how participants are invited, and how other roles are defined will have a powerful influence on the program's success. The manager should think through necessary tasks and then consider the most constructive way to complete them. Attention paid to details at the beginning may save agony later on.

Preparing a Description of the Process

The manager should prepare a written description of the process that can be given to interested individuals and organizations. A process description provides a common language that parties can use to explain the program to other people. Without it, parties will impose their own explanations, and they may not convey accurately a program's purpose and approach. A program description includes a statement of the problem, the goals of the effort, suggested process steps, the categories of participating parties, and a time frame. The description is refined as a process evolves, but a common statement at the beginning helps to minimize misunderstanding about a program's purpose and structure.

Securing Funding

A manager must be sparing about the resources committed to setting up a process until he or she knows whether funding will be available. The manager will need to talk with funding sources identified during the design phase and ask for a firm financial commitment or in-kind contributions and organizational support.

Developing Ground Rules

If ground rules will be used, they should be prepared at this point and circulated to participants for their review. Ground rules are usually presented for adoption at the first formal session. Parties should be given an opportunity to read and comment on the rules prior to convening. If they disagree about the use of a rule, they can discuss their differences when they convene (see Chapter Six for information about developing ground rules).

Inviting Participants

The list of potential participants compiled during the design phase should be used as the basis for inviting representatives. Participants should be invited orally and the invitation confirmed in writing, restating the purpose of the program and the role they will be expected to play. They should understand clearly whether they are representing their constituency group or participating as an individual with a particular perspective. They should be told how much time the process is expected to take, how frequently the group will meet, and what additional time commitments are expected between sessions. They should also be given a copy of the proposed ground rules for their comment and a written description of the process steps. Occasionally an individual will decline to participate for personal or professional reasons, so the manager should be prepared to find an acceptable alternative from a list of suggestions provided by the parties or to check back with key players for additional ideas.

Confirming Roles

The manager should ask individuals to serve specific roles in the process, using the list of roles and suggested people that were developed in the design phase. He or she should be prepared to give a detailed explanation of what individuals are being asked to do and should answer any questions they may have about the program. An oral conversation should be followed up with a letter restating the request. A sheet describing all the roles should be prepared so that all parties have a common understanding of the responsibilities of each person.

Notifying Interested Groups

Some people will express an interest in the process, recognizing, however, that they are not appropriate participants. Such individuals should be sent a packet of materials that include a statement of the problem, the program's goals, the process description, and the list of participants. The manager should establish a mailing list of interested individuals and organizations who should be kept informed and add to it the names of individuals who ask to receive regular briefings.

Dealing with the News Media

Most public controversies attract news media attention. To help avoid inaccurate reporting, a press kit should be compiled that includes a description of the problem, the statement of goals, an overview of the process, a list of people who will be involved in the discussions, and the name of a person who can be contacted for additional information.

Earlier discussions with parties will suggest whether the meetings should be open or closed to the press. If the meetings are open, the manager should bring copies of the press kit to the first session and designate a person to answer press questions. If the meetings are closed and the press demands to know what is happening, the manager should arrange to visit with the appropriate reporter or the editor to explain the program (see "Working with the News Media" in Chapter Eight).

Assembling Background Materials

The manager should assemble materials about the issue as a reference library for participants. These materials should include background papers on the problem, rules and regulations that relate to the issue, staff reports, historical documents, newspaper clippings, and any other relevant printed material. Also available should be the statement of the problem, the goals, copies of the ground rules, and descriptions of the process steps that were sent to participants. This collection of materials will be valuable as people begin to discuss the problems and seek clarification of an issue. A reference library should be maintained throughout a conflict management program.

Finally, a list of the participants, official observers, and staff people should be compiled to hand out at the first meeting. The list should include not only the names of individuals but also their titles, affiliations, addresses, and telephone numbers so that people can contact one another and project staff members between sessions.

Arranging the First Meeting

The first meeting is critical to the success of the process. If it is not carefully thought through, people may decide that the effort is not worth their time and drop out. Some details to consider when planning the session include preparing an agenda, locating a comfortable and convenient meeting facility, determining how the room should be arranged, preparing and sending a mailing to participants well in advance of the session, organizing support materials to be used at the meeting, and arranging for audiovisual equipment, if needed. People's schedules should be checked to be sure that everyone can attend the session. A four-week lead time is often necessary to find a free date, and even more notice may be required if many parties are involved.

Usually the first meeting covers introductions, procedural issues, and organizational details. Parties review and discuss the proposed process and accompanying ground rules. The manager should arrange for a presentation that outlines the history and context of the problem. It is important to avoid trying to make important decisions about substantive issues until parties have reached agreements about procedures.

The three preparatory steps we have outlined—analyzing a conflict, designing a strategy, and setting up a program—are general guidelines for planning and organizing a conflict management program. The actual preparation phase will vary in its formality. The preparation phase of the water roundtable took three months to complete. It involved over forty formal interviews and extensive discussions with the parties about the scope of the issues, the categories and numbers of participants, and the operating procedures. Preparation for dealing with the town and the park dispute involved only a few days of informal discussions, since many of the design considerations had already been decided by the community. In that case, the facilitators simply reviewed the current plans to determine whether any important factors had been overlooked and suggested an agenda.

6

Adopting Procedures, Educating Parties, and Developing Options

"Let's get together and talk about it" is a good way to plan the next fishing trip but a bad way for more than a few people to address a controversial topic. A clearly defined process is useful anytime people meet to exchange views, but it is *essential* when the subject is contentious. The manager's problem is that generally there are no formal mechanisms for convening parties or for conducting discussions in public disputes. Often a process must be created from scratch to enable parties to work together productively. Yet it must be done, because only when they have a procedure to follow—one they understand and support—can the parties turn their attention to solving a problem and away from questions of how they will deal with each other.

In the process for managing public disputes presented in Exhibit 1, we suggest four sequential steps for conducting a program: adopting procedures, educating parties, developing options, and reaching agreements. The nature and complexity of the conflict will determine how much time and what type of attention should be devoted to each step—a two-day negotiation will be quite different from a two-year program—but the same four steps will be used. This chapter addresses methods for conducting the first three steps, and the next chapter discusses the final step.

Each step should be followed in order, tailoring the precise methods to the peculiarities of the problem. Remember that a conflict management program takes on a life of its own after

116

the first session. Issues unfold, personalities of participants assert themselves, and unexpected events occur. No amount of careful preparation can anticipate exactly how the process will develop. Problems that seemed difficult to handle turn out to be easy, and simple routine matters become major battlegrounds.

Surprises are regular occurrences. A party surfaces apparently from nowhere and demands the right to participate in a session. Another party threatens to leave. One group demands access to confidential information, and others want to hire an expensive consultant. All of these situations require working with the group to establish criteria for making decisions about questions such as "What should be the basis for adding a new person?" and "Should a task group be set up to deal with questions of data?" When special problems arise, the group will need to identify several ways to handle the situation and choose the most constructive alternative (see Chapters Ten and Eleven for ways of dealing with special problems).

Adopting Procedures

One way to improve the effectiveness of a program at the outset is to explain to all participants the procedures that will be used. When procedures are made explicit, they create an atmosphere of predictability by offering process guidelines and by defining specific rules for all participants to adopt and monitor. Clearly stated procedures protect everyone from unpleasant surprises by investing the entire group with the responsibility for making the program work. Procedures provide an essential framework for conducting business.

Reviewing General Procedures

General procedures should be presented and approved at the first meeting of the parties. General procedures include:

- The statement of the problem.
- The goals of the program.
- The proposed process steps.

- The method by which decisions will be made.
- The amount of time the process is expected to take.

Anyone who is confused or has a problem with the proposal should be encouraged to express it at this point, rather than waiting until parties are further into their discussions and less willing to make changes. The manager should be sure that everyone understands the process and the logic behind the steps.

Some people will be anxious to get on with the discussions. Common reactions are "I don't see why we can't discuss solutions right away" and "Why can't this take three months rather than the six that you have proposed?" Busy people want to feel that they are being efficient. They should be reminded that their goal is to solve a problem and that following this sequence of steps will lead to more secure agreements than will leaping prematurely to solutions.

Agreeing on Ground Rules

Ground rules are the rules of conduct by which all participants abide during a negotiation or other form of conflict management activity. People in a conflict need explicit guidelines when they are embarking on something as unfamiliar as problem solving with others with whom they are unfamiliar or whom they consider to be adversaries.

The concept of ground rules is based on the belief that a negotiation process should treat all parties equally and fairly. Ground rules explicitly spell out behavior and procedures that people normally consider to be fair but sometimes abandon in carrying on a fight. They apply to everyone who is involved in the process. No one is permitted to dominate a discussion or hold special privilege unless the entire group agrees to grant it. Each person has his or her turn to speak and present a case. People who feel that they have been treated unfairly in the past are protected by an explicit set of guidelines for everyone to follow. Nearly every managed program dealing with public disputes uses some form of ground rules (Murray, 1978; Wessel, 1976).

Types of Ground Rules. Rules may be designed to cover several aspects of a negotiation. Some ground rules define the *behaviors* of individual participants, such as, "Individuals will treat each other with respect" or "Stereotypical language will not be permitted." Behavioral ground rules prohibit attacking other people's motives or values.

Other rules apply to *procedures* to be used by the group, such as "All decisions will be made by consensus" or "Representatives will not be allowed to send substitutes to the negotiation." Procedural ground rules define the functions of the person in charge of the meeting, the responsibilities of the group, the role of observers, the open or closed nature of the meetings, and ways to deal with the news media.

Finally, ground rules may define the boundaries of the *substantive* discussions: for example, "The discussions will address housing needs within the city border but will not look at suburban needs." Substantive ground rules may also address the types of data that will be used and the methods by which data will be obtained.

Forms of Ground Rules. Ground rules may be committed to writing or conveyed orally. Parties use written ground rules when they will be working with each other over an extended period of time and especially when the level of trust among participants is low. Oral ground rules are often used when parties have established positive working relationships. They also may be proposed when an unexpected problem arises and the group can benefit from a specific guideline to address the problem. Oral rules are often used when the group plans to meet only once or twice.

The negotiators in the case of the old railroad (Chapter Two) knew each other well and, in general, understood the motives of the other participants. However, the problem had continued so long that they had begun to wonder about the willingness of the other parties to carry out any commitments that the group might make. Two ground rules, "No one will impugn anyone else's motives" and "No one will make personal attacks," were suggested verbally to the group to keep that uncertainty from becoming an issue in itself until the parties made progress on other issues. The participants wanted to avoid abrasive exchanges, and they accepted the suggestion with no further discussion.

Designing and Applying Ground Rules

Initiating Rules. Ground rules are usually developed before the first meeting and are sent in draft form to the parties for their review. If time permits, the program manager talks to each participant about the rules before the first session and asks that everyone come prepared to discuss them.

In the game damage project (Chapter Two), all the parties received a draft agenda for the first meeting, a proposed set of ground rules that contained guidelines for constructive discussion, and an explanation of the use of consensus in making decisions. Telephone calls followed to be sure that the purpose and content of the rules were clearly understood.

Ground rules are usually developed by the person responsible for setting up a program. They are based on the person's experience and on concerns raised by the parties during analysis interviews and in other discussions. Sometimes parties are asked directly to suggest ground rules that would be useful to the process. For example, a forest service manager in a preliminary interview indicated that earlier public discussions had been quite confrontational. He said he would come to a meeting but that he had no intention of enduring a "roast the ranger" session. The meeting organizers proposed, and the group accepted, a ground rule forbidding personal attacks. Most meeting managers use a combination of the two approaches, asking participants for their suggestions and offering some of their own ideas.

Approving Rules. Ground rules work when all parties agree to use them. If ground rules are presented to the group at the first session without prior consultation, the person conducting the program must be prepared to spend more time in the meeting explaining the rules. Parties sometimes request additional time after the meeting to consider the rules.

If possible, the ground rules should be adopted by the group at the first or second session. The meeting manager asks, "Does anyone have any questions or concerns about the ground rules?" If parties still have questions, they should be addressed at this time. He or she then asks, "Can the group agree to accept these rules for the duration of our negotiations?" It is important that *all* parties accept the ground rules, because if any individual or group refuses to abide by them, the rules become meaningless to everyone else.

Some ground rules may be more difficult for the group to accept than others. The question of whether the meeting should be open or closed to the public, for example, can be a sticky one for elected officials accustomed to conducting their business in the public arena. Many of these officials are regulated by sunshine laws requiring that certain meetings be open. Nonetheless, a satisfactory resolution must be found and agreement reached.

The exercise of adopting procedures gives parties an opportunity to reach agreements early in the discussions. Success at this point demonstrates to skeptical parties that they can reach accord and opens up the possibility of reaching agreements on more difficult problems.

Applying Rules. Whether the ground rules are written or oral, the parties should be reminded at the beginning of each meeting that they have agreed to observe them. If the rules are written, participants should refer to their own copies; if the rules are oral, the meeting manager should repeat the rules for everyone to hear at the beginning of each session and should remind the participants that it is everyone's responsibility to observe the rules and enforce them within the group.

Enforcing Rules. Even though everyone has agreed to observe the rules, violations will occur, whether because someone misinterprets a rule, forgets a rule in the height of an emotional discussion, or intentionally violates a rule.

Either the chairperson or a participant may acknowledge the infraction. The first acknowledgment can be phrased as a re-

minder: "Mr. Jones, remember that the group has agreed that
it will not question another person's motives." If the chairperson does not comment promptly, a participant can bring the
infraction to the group's attention, "I thought that we all
agreed not to attack each other's motives."

If additional violations of the same rule occur, the re-
minders become more forceful: "Mr. Jones, you have violated
the ground rule which states that no one will question the motives of another individual. I ask you to refrain from such comments." If the violation continues beyond a second reminder,
the chairperson can ask the participant to leave the session. The
chair may also try to catch the individual at a break during the
meeting or between meetings to discuss the matter. In rare cases
an individual may be asked by the group to drop out of a process altogether because he or she is destroying the productivity
of the group.

Changing Rules. From time to time a group changes
ground rules midway in the course of a negotiation. It may be
necessary to add a rule, to modify an existing one, or, more
rarely, to drop a rule. Any participant can propose a change,
but the entire group must approve the change before it is
adopted.

In one project, the group decided that the number of observers should be limited to a few individuals so as to minimize
grandstanding by negotiators and coaching of the negotiators by
observers. In addition, a ground rule was instituted to prohibit
observers from participating in the discussions. Later in the
negotiations the discussion focused on technical matters and
public policy decisions, and it became desirable for the observers
to offer comments when no one at the table could offer the
same information. The ground rules were changed to reflect the
evolution in the process.

Exhibit 6 is an example of a set of ground rules that a
group might adopt for a complex negotiation. These rules were
used by the water roundtable (Chapter Two) in its eighteen-
month negotiation. The ground rules were drafted by the facilitators with the help of the participants and were adopted by the
parties as their operating framework.

Exhibit 6. Sample Set of Ground Rules.

General

1. The Roundtable is responsible for the overall conduct and outcome of this project. After initial information-sharing meetings, the Roundtable will determine the issues to be discussed and the timeline for its work.
2. The Roundtable may create committees of its own members or form task groups that include others who are not Roundtable participants for detailed study or discussion of specific topics. Final decision-making authority rests with the Roundtable participants.
3. Since the success of the Roundtable depends upon cooperation among participants, Roundtable participants will observe the following guidelines:
    a. Personal attacks will not be tolerated.
    b. The motivations and intentions of participants will not be impugned.
    c. The personal integrity and values of participants will be respected. Stereotyping will be avoided.
    d. Commitments will not be made lightly and will be kept. Delay will not be employed as a tactic to avoid an undesired result.
    e. Disagreements will be regarded as problems to be solved rather than as battles to be won.

Substitutes and Observers

1. Because the success of the Roundtable will ultimately depend upon personal relationships and trust, there will be no substitutes permitted for participants.
2. Before a decision is requested on any matter, sufficient time will be provided for participants to seek advice from constituents, counsel, or other experts. Technical advisors or resource people may be invited by the Roundtable to provide information. Only recognized and invited observers will be allowed to attend.
3. If a Roundtable participant determines he or she can no longer participate effectively, a permanent substitute may be selected. The Roundtable will be advised of the request.

Information

1. Roundtable participants will provide pertinent information.
2. Information used to support positions will be shared in advance.
3. Claims of privilege will not be asserted lightly. Any participant claiming privilege must establish good cause.
4. Tentative or sensitive data will be respected as such.
5. Information will not be withheld for tactical advantage.
6. All statements, documents, and other communications used in the course of Roundtable meetings will not be offered or utilized as evidence in any administrative or judicial proceeding.

(continued on next page)

Exhibit 6. Sample Set of Ground Rules, Cont'd.

Ongoing Activities

1. It is recognized that some Roundtable participants are associated with operating agencies and have an obligation to make management decisions and take actions necessary for the proper functioning of their agencies. Participants will advise the Roundtable of pending decisions of their agencies that are within the scope of Roundtable discussion unless such prior disclosure would jeopardize consummation of the decisions. In those cases, Roundtable participants will be notified of the decision as soon as practical. It is the intention of this ground rule that irrevocable financial or policy commitments will be disclosed while still pending and before the opportunity for discussion by the Roundtable has been foreclosed.
2. Legal rights or remedies are not abrogated by virtue of participation in the Roundtable. However, participants should be aware that litigation could jeopardize the Roundtable process and their ability to participate effectively in it.

Media Contacts

1. All meetings of the Roundtable are closed to members of the press. A statement or press release will be issued following Roundtable meetings. The Roundtable will approve the content of these statements prior to their release. Participants will receive copies of all releases.
2. When discussing the Roundtable with reporters, participants should be careful to present only their own views and not those of other participants or of the Roundtable. The temptation to discuss someone else's statement or position should be avoided.
3. While the Roundtable is studying, negotiating, or evaluating issues, Roundtable participants will not make public statements prejudging the outcome. Such statements could jeopardize constructive discussion and could reduce participants' ability to accept or modify a proposal.
4. Some reporters tend to emphasize the negative or divisive aspects of a project; participants should convey a positive tone whenever possible.

Enforcement

It is the joint responsibility of Roundtable participants, the Chairman, and the meeting facilitators to assure that these ground rules are observed. Participants are free to question, in good faith, actions of others that may come within the scope of these ground rules.

Educating Parties

The second step in running a program is educating the parties. They educate each other, describing their perceptions of the problem, identifying and discussing issues, explaining their concerns, and listing their assumptions and the sources of information they have used to draw conclusions. Education is time-consuming, and to some it will seem unnecessary. Inexperienced negotiators in particular may treat this step as the most easily expendable portion of a conflict management program. Individuals will say, "Can't someone just summarize all the issues so we can move on?" But the more time the parties invest in educating each other, the greater chance they will have of developing options and reaching agreements.

Education serves the important function of letting parties describe, many for the first time, their side of the story directly, face to face, to other groups. If information has been exchanged before, it is likely to have been in writing—letters, statements, reports, legal documents, and stories in the newspapers. Education provides an opportunity for individuals to gain information from other sides *and* to tell others how they see the situation and what effect they think the conflict or a proposed change will have on everyone concerned. Each side gains the satisfaction of knowing that the other side has been exposed to its perception of the situation (Curle, 1971).

All participants are asked to identify the important issues, which provide the framework around which solutions are fashioned. They also identify and explain their concerns about each issue. The collective list of interests provides the basis for developing options.

The education phase provides an opportunity for everyone to examine data together. In most conflicts, parties generate their own sets of figures to support their case. They may also use the same set of facts as their adversaries but reach different conclusions about them. If data do play a role in a dispute, parties must examine each other's statistics and agree on a common set of figures. A common data base provides a standard by which the parties develop and assess solutions (see "Negotiating Differences in Data" in Chapter Eleven).

A carefully managed education phase also provides a nonthreatening way for people to interact with each other. Participants focus their attention on gathering and conveying information, which is a much less stressful occupation than trying to reach agreements. If parties observe each other acting in good faith—sharing information, asking candid questions, trying to understand what the other side has been saying—they gain tangible evidence, not just promises, that the conflict management process and perhaps even the other side may merit their trust. Trust is essential to reaching agreements.

Reviewing the History and Context of the Problem

The process of education begins with an explanation of the history and context of the problem, in which one individual or a representative from each party presents his or her view of the general situation. If the dispute is over a proposal for a new project, the sponsoring agency or company describes its reasons for proposing the program, what it hopes to accomplish, and how it plans to achieve its goals. Because this is likely to be the first opportunity some of the parties will have to gain specific details directly from the project proponent, people are encouraged to ask questions to clarify their understanding, but not to challenge the validity of the proposal at this point.

An alternative approach is for each party to recount its *own involvement in the conflict,* citing its view of the origin, describing what events led up to the problem, discussing its role, and presenting reasons why the problem is significant. In the town and the park situation (see Chapter Two), each side described its views of what had happened earlier and its feelings about it. This was the first time that park officials and conservation group representatives had heard directly from town residents how they perceived the events that had led to the meeting.

If the conflict involves complex technical issues, it is useful to have a resource person describe the evolution of the problem and explain the technical background or legal setting. But selecting a resource person can be a far more perilous matter than it may first appear. During the water roundtable negotiation, the members agreed that they needed technical advice on the geology of several optional sites for the proposed dam. A large consulting firm had been doing investigative work of this kind for the city, so it seemed logical and expeditious to ask someone from the firm to present the facts. Unfortunately, the engineer presenting the material was much more interested in pleasing his primary client than in being scientifically objective about the data and proceeded to eulogize the city for its wisdom in choosing its preferred site. This, of course, infuriated the other participants and made using technical experts much more difficult in the future.

The knowledge of technical experts can be an essential ingredient in negotiation of technical issues, but their behavior can be a disaster if their presentations are biased or if they speak condescendingly or abrasively, as technical people are occasionally apt to do. Parties in a dispute are more likely to trust the statements of an expert with no connection with either side, but it is entirely possible to use a technician employed by one of the parties if the other representatives recognize the person's knowledge and if his or her contribution is a straightforward presentation of the facts as the person sees them.

Identifying the Issues

After talking about the history and context of the dispute, the parties should identify the issues that are most important to them. An *issue* is a matter or question that must be addressed if a conflict is to be resolved. It can best be stated as a problem to be solved, such as "How can the safety of workers be protected?" Issues can involve tangible items (money and resources), appropriate procedures (who does what, when), and the effect of an action on intangible factors, such as reputation and status. In developing a composite list of issues, the parties should distinguish between those they consider to be of primary importance and those they consider to be secondary. For example, issues associated with a dispute over where to locate a new convention center may include zoning (How are the pieces of land under consideration zoned at present?), access (What road system will be needed to support the volume of traffic that will be created? What type of public transportation is available?), economics (What land and property costs will be associated with the new facility?), and effect on the area (What effect will the new facility have on the adjacent properties and neighborhoods?). The parties must decide which topics to address first.

If a thorough conflict analysis has been done before the first meeting, the chairperson can begin by presenting to the negotiators the issues identified in the individual interviews. Issues are clustered by topic and generalized so that individual parties are not identified with a particular issue. The list of issues is presented solely as a starting point for further discussion, and the participants are encouraged to add to the list or modify it until they feel it accurately reflects all the issues they are concerned about. This method is used primarily when time is short.

Another approach, one that more effectively involves the parties in the initial stages of discussion, is to ask each person to describe his or her issues to the other parties. This method gives everyone an opportunity to lay out an explanation of an issue and say why it is important. As participants listen to these explanations, they may ask questions for clarification, but they must not be allowed to comment on the validity of the content. Emphasis is placed on conveying and understanding each party's list of issues.

It is essential that representatives work with their constituents to identify the items that should be on the list, because the participants must receive a full explanation of all the issues that are important to the constituency group and not just those that are of particular interest to the representative. The conflict manager should emphasize this point, because failing to capture all matters of importance will give the negotiators a false impression of the dimensions of the dispute. When representatives check with their constituents about issues for discussion, they also begin the important process of consulting with them on matters of significance, a task that must continue throughout the negotiation.

Another way for parties to build a list of issues is to ask each group to present a single issue until every party has had a chance to present one item. A second round begins, and each party offers another issue. The process continues until all parties have listed all their topics. The chairperson keeps a record in handwritten notes or on newsprint wall sheets.

Discussing Interests

Interests are the key to identifying workable solutions. An *interest* is a specific need or condition that a party considers to be important to a satisfactory agreement. For example, if a community is faced with a conflict over where to locate a new health facility, the issues can include size (how large the physical structure should be), service (what types of services should be offered), and facilities (how parking can be accommodated). Under the question of size, parties' interests may include the structure's compatibility with local surroundings. On the issue of services, some will want the clinic to offer medical services tailored to the elderly, while others will be concerned about the hours the services will be available. Interests associated with the issue of parking may include assurance that clients will have adequate space to park and that local residents will not lose their curbside parking. Parties can begin with a general discussion of their interests and progress to more detailed descriptions as specific issues are identified. The more interests they identify, the more prepared they will be to develop options later.

People who have difficulty in describing their issues or their interests may find it easier to talk about why they are *concerned* about the problem. Because people tend to offer solutions rather than describe their interests, the chairperson should be prepared to remind them to describe their specific concerns about the problem. It is also helpful to provide examples of interests so that people will understand how to phrase their concerns. Better yet, people should be asked to think about their interests before attending the meeting. They will then have a chance to develop a more complete list than they would otherwise be able to offer.

The chairperson often redirects questions to get people to describe their interests rather than solutions. Here is a sample conversation:

Chairperson: I want to know what concerns you have about the proposed new airport.

Citizen: I think they should have chosen the site ten miles out of town, not the one they did. (This is a solution.)

Chairperson: Why don't you like the site they are recommending?

Citizen: There will be too much noise in the neighborhoods. (Noise level is an issue. Not wanting too much noise is an interest.)

Chairperson: What type of noise are you worried about?

Citizen: Those planes will probably take off and land right over our homes. We won't be able to hear each other talk in our own living rooms. (Takeoffs and landing patterns are another issue. Keeping the noise level down is an interest.)

Chairperson: Is that your primary concern about noise?

Citizen: Well, I want to get a good night's sleep.

Chairperson: Can you be more specific?

Citizen: I don't want planes flying over my house early in the morning. (Timing of plane traffic is an issue. No early morning noise is an interest.)

If more than twenty-five participants are involved, they should be asked to divide into small groups so that everyone can participate in the discussion. This procedure has the drawback that not all participants will hear what everyone has to say, but, on balance, it is more important to be sure that everyone, the shy and retiring as well as the eloquent, speaks his or her piece. Each small group should select or be provided a recorder who makes a visible record of the discussion on newsprint and reports a summary to the general session. In the water roundtable, after small groups presented their interests to the general session a task group was appointed to combine the lists into one composite record for future reference. In this case participants worked in small assigned groups of diverse interests. In other programs parties of *similar interests* have worked together to identify issues. The identification of issues and interests is frequently blended into one discussion.

Agreeing on Data

Public disputes are waged within a context of facts and figures about technical matters and policy issues, so early in a negotiation the group should identify *categories* of data related to their problem. They may gather information by assembling materials, by inviting resource people to address key topics, and by interviewing technical experts for information. Working together, often in task groups, they assemble and assess the data, and they report their findings to the whole group, which develops a common set of figures that is used to identify and evaluate solutions.

When differences in data or their interpretation occur, participants must discuss the discrepancies—the sources of information, the assumptions on which the data are based, and the methodologies that have been used to draw conclusions. If one of the parties has presented controversial figures, the others should ask questions to increase their understanding of how the facts were derived. If an outside person or organization is responsible for the data, he or she should be available for questioning as well.

Discussion of disagreements over data is effective when the material does not require specialized training to understand its significance. If data are highly technical, parties can hire an impartial expert to review and comment on the figures in question, or they can delegate the resolution of differences to a small task group of knowledgeable participants for detailed discussions. A third option is to settle for a reasonable *range* of figures rather than trying to agree on one specific number. It is essential that parties not proceed if they disagree on the basic facts, because both the negotiating process and the solutions may be flawed and open to challenge. If one party does not have resources to acquire data it considers essential, provision must be made to acquire them. The manager will need to find either staff people who can brief participants or some way of paying for outside technical help (see "Negotiating Differences in Data" in Chapter Eleven).

The meeting manager should capture in writing what parties have learned about the problem. Copies of lists of issues and interests and general information and data reports should be distributed for reference when parties begin to develop solutions and seek final agreements. All conflict management programs go through cycles of productivity. Negotiators alternate between feeling that progress is being made and wondering whether anything is ever going to get resolved. Written records that summarize topics parties have already covered help them remember how much work they have completed and, in spite of their frustrations, that they are making progress.

Developing Options

In the third step, developing options, negotiators use the information they have gathered about issues, interests, and data to identify options for solving the problem. They are encouraged to create multiple proposals, but they are not yet permitted to assess the solutions, even though some of the parties will push for settling on one. At this stage the goal is to produce the broadest possible selection of alternatives.

This approach, separating the development of options from the choice of a solution, differs markedly from the conventional way of doing things, in which disputing parties come together with their positions already developed. The trouble with the latter process is that positions, most or all of which have been proposed before and failed, become more rigid as a dispute intensifies. The parties focus more and more on advocating the merits of their respective positions and trying to win concessions. And their constituents follow along as positions become increasingly inflexible, forming an unyielding mass that must be reckoned with if the parties want to turn to a more cooperative form of negotiation.

Among the drawbacks of a system of bargaining in which the parties attempt to prevail over each other is the risk of one party winning nearly everything and the other party losing nearly everything but not disappearing afterward, with the uncertain consequences we discuss in other parts of this book. Another is that they may turn to a familiar form of compromise in which the parties realize that the options before them are unsatisfactory and that neither side can win, but they feel they have to do something. They then proceed to make concessions in exchange for concessions from the other side, progressively giving up things they wanted to keep. People offer downgrading concessions when no better alternatives are available to them. In contrast, an alternative approach encourages people to move beyond simple advocating of fixed positions into a search for alternatives that satisfy the interests of all parties and that conceivably no one has thought of before (Fisher and Ury, 1981; Walton and McKersie, 1965).

After defining their interests, the parties have the basis for recognizing which options will address their needs and which will not. They may also be more receptive to proposals other than their own and more open to discussing additional ways to resolve their differences.

They create options in a variety of ways. The entire group of negotiators may be involved in the development of a solution, or they may work on some issues together and have a task group of technical experts address others. In the remainder of this chapter we look at how groups go about creating options and the forms the alternatives can take. All of the approaches listed have two traits in common. First, the parties refrain from evaluating options while they are developing them. Evaluation occurs in the next step, when parties jointly establish and apply criteria for assessing each option. Second, parties develop options based on what they have said they need in an agreement, not on their stated positions. The chairperson refers them to a written list of interests, or verbally reviews the list, once again asking participants to add to it and refine the summary list.

Organizing to Produce Options

All Parties Work Together. Negotiators can work as a group to develop options, on the expectation that more people will produce more options. They can brainstorm solutions, coming up with as many ideas as they can in a specified period of time. Brainstorming is an effective tool for getting people out of blind alleys in negotiation and encouraging them to explore all possibilities for an answer. They are told not to worry about how outrageous an idea might sound, since an impractical idea may stimulate another, more workable solution. All ideas are listed on newsprint paper in front of the group. Participants are then encouraged to review the list of ideas as it is developed to see whether any new suggestions occur to them. They are reminded not to evaluate ideas at this time. Groups larger than twenty-five should be divided into smaller segments and their ideas presented later to the entire group for review (Delbecq, Vandeven, and Gustafson, 1975; Doyle and Straus, 1976).

Task Groups. In many disputes, issues can be divided into logical categories, such as options for design, legal mechanisms, funding strategies, and mitigation measures. Separate task groups can be created to identify options for each category. Individuals participate in one or more groups according to their interests and skills. The same techniques used to generate options in a large group are used in a task group. Task groups are generally effective when many issues are involved and the solution requires knowledge and expertise in specialized areas. Remember that the job of the task group is to come up with options, not to select the best one. The entire group will decide what options are acceptable. Task groups are frequently used in conjunction with other means of producing options.

Outside Experts. Experts who are not directly involved in the controversy can supplement the group's own thinking and expand the number of options on the table. When mistrust runs high among the parties, they will be more receptive to ideas coming from an impartial source than from each other. Outside experts can submit written descriptions of how other problems have been solved in similar circumstances, or they can come before the group with specific ideas and explain how these solutions have been implemented by other groups. The latter approach is preferable because the parties gain a more detailed picture of the alternatives and how they might apply to the situation at hand.

An expert is called on to offer options in technical areas when representatives do not have enough knowledge about the subject matter to develop their own proposals. The challenge of using outside experts is to find people who are not aligned with one side in a controversy. As mentioned earlier in this chapter, this is not always an easy task, because often people who are experts in a specialized area have been employed by one or more of the organizations participating in the program. If the parties cannot find an impartial individual, they can invite several people who represent different perspectives to offer suggestions for review by the negotiators.

Each Party Develops a Proposal. In a traditional negotiation each participant presents a proposal that reflects only the interests of its own constituency. An alternative approach after completing the education step is to ask each party to develop a proposal, considering not only its own interests but those of the other parties as well. The parties are not asked to compromise their goals but to find creative ways that their needs can be met along with those of the other parties. In doing so they must, of course, have a thorough understanding of each others' interests.

An Intermediary Gathers Options. A respected individual, often the chairperson, might conduct independent brainstorming sessions with each party. A list of all the ideas that come out of these sessions can then be presented to the group for discussion, with the assurance that no idea will be attributed to any one party. The intermediary approach is useful when parties remain suspicious of each other's motives and are therefore reluctant to suggest anything but their own position in front of others. Because suggestions are not linked to any one side, participants are more willing to risk offering and considering new and different ideas. This procedure also works well when representatives are highly visible political figures in a community. Here, trust is not the issue. Instead, they do not want to be associated by the press with a roughly formed, preliminary idea that is tossed out for public discussion and disturbs some constituents. The person collecting the ideas must be trusted by all the parties and must have the ability to keep the discussion within each group confidential.

Two Forms of Options

We have suggested a variety of ways the parties can organize their efforts to develop the options that will eventually form the basis of a solution. The form of the options themselves will be determined by the nature of the problem.

Options will take one of two general forms. In the first, the parties develop a number of options for each of the major issues they have identified in their discussions. The chairperson encourages them to produce as many alternatives for each issue as possible. Generating multiple options helps the parties break away from rigid adherence to their favorite solution. In the next step, when they begin to seek agreements, they will review all the options that have been developed for one issue and select the most desirable alternative.

The second approach is for parties to develop several comprehensive proposals that address all key issues. The advantage of this approach is that parties can create different combinations of options that they will evaluate in the next step, reaching agreements. This form works best when issues are not numerous and complex.

7

Reaching and
Carrying Out Agreements

Reaching agreements is the *last* step parties take to resolve their differences (see Exhibit 1, p. 67). Groups that begin discussing solutions without identifying issues or developing options discover, to their dismay, how difficult it is to reach closure. The parties thrash around, pushing with increased intensity for their position because they do not understand how others see the problem and do not recognize when a new proposal may serve their interests. They begin to view the process as a waste of time, which it usually is, and consider the other parties to be stubborn and unreasonable. The harder they seek agreements, the more elusive the agreements become.

On the other hand, when negotiators follow the steps of adopting procedures, educating themselves, and developing options, they prepare themselves to recognize workable solutions. They understand what interests of their constituents must be satisfied, and they have explored different ways to address them. If the possibility for reaching an agreement exists at all, parties who have walked through these steps are far more likely to fashion a better solution and to reach closure than those who do not.

General Approaches to Reaching Agreements

Negotiators reach agreements by one of three general approaches: (1) developing a framework that outlines how the problem should be resolved in general terms (agreements in principle) and then proceeding to work out details for each issue, (2) negotiating and reaching closure on each issue separately (the building block approach), or (3) blending comprehensive proposals developed by the parties separately into a final agreement.

Using a Framework of General Agreements to Reach Specific Agreements. With the agreements in principle approach, parties reach general agreements about a problem and then work toward agreements on specific issues. Agreements in principle affirm goals of the group and specify principles to be followed in subsequent discussions. Agreements in principle are easier to reach than detailed agreements on each issue, and they enable the parties to experience success in reaching agreements. They can be developed by asking parties to suggest a principle that everyone will accept. The group develops a list of possible agreements and then reviews and refines the list by dropping some suggestions and combining and rewording others.

Another method is to have a small representative group draft agreements in principle. The small group is convened after the whole group has discussed possible agreements, or it is charged with the responsibility of talking with each member of the negotiation to gather suggestions. The product of the small group is presented to the whole group for discussion and approval.

After the water roundtable members had agreed upon data regarding the options for providing water to the city, they were asked to identify areas of general agreement. In this case, two of the mediators interviewed individual participants for their suggestions. The results were compiled into a three-page statement of agreements, including:

- The city faces a genuine water shortage in coming years if measures are not taken to increase supply and use of water more efficiently. Roundtable members agree that this situation is serious and requires immediate action.
- Decisions regarding water development and supply should not be used as a means to control population growth in the metropolitan area.
- Any east slope storage should address the expansion of exist-

ing facilities where economically or institutionally feasible; reexamine the management practices of east slope reservoirs to maximize the amount of water available from existing facilities where feasible; environmental impact mitigation, and the creation of a plan to maximize efficient use of water.

• Any water use efficiency recommendations should address a water conservation education and awareness program and a commitment to thorough planning and implementation of water conservation techniques and measures.

These agreements in principle became the pillars for building a more detailed set of agreements nine months later. Figure 5 illustrates the process of moving from general to specific agreements.

Figure 5. Agreements in Principle Approach.

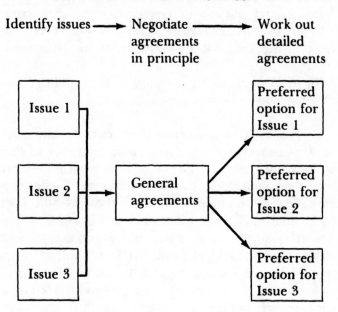

Negotiating Issues Separately. In the building block approach, parties agree on specific issues to be negotiated. Each issue is discussed, and solutions are proposed for it independently of other issues. The results are put together in a final overall agreement. Resolving pieces of the problem is more manageable than finding a comprehensive solution. Because agreement on all issues is not required and each solution stands on its own, the parties can make progress by moving forward on issues where agreement can be reached, without having to wait for closure on everything. They can handle issues where no agreement is reached by bringing in additional people to offer ideas, by tabling the issue for a defined period of time, or by submitting the single issue to arbitration.

Negotiators can work sequentially or simultaneously on issues. If they decide to work sequentially, they may choose to work on the easier issues first. This strategy has the benefit of giving parties a sense of accomplishment when they reach agreement, thus encouraging them to tackle the more difficult problems. Parties choose to negotiate issues simultaneously when each group has enough representatives to cover each discussion or when only some of the topics are of interest to a group.

Figure 6 provides an overview of the building block approach.

Combining Comprehensive Proposals. If each party has prepared its own comprehensive proposal as a way of developing options, then all participants together must review each of the proposals, applying evaluation criteria and finding ways to combine ideas from one proposal with those of others. Parties use a combination of persuasion, accommodation, and imagination to arrive at a joint proposal that all can accept. Figure 7 illustrates this approach. The final agreement reflects Party B's ability to persuade Party A to accept Option 4 instead of Option 1 for a solution to Issue 1. Both groups included Option 2 in their proposals and it became part of the final agreement. Option 6 grew out of their discussions about how to deal with the third issue. In this latter case neither Option 3 or Option 5 was acceptable to the other side.

These three methods are not mutually exclusive. On the

Figure 6. Building Block Approach.

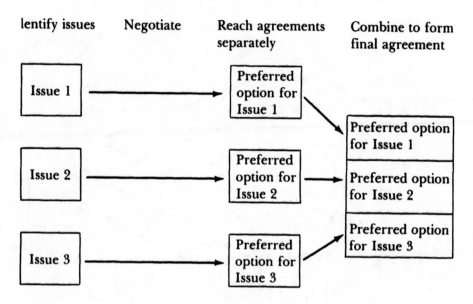

contrary, parties in complex situations will use a combination of approaches. The water roundtable members developed agreements in principle and then went on to work out three comprehensive proposals that eventually blended into a final agreement. Several side issues were also negotiated separately from the final agreements.

The Steps to Reaching Agreements

Negotiators will approach the problem of reaching agreements in different ways, but each should follow the same basic sequence of steps:

1. Establish objective criteria.
2. Apply criteria to existing options.
3. Reach consensus on options.

Figure 7. Combining Proposals.

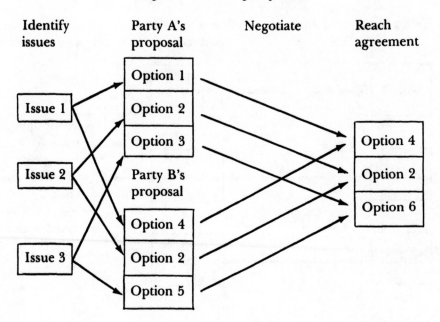

| Identify issues | Party A's proposal | Negotiate | Reach agreement |

4. Produce a draft agreement.
5. Present the draft to constituency groups for review and approval.
6. Reach final agreement.

Establish Objective Criteria. When negotiators move into the phase of reaching agreements, they must first establish guidelines for measuring the appropriateness and acceptability of each alternative. They need to work together to develop and agree upon a list of criteria, by reviewing their list of interests and proposing other factors that should be considered when options are evaluated. Criteria can be general or specific. For example, general criteria for siting a new urban park could include: (1) the proposal should be cost-effective, (2) it should include mitigation measures for any adverse effects on local residents, (3) it should be legally feasible, and (4) it should be manageable within current organizational capabilities. More specific criteria might be: (1) the park cannot cost more than $100,000, (2) adequate parking must be available, and (3) zoning variances must be obtainable. This approach is in stark contrast to traditional decision making, in which each party evaluates each proposal by assessing how closely it matches its own proposal.

Apply Criteria to Existing Options. If parties are working with several comprehensive proposals, they proceed to evaluate each one, applying their agreed-upon criteria. If parties have generated ideas for each issue, they must decide whether the whole group will evaluate them sequentially or whether they want to divide the issues into categories and assess the categories simultaneously, a decision that will depend on the number and the nature of the issues involved.

Applying the criteria to each option helps identify which options the group is ready to accept, which ones require further discussion by the parties, and which should be eliminated from further consideration.

In some cases, it will be obvious to the group that it has already reached an agreement on one or more of the issues. Usually someone in the group says, "I think that we agree that we want to separate the cross-country ski trails from the snowmobile routes. Am I right?" If the group responds affirmatively, they can move on to the next issue. If one party is not prepared to agree completely and answers, "I think I'm in favor of the option, but I would like to see how we come out on some of the other issues before I say yes," the group can return to this issue later and then test for agreement.

It may be necessary to drop options that no one thinks are workable. Parties were encouraged during brainstorming to come up with as many options as possible, because a suggestion that seemed far out of reality might actually help someone think of an entirely new way to handle a problem. Now it is time to eliminate as many ideas as possible, dropping those that all the parties agree to cut. The chairperson should ask questions such as "Are there any suggestions for funding the program that you all agree should be eliminated?" If someone suggests an option to be dropped, the chairperson should check it out with the group: "Do the rest of you agree?" If all heads nod yes, the suggestion is accepted. If some people do not respond, each individual should be asked directly: "Peter, do you support eliminating that last option?" Silence should not be confused with agreement. Everyone must answer with a "yes" or "no." The group can then proceed to evaluate all remaining options.

The group can also review the list of options by identifying their advantages and disadvantages. This method of evaluating is done along with or as an alternative to establishing and applying criteria. Negotiators list options on a sheet of paper and draw two vertical columns to the right of the list. The heading for one column is Advantages and the heading for the other is Disadvantages. The headings Costs and Benefits can also be used. Parties discuss each option's advantages and disadvantages in relation to the interests that must be addressed. After all the options for one issue have been discussed, the participants review the list to see whether any items can be eliminated. The group's discussion often makes it clear that certain options are unworkable or are less desirable than others and also highlights the most promising alternatives.

Reach Consensus on Options. The group now reviews options that look promising, either working with one issue at a time until consensus is reached or considering each general proposal that includes solutions to several issues. Consensus may require combining or synthesizing acceptable options, linking and trading off solutions, or agreeing to drop an issue altogether. When parties recognize that they are not going to reach an agreement on an issue, they can agree to drop it (Doyle and Straus, 1976; Moore, 1986).

When a group seems close to agreement, the chairperson tests for closure by restating agreements that he or she thinks the group has reached. Periodic testing makes any disagreements explicit and thus avoids surprises later on. A tentative consensus initially should be stated in question form: "Are we in agreement that . . . ?" If there is consensus, the chairperson restates the final agreement. Occasionally, a chairperson states the consensus in the negative—"Is there anyone who feels strongly opposed to . . . ?"—which requires dissenters to speak up. This practice is not recommended, except in circumstances when the parties seem completely stuck, because it puts pressure on parties to agree even though they may have reservations about the suggestion.

If agreement cannot be reached on an issue, negotiators can look for less complete forms of agreement. If they cannot reach a substantive agreement, they can look for a procedural one. If they have a problem agreeing on who should administer and pay for a program, for example, they can establish a committee to come back to the parties with a recommendation at a later time. Other weaker forms of agreement include writing provisional rather than permanent solutions and contingent rather than unconditional agreements (Fisher and Ury, 1981).

Produce a Draft Agreement. Generally, one individual or a small team of negotiators is assigned the task of preparing a draft agreement. If the agreement contains specialized information, such as complex legal or scientific language, the job of drafting it may be assigned to a subgroup of negotiators who are familiar with the substantive information. Parties should review the document for substance to see whether it precisely reflects the oral agreements, and for wording to be sure that the content is expressed in a way acceptable to their constituents. Some people will want an agreement to be stated generally, while others will push for explicit, detailed language to prevent confusion on an issue. Parties must maintain active communication with their constituents throughout the consensus building and drafting of agreements.

When they have difficulty reaching an agreement, the negotiators can consider using a mediator to help them work out their differences and to assist them in drafting an agreement (see "Using a Third Party" in Chapter Eight). If parties have a history of bitter fighting and deep mistrust and refuse to meet together, a mediator can move things along by preparing a draft of agreements based on what each side says it needs. Rather than convening parties, a mediator submits a draft to one party for its comments, incorporates those suggestions, and then delivers the draft to the second party for its reactions. The working draft continues to move back and forth between the parties for their revisions until everyone is satisfied with its content. This approach is known as a one-text negotiation. The system also works well when a large number of parties makes face-to-face negotiation difficult (Fisher and Ury, 1981; Raiffa, 1982; Sebenius, 1984).

Present the Draft to Constituency Groups for Review and Approval. When parties have created an acceptable draft agreement, they must take their product back to their respective constituents for approval. If representatives have done a good job of keeping their constituents informed throughout the negotiation, there should be few surprises in the final document. Too often, however, negotiators fail to keep their members briefed on their progress. In particular, they fail to describe the interests of each side and the range of options available. At best, uninformed constituents will be puzzled by the draft agreements, and at worst they will be angry because they feel that they have been betrayed and they will reject the agreement. Without the support of the constituents, agreements have little chance of being implemented.

Describing all the dynamics that occur at a negotiating table is a difficult task for a representative, and it is no wonder that constituents frequently do not understand the substantive trade-offs that are made. Nor do they have a chance to develop better understanding of the other individuals involved and the evolving relationships. Parties should be clear in the beginning of the negotiating process about the procedures they will use to keep their constituents informed (see "Involving Constituents" in Chapter Eight). Working with constituents takes time, particularly when the membership of an organization is large and geographically dispersed and when individuals hold differing opinions about how their organizations should proceed. Nothing is more frustrating to other parties at the table than to commit the time and resources to a negotiation and then have one of the constituent groups refuse to accept the final draft. Rejection of an agreement that everyone else thinks is reasonable produces additional conflict and tension among parties and makes further attempts to resolve differences even more difficult.

Constituency groups can raise two types of objections. They can disagree with the content of the agreement, or they can object to the wording. They may dislike a particular option or the process proposed for implementing an option, such as the timing of a proposed action, or they may feel that groups designated to be responsible for conducting implementation activities are inappropriate. In other cases parties are willing to accept the substance but are concerned about the words used in the document. The language may be confusing or too vague and may need to be sharpened. Constituents can help improve the final product by suggesting alternative wording or by asking the parties to clarify certain sections. Suggestions for changes are then brought back to the other negotiators for discussion.

Reach Final Agreement. Parties return to the table with the comments they have received from their respective organizations. Negotiators address the issues that were raised and decide how to handle requests for change. Changes in the content do occur, but the negotiators should be made to realize the consequences of requesting substantial changes. Parties feel they have been negotiating in good faith, and if one of the parties at the last minute finds one section unacceptable, the entire agreement can be thrown into question. Agreements represent a series of trade-offs, and tampering with one component can affect the willingness of parties to support other sections in the agreement. The sensitivity of these trade-offs is not going to be obvious to an outside constituent, nor is the possibility that a change may render the entire agreement unacceptable.

Proposals for changes in content should be addressed by the entire group. If the participants agree to make changes, the new agreements must be returned to constituents for their approval. A negotiator should know the boundaries of what his or her group is prepared to accept on each issue and therefore whether a suggested change is realistic. Constituency groups must be given an opportunity to look over the final draft, no matter how many times it takes to go back and forth between them and the parties at the table.

Representatives should refine the language after they have agreed on the general content. For many people, this final phase can be tedious and frustrating, and some parties will spend what seems to be inordinate amounts of time adjusting the precise wording. Unfortunately, this is a necessary part of the process. One way to handle wording changes is to have everyone who wants to offer a suggestion describe it to the entire group. Someone is designated to record all the suggestions and reactions to them, and an individual or a team of two or three people is assigned to redraft the agreements to incorporate the specific suggestions. People who feel the most strongly about changes are put together with individuals who represent the broader interests of the group to revise the language.

It is customary for each party that participates in the discussion to sign the agreement. This is more a symbolic gesture than a legal requirement, since agreements are only as good as the intentions of the people who make them. In a few cases, a court, by prior arrangement, will agree to enforce an agreement because it ordered the parties to sit down and negotiate in the first place. The parties may also seek assurance that their efforts will be backed by an institution with enforcement capabilities as a condition for negotiating, but the real success of a negotiation depends on people acting in good faith.

Coming up with an agreement is only the first half of solving a problem. The other half is carrying out the agreement. Parties too often walk away in exhaustion and neglect to specify how the plan will be implemented. Many carefully crafted agreements are lost because parties do not translate their agreements into action. A good document will spell out who will do what and by what time and who is responsible for overseeing the activities.

Carrying Out Agreements

Reaching an accord with adversaries after weeks, months, or years of fighting is a heady experience. In fact, the expres-

sions of surprise and relief that one so often hears after successful conclusion of a hard-fought negotiation are compelling evidence that most people prefer to act fairly and reasonably if
they are given a chance to do so without harming themselves.
Alternative conflict management techniques are based on this
belief. The negotiators push back their chairs from the table,
stand up, shake hands, and congratulate each other. "A year ago
I would not have believed we could even sit at the same table
together, and here we are agreeing on a solution."

What they do next may determine whether they would
have been better off staying away from the table in the first
place, because agreements reached but not carried out can create a feeling of betrayal among the parties and resentment
about resources spent in negotiation that apparently have been
wasted. If all the effort goes for naught, the parties may end up
even angrier with each other than they were before (Aggerholm,
1983; Bingham, 1984; McCarthy, with Shorett, 1984). Thus,
the important final phase of managing a public dispute is carrying out agreements (see Exhibit 1, p. 67).

Defining Implementation Procedures

The key to carrying out agreements is to include a plan
for implementation *in* the final agreement, not produce one as
an afterthought. The parties must realize that a negotiation is
not successful until they have mapped out methods for achieving their goals. This is true for two reasons. First, something *will*
go wrong. Someone will misunderstand what someone else says
or find that he or she cannot carry out a promise, or in some
other way conditions will change after agreements are reached.
It is vital, therefore, that procedures be stipulated in advance to
handle unexpected setbacks. Second, although the participants
understand their adversaries better and almost certainly have
achieved greater tolerance about their differences, they usually
remain adversaries over the issue negotiated. It would be highly
unusual for all the differences of opinion and the competition
over resources to disappear completely during the course of discussion. Furthermore, although some of the people may like
each other better and may even have formed new friendships

among their adversaries, trust will still be centered in the process and not in the individuals. Trust in a negotiating process often begins to dissolve when regular direct contact among the parties ceases, and, if the parties lose confidence in the durability of their work, they are likely to return to their old ways of dealing with each other. They must, therefore, have visible, predictable procedures for executing their agreements (Bacow and Wheeler, 1984; Clark-McGlennon Associates, 1982; Fisher, 1969; Moore, 1986).

The nature of these procedures will vary widely, depending on the complexity of the dispute and the frequency of contact among the parties. In this book, we advocate the use of conflict management techniques in a manager's day-to-day work. Most of the time, he or she will apply these procedures in relatively uncomplicated situations where the public is involved in some way but the disagreement is limited to a single issue, and, using effective methods, the manager finds a satisfactory answer. In these situations, by far the most frequent of managed controversies, elaborate forms of signed agreements would be out of place. The parties will know whether final agreements are carried out because they are in day-to-day contact with each other and with their original problem. Consider, for example, a quarrel between county officials and a company manager over the amount and timing of communication provided by the company. County officials tell the manager that he or she is not passing along new project information quickly enough. They sit down and negotiate a weekly schedule of meetings in which they share information. Everyone will know immediately if the meetings are not actually held. The schedule is clear and the solution is so straightforward that the parties assume they understand everything they have agreed to do. But this is the point where many successful negotiations fall apart. Even in the simplest of controversies people remember conversations differently. It is essential, therefore, that the agreements be stated clearly, in writing, so there are no misunderstandings among the participants at the negotiating table or among new individuals who replace them in their organizations. The form varies with the need, ranging from signed statements of agreement, each word of which is also negotiated, to minutes of a meeting distributed to all the parties. The essential point is that the accord not be solely oral and thus left to the memories of the people who were there.

Representatives of the government agencies and citizen groups understood what each was to do to solve the problem of the old railroad (see Chapter Two). As in so many disputes, the parties shared similar goals, and all they had needed was a method for breaking off their disagreements and joining forces to solve their problem. Even so, in their final meeting, they listed their assignments and confirmed them in written minutes of the meeting.

Negotiators in the oil and gas conflict (Chapter Two) had more difficult factors with which to contend. While the issue itself was relatively simple, two federal agencies were involved, there was lots of tension between the parties, and large national organizations were looking on. The parties drew up a signed summary of agreement and wrote a "joint letter" to the lead agency manager outlining their recommendations, which included an expanded notification procedure, a request for monitoring of the agreement by the agency, and a "sunset" clause. Notification was to be extended from a primary list of affected parties to a broader list of interested parties. The letter named a trusted individual in the agency to do the monitoring and asked that he be appointed. Finally, the letter suggested that the citizens group assert their continuing need for the procedure one year from the date of the agreement, and if they failed to do so, the agency should discontinue its notification procedures.

Components of Implementation

Any effort to carry out negotiated agreements should involve, in one form or another, four main elements: a monitoring system, a plan for working out details of the agreement, a system for renegotiating parts of the agreement, and procedures for dealing with violations.

Establishing a Monitoring System. Parties must agree on a predictable system for ensuring that the agreements are carried out. Monitoring can be conducted by a political official such as a mayor or governor, a government agency, or a committee made up of representatives involved in the negotiation. Generally, if an agency assumes the responsibility, it will convene a small advisory group of diverse interests to oversee implementation activities. A monitoring system provides a central point where all parties can direct their concerns and suggestions. The committee establishes specific tasks associated with implementation and sets reasonable deadlines for completing them. It also keeps the other parties informed of its progress. If the spirit of the agreement is not followed or if an overt violation occurs, the monitoring committee decides what action is appropriate to get activities back on course.

When the water roundtable finished its work and reached agreements on many separate issues, it asked the governor to appoint a steering committee to oversee implementation. The governor also expanded two existing committees and established two additional groups, the conservation committee and the exchange project team, to work on specific components of the agreements. Roundtable committees continued to work with the lead federal agency to help it incorporate portions of the agreements into its environmental impact statement. The entire roundtable reconvened every three months to review the implementation activities of its committees.

Working Out the Details. Ideally, an agreement will specify precise steps, identify responsible individuals, and define a reasonable time frame for the completion of activities. Most agreements, however, are a mixture of general statements and specific actions, providing a broad framework for parties to follow but leaving the details to be worked out later. It is crucial in these situations that the parties continue to work together to sharpen their understanding of what should be done and support the efforts of individuals who are responsible for implementation. Negotiators who are not part of the monitoring committee must be kept informed of committee activities. This communication can be in the form of a periodic letter that explains what activities have occurred and describes plans for the future. Responsible parties or committees can hold periodic briefing sessions with the original participants. Parties can also choose to reconvene as a group as frequently as necessary to stay in touch with what is happening. Negotiations at this stage can become extremely time-consuming and trying, especially if the agreements include additional policy discussions or many technical details. This is a good time to consider using a third party if discussions are bogging down and the parties are becoming frustrated.

Renegotiating Sections. Sometimes parties will find it necessary to renegotiate a section of an agreement. New information becomes available that alters the desirability of an alternative, or conditions change for a party and it decides it cannot live with an alternative that had been acceptable before. The parties must decide what process they will use to renegotiate a section of an agreement, preferably as a part of their agreement itself. A monitoring committee can work out a new agreement and then discuss the changes with the original participants and seek their approval, or the entire negotiating group can choose to reconvene and work out a new statement. If the final agreement does not spell out how items will be renegotiated, then all the original parties should be asked for their advice on how to proceed. Their decision will depend on the nature of the topic being considered—the more directly the issue affects their interests, the more likely it is that they will want to be involved personally in the renegotiation.

Agreements regarding public disputes are reached in the context of a large framework of policies and programs that are themselves subject to challenge and change. Parties should not be alarmed when adjustments in their agreement are required.

Handling Violations. Violations do occur. Public disputes involve organizations, and organizations change their personnel and their policies. One party in a settlement may discover that a program it promised to initiate is going to be much more expensive than it anticipated and top management says no. Or an organization's goals and priorities change. The person in the organization responsible for carrying out an agreement leaves and no one is left to implement the organization's commitment. In another situation, the parties may have an argument after the close of negotiations and a representative may become so angry that he or she decides to renege on promises made earlier.

The monitoring committee must take responsibility for naming the violation, regardless of whether it has identified the problem or someone else has brought it to the committee's attention. The committee should explore with the offending party the reasons for the infraction and, if the reasons are legitimate, examine alternative methods to solve the problem. However, if a party is simply being irresponsible, pressure must be applied by the other parties through their monitoring committee to compel it to comply. If the negotiators anticipated the possibility that violations would occur and established sanctions that could be invoked if necessary, the job of the committee is easier. The committee proceeds to act according to its instructions, perhaps applying monetary penalties or removing privileges. If the negotiators did not decide on sanctions in advance, as is so often the case, the parties will turn to peer pressure or the force of public opinion. Whatever course they take, they must act incisively or other members will also begin to avoid tasks they agreed to but have found to be uncomfortable or more expensive than expected. Both for survival of the agreements and out of fairness to the other parties, the negotiators must do everything they can to make certain that all parties fulfill their obligations.

Part Three

Ensuring the Success
of Conflict Management

  Part Three is devoted to making the process work by anticipating problems, preventing them from happening where possible, and dealing with setbacks when things go wrong. Chapter Eight explores procedural problems that arise in public disputes, such as managing effective meetings, involving constituents, and handling the news media. The chapter also discusses the use of third parties in part or all of a conflict management program.

Chapter Nine examines the influence on negotiations of competing values and of trust and mistrust. Techniques for identifying and handling complex power relationships among the parties are suggested in this chapter. Chapter Ten considers the human side of the process, including such issues as bringing people to the table and keeping them there and handling situations in which intense emotions dominate discussions. Chapter Eleven addresses two all-too-familiar problems in public disputes: the difficulty of getting people to agree on a common base of information for their negotiations and what to do when discussions reach an impasse.

8

Guidelines for Making
the Program Work

The activities described in this chapter demand some measure of attention in practically all public disputes. The subject of holding productive meetings comes first because it is an essential and often disregarded consideration in managing conflict. The next topic, activities between meetings, is as important as the meetings themselves. Our discussions on involving constituents, informing the public, and working with the news media highlight the importance of the other people outside the negotiation who have a strong interest in what is going on. The last part of the chapter is devoted to a discussion of third parties—when they can be useful and how to take advantage of the skills they offer.

Holding Productive Meetings

When the adversaries in a dispute gather in one room, their convener assumes a substantial responsibility. The meeting can be the first step in improving relationships and moving toward a solution to the problem, or it can be disastrous. A great deal depends on how carefully and thoroughly the steps described in earlier chapters have been followed. But now the negotiators are together, and it is up to the people responsible for managing the meeting to establish a setting in which the parties can work out their problems.

The person conducting the meeting can be a representative—a manager or staff professional—from the organization that called the meeting. If the organization is considered to be one of the parties, then at least one other person should represent

157

the agency on substantive matters, freeing the manager to concentrate on running a productive meeting. A manager can also
arrange to have a neutral facilitator run a difficult session. The
following suggestions will help the person conducting a meeting
to hold a productive session (Doyle and Straus, 1976; Maier,
1963).

Establish an Agenda. The agenda should be available for
all participants to see throughout the meeting. It can be type-
written and distributed or written on a large piece of newsprint
and posted on a wall in front of the group. The agenda should
list in order the items to be covered in the meeting and should
indicate the amount of time each item is expected to take. An
agenda is a plan for a meeting, an outline that can be modified
when necessary with the approval of the participants. It tells
people what specific tasks the meeting is expected to accomplish, such as "discuss the association's report," "identify issues
to be studied," and "select options." An agenda tells people
whether issues they are concerned about will be discussed and
helps the manager of the meeting and the participants focus on
the subjects they came to consider.

It is desirable to prepare an agenda before a meeting and
to check it out with the key participants, asking them to say
whether they think the items are appropriate, whether enough
time has been allotted, whether any issues have been forgotten,
and whether the sequence of discussion topics makes sense. If
there is not enough time to work out an agenda before a meeting, time at the beginning should be allotted for asking participants these questions. It is important that they accept the
agenda as a workable plan.

At the conclusion of the meeting it is useful to review
and assess the group's progress. Did it get through all of the
agenda items? Is more discussion or information required on
some issues? Were new topics suggested for subsequent sessions?
After the review of progress, parties should be asked what topics they think should be covered at the next meeting.

Keep the Discussion Focused on the Agenda. Nothing is
more tempting in a conflict situation than for one party to di-

gress into a lengthy exposé of the grave injustices inflicted upon it by another party. While impassioned recounting of war stories may feel good to the teller, it generally serves no useful purpose. Rather, it annoys other participants, who have come to solve problems. And others may respond by telling a few tales of their own.

The discussion can be kept on track by reminding people about the purpose of the particular agenda item they are discussing: "Mr. Marquet, remember that the purpose of this portion of our meeting is to comment on the planning staff's draft proposal."

Sometimes people move to an item that appears later on an agenda, describing, for example, their favorite solutions before parties have finished discussing possible options. They should be reminded that they will have an opportunity to express their preference for solutions later in the meeting.

The manager should listen carefully to the discussion, allowing items that are consistent with the agenda to proceed. If a comment does not appear to be relevant, the manager can ask the individual about it: "I don't understand how your comments relate to the agenda item." The individual then has the opportunity to explain the relationship and tighten the connection if there is one.

Clarify Statements. Clear communication is absolutely critical in resolving conflicts. If someone's idea is confusing to the meeting manager, chances are that it is unclear to others as well. The manager can ask a speaker to clarify a statement ("Mrs. Wells, I'm not sure that I understand what you were saying; can you please explain that again?") or try to restate it ("If I understand you correctly, you are saying that . . . ").

The meeting manager should watch for situations in which the discussion is clear to some people because of their familiarity with the topic, while others in the group are sitting with puzzled looks on their faces. When this happens, the manager should stop and clarify what is being discussed so that everyone can keep up with the discussion. He or she can try something like, "Can you review what you have just said, just to make sure that we all understand?" The manager can then ask the group, "Are there any additional questions you would like to ask?"

Summarize Statements. Periodically summarizing what has been discussed helps to assure that everyone is on the same track. Summarizing the key points sharpens what has happened and provides the basis for determining the direction in which the group should be moving. The manager should summarize after major presentations and at the completion of individual agenda items and should check back with the group to see whether any key points have been left out.

If a member of the group has volunteered to do the summarizing, he or she can ask the group whether anyone has anything they would like to add to the discussion. Advising the group in advance that someone will later be asked to summarize has the added advantage of encouraging the parties to listen attentively.

Explore Ideas. In public disputes, citizens not accustomed to speaking in public are sometimes pitted against articulate lawyers representing another party. The citizens, angry for good reason when they arrive, are intimidated by the lawyers and have difficulty expressing their ideas before the group, which makes them even madder.

When confronted by an incoherently expressed idea, meeting managers commonly dismiss it with a brisk "thank you" and move on to the next speaker. Such a momentary lapse in courtesy can have lasting consequences if friends and neighbors of the person trying to get out a thought feel that he or she has been insulted. They may quickly turn into a hostile audience. It is far better to try to draw the speaker out by saying, "Can you tell us a little more about what you mean? I am not sure how it applies to our situation." With this encouragement, the person has a second chance to correct the original statement, and the audience will see that the manager has tried to be fair.

Encourage All Members of the Group to Participate. In every meeting, some people are more vocal than others, and they will dominate the discussion if other, less assertive people are not encouraged to speak. Statements such as "Several of you have not said anything during this discussion; I'm wondering if you have any comments you would like to make at this time" encourage quieter members to speak up and remind the more active participants that they should give everyone a chance to express their views.

In some cases, people will be content with the discussion, usually because someone else is articulating their ideas and they feel no need to join in. In other cases, however, they may be reluctant to say anything even if they have opinions that they want to express, perhaps because they distrust or are uncomfortable with other members of the group. They may be afraid of not being able to express their views well, or they may be dissatisfied with the progress of the talks in general. The meeting manager must be careful about the silence of some members. They may or may not agree with statements that have been made, and it is discouraging to spend three hours discussing a topic, thinking that everyone is close to reaching an agreement, only to discover at the end that the silent party strongly objects to a proposal that everyone else has worked hard to develop. Periodic checks avoid last-minute frustrations.

Maintain a Positive Tone. Negotiators become frustrated when progress slows down or when parties walk tediously through a technical issue. They need the reassurance that their frustration is normal and that it takes time to reach agreements. The parties need to be reminded of what they have accomplished to date, such as earlier agreements on ground rules or issues to discuss, which can be precedents for reaching agreements in more difficult substantive areas (see "Keeping People at the Table" in Chapter Ten).

Enforce the Ground Rules. Ground rules must be scrupulously observed or they become meaningless. Prompt action is necessary when an infraction occurs. When people see that the ground rules are taken seriously and administered fairly, they usually relax and business can continue (see Chapter Six).

Describe What Is Happening. Participants naturally focus on their own concerns during a meeting. They are not accustomed to thinking about the dynamics of what is happening. People know when progress is faltering and feel uncomfortable when relationships become tense, but they do not know what to do about it. When something is happening that is hurting the discussions, the meeting manager should name what is going on and ask the members of the group whether they agree. He or she can make process observations, such as "We seem to be going very quickly through this report. Is this pace comfortable, or should we be slowing down?" Comments can also be made about the human dynamics and about the content of the discussion: "It doesn't seem that the mayor's office is answering the neighborhood representative's questions. Is that correct?" The neighborhood person may be getting enough of an answer to be satisfied and will say so. If not, the mayor's office is given a chance to provide a more direct answer or to explain why one is not possible at this time. "The issue of financing seems to be the stumbling block in this discussion. Is that right?" The group will confirm or correct the perception. (Financing may not be the problem. Rather, it may be a smoke screen for a different and more delicate issue, such as the question of who administers the funds.)

When something is blocking the progress of a meeting, the manager might describe it to the group, ask whether participants agree with the assessment, and then offer a procedural suggestion to remedy the situation. Or this may be an occasion for the group to assume more responsibility, and members should be asked what they think should be done.

Offer Process Suggestions. A meeting manager continually assesses the steps being used to achieve a meeting goal and, if they are not productive, suggests alternative methods. If, for example, a group is stuck in a discussion, it may be mixing too many topics together. The manager might suggest that the group divide the subject into three subtopics and discuss each one separately. The manager should always test the suggestion with the group: "This discussion seems to be getting bogged down. Would it make sense to divide it into three subtopics and discuss each one separately?"

Other examples of process suggestions include "The group seems to be getting restless [description of what is happening]; would it make sense to take a ten-minute break?" and "The issue of traffic seems to be a stumbling block in this discussion; should we set up a subcommittee that will try to resolve this issue before our next meeting?" The participants can answer "yes" or "no" depending on their perceptions of the problem. For example, someone may suggest that the group is restless because it does not have enough information to engage in a productive discussion and may recommend that further discussion of the topic be postponed until everyone has had a chance to read related background material.

Supervise Record Keeping. Record keeping is an important function in conflict resolution meetings. Accurate notes must be kept on the topics covered and actions taken. Usually someone is designated to record at least the sequence of topics that have been covered and any decisions that have been made. If the group wants a more thorough documentation of the discussion, it should request it at the beginning of the meeting. If someone wants to tape record a session, the permission of the group should be obtained before any recording is done. It is essential that any summary or minutes of the meeting be submitted to the group for review and approval.

An effective method for capturing key ideas, phrases, and agreements as the discussion goes along is to record them on newsprint posted on walls in front of the group. This highly useful procedure, called "group memory" (Doyle and Straus, 1976), shifts the focus of the problem to the wall and away from individual participants. It helps the group develop a common perception of the direction the meeting is moving and documents progress as it is made. It also gives tangible evidence that each person is being heard. One person is designated to be a wall recorder for a session. Completed charts should be displayed on the wall throughout a meeting so that participants can refer back to any topic, check to see whether points were covered, and determine whether additional items should be added.

Test for Agreements. When parties appear to be close to an agreement, every effort should be made to reach closure. Too often, they narrow their differences, but no one acknowledges that they are near an agreement, and a possible solution slips away. The manager should test the group to see whether they think they have reached agreement. He or she can ask the group to sharpen the wording to ensure the acceptability of the final statement. In some situations the parties will not be as near closure as they appear to be, and they will say so. When the discussion is completed and refinements are made, the manager should restate the agreement in precise terms. The wording should be recorded exactly as it is stated to the group so that a written version can be referred to later if there is any question about accuracy. Writing an agreement on newsprint in front of the group is a good way of ensuring accuracy. Since silence does not equal agreement, the manager should press for affirmative statements or signals, such as a positive nod from all parties.

Managing Activities Between Meetings

Important as they are, meetings represent only a small portion of the activity that goes on during a conflict management program. People on the outside of a process may look at a successful outcome and say, "They solved the problem in only four meetings." This statement may be accurate as far as it goes, but it misses the really important part of the effort—the time spent between negotiating sessions. Parties in a negotiation normally spend far more hours working between sessions than in the meetings themselves.

Between meetings, parties confer with their constituents, describing what happened at the last meeting and developing strategies for the next session. They confer with other parties to sharpen their understanding of a problem or to test an idea informally before suggesting it to the entire group. Subcommittees are frequently convened to discuss a technical issue or to deal with an issue that concerns only a few of the parties. The person responsible for conducting the meeting also has an important part in the activities taking place between meetings. Some suggestions for managing activities between meetings follow.

Talk with the Parties Individually. The manager should talk with key actors between sessions to find out how they thought the last meeting went and what actions are appropriate for the group to take next. Individuals who have been reluctant to express their concerns before the entire group, because their statements reflect adversely on someone else's judgment or on a superior, are far more likely to share their thoughts in private. The manager should check with the parties between meetings to detect problems that did not come out in open session. For example, if someone was particularly quiet at the last meeting, the manager could call and ask what he or she thought of the session. The answer may be a comment about the meeting itself, such as about the way one person was treating another, or it may reflect the person's concern about something totally outside the negotiation. Either way, the message has been conveyed that the person's part in the negotiation is important.

Some people agree to participate in a negotiation but remain skeptical about the process and the people in it. They are a hazard and deserve close attention as long as they remain uncommitted. Talking with these people can head off misunderstandings they may have about the actions and motives of other parties and can make it clear that they are encouraged to have an active part in the program.

Clarify the Parties' Perceptions of Each Other. In the stress of conflict, people leap quickly and easily to the most negative interpretation of what their adversaries say or do. They come to the table with different and often competing interests. They have varying styles of interacting with people, have different agendas, and are under stress, so the slightest breach of good behavior or any hint of a failure to keep a promise can trigger a harsh response.

In one case, the staff of an electric utility was asked to make a presentation to a diverse group of consumers about the company's system for supplying electricity. The staff agonized over how technical the discussion should be, recognizing that the audience's familiarity with the topic ranged from that of un-informed homeowners to that of highly sophisticated engineers. The company decided to give a general overview for the benefit of parties not familiar with the industry's terminology and con-cepts. Unfortunately, the better-informed participants were outraged. They felt that the presentation was condescending and that the company should have given a much more technical review. One individual got up and left the meeting in disgust. Others sat silently through the session but expressed their anger as soon as the meeting was over. Over the next several days the meeting manager talked with people who were upset about the meeting, describing how much thought the company had given to the level of the presentation and explaining the company's reasoning. Damage control of this kind may be necessary when a difficult session goes off track. Calls to correct misconcep-tions may take hours of time, but they will enable the process to continue and prevent more serious problems later on.

Communicate New Information. Since most representa-tives in a negotiation are busy people with other problems to worry about, meetings are usually held no more often than once a month or once every three weeks. During that time, new de-velopments often occur that will affect the agenda for the next meeting. The information may have to do with a government decision that relates to the issues being discussed; it may be the release of a report that has bearing on options being considered; or one party may have changed its stance on an issue in a way that will alter how other parties proceed in the negotiation. It is important to convey essential new information to the parties promptly, because some will discover new information through their normal contacts and others will not. Those who are not in-formed will feel left out and resentful, which will add more tensions to what may already be a touchy situation. Conveying the same information directly to everyone minimizes the distortion that always occurs when one party describes the situation to another, imposing his or her own values and perceptions on the material or leaving out critical pieces.

Test New Ideas. Because people will give a more candid assessment in a private discussion than they will before a large group, the period between sessions is also an excellent time to try out new ideas. Someone may think of a new proposal but will be hesitant to suggest it in the whole group. For example, a developer may realize that there is a workable alternative to controversial proposals on the table but may feel that if she suggests it, her opponents will be suspicious of her motives. The developer may approach the chairperson between meetings, describe the idea, and ask that it be tested with other parties by asking them for opinions, without identifying the source. If there is sufficient support, the chairperson can look for an acceptable party to introduce the idea or can suggest it by saying, "I would like to throw out an idea that evolved in my discussions with a number of you over the past few weeks. I am curious to see what you think of it."

Another reason to test ideas between sessions is that people may not be able to support an idea for reasons that have nothing to do with the soundness of the proposal. For example, one group may propose that a government agency take the primary responsibility for administering a program, but several people are clearly uncomfortable with the suggestion even though it is a logical idea. In private discussions they explain that they are not opposed in principle to the agency handling the program but are deeply concerned about the ability of the particular individual who would most likely be responsible for it, an objection that is difficult to express in public. Once this message is conveyed in private, some alternative way to administer the program can be explored without having to criticize individuals publicly.

Arrange for Technical Assistance When Necessary. Negotiators must have access to relevant technical information to pursue an intelligent discussion, and they must be able to understand the implications of the material that is provided. They may therefore request background briefing papers that explain complex issues in lay terms, or request the presence of a technical resource person. The manager arranges for technical assistance when requested to do so.

Plan for the Next Meeting. An important task between meetings is to determine the purpose of the upcoming session and to develop an appropriate agenda, including the substantive topics to be covered and necessary actions. The manager will need to work with the parties to decide what topics to cover, determine a logical order for the topics, and select the best method for covering each item, such as small group discussions, written reports, or oral presentations. The manager should determine how much time to allot to each item, allowing adequate time for discussions after presentations. Finally, the manager will need to identify the person who should be responsible for handling each agenda item and be sure that he or she is notified before the meeting.

After the goals of the meeting have been determined, a decision must be made as to who should be present as representatives, as resource people, and as observers. If the meeting is open to the public, appropriate groups will need to be notified well in advance. It is also important to consider what materials parties will want to use during the next session and to determine whether these materials should be sent out before the session so that parties have an opportunity to review them. The manager should collect reference documents—all previous handouts given to the participants and other reports or studies—that parties might want to use and be sure to have copies of minutes of the previous meeting for review and approval of the participants.

Involving Constituents

"I believe you when you say you will keep this agreement, but can you deliver your group?"

At meetings, negotiators discuss and agree, and observers

watch and comment. Constituents do not even attend meetings as a general rule, but *they* decide whether negotiations will succeed or fail. They have this power because the vast majority of negotiations over public disputes are voluntary and impromptu. Representatives of the parties have standing only so long as their constituents allow them to have it. This is true whether the parties are long-established, well-funded, professionally managed organizations such as trade associations and citizen federations with headquarters in Washington, D.C., or ad hoc, loosely aggregated assemblages of concerned citizens with ambiguous accountability and shifting leadership. Whatever their structure, constituencies have final authority to make or break a negotiated solution.

Negotiators take their power from their constituents. The word *constituent* is defined in dictionaries as a person who elects officials, but in conflict management parlance it has come to mean a person to whom representatives are responsible and whose support is required if agreements reached in negotiation are to be implemented. Not only do constituents have final and often unpredictable influence on negotiations, but they also determine the amount of personal risk incurred by participants. If a representative gets too far out in front of his or her supporters, they may become hesitant, cease to endorse agreements, and give conflicting signals to their representative. The representative may then be forced to change his or her position in succeeding negotiating sessions, an extremely frustrating development for the others at the table. Other negotiators may then raise the pivotal questions, "Will your group support you? Can you deliver what you've promised?"

Factors Affecting a Constituency's
Support of Negotiation

A manager takes a careful look at the ability of all of the parties to function as constituencies for their representatives. It is not enough that the leaders of the key parties support the idea of negotiation. The important question is whether their constituents will back them up.

Factors that should be considered are:

1. *Coalitions.* How large is the group? If it is very large, it may be hard to synthesize divergent views into one negotiating strategy. How far apart are the extremes? Are there clearly understood central goals that bind the people with separate views together in support of their representative?

2. *Leadership.* Are leaders available who are capable of dealing in good faith with their adversaries? Will members accept a representative who is willing to reason with the other side?

3. *Decision making within the group.* Do they reach agreement by consensus or by majority rule? If they vote, will minorities abide by decisions or bolt? Are enough organizational levels involved?

4. *Communication.* What forms of communication are used within the group? Will members attend and participate in briefing sessions? Will they read reports? Will someone write reports? What are the most effective methods of keeping members abreast of developments?

5. *Outsiders.* How much influence do outside individuals and organizations have? Is the influence consistent or inconsistent with the goals of a party *in this negotiation?* For example, is a national organization intent on total victory, with no concessions, so that it can establish a legal precedent? Will members permit outsiders to impose their own agendas?

6. *Experience in negotiation.* How familiar are members with the concepts of good faith negotiation? If they are not familiar, what can be done to educate them so they will understand the actions of their representatives?

7. *Personal risk.* How much risk to personal standing or professional career is a representative taking? In a hierarchical organization, will superiors support their subordinates? Will representatives be forced to leave a negotiation to protect themselves from attack within their group?

The Water Roundtable

Although most of the thirty participants of the water roundtable (see Chapter Two) were officials or executives of

public bodies or established organizations, some represented coalitions of interests having generally similar goals but widely differing perspectives on how to achieve them. The mediators advised the groups on methods for choosing their representatives
and informing themselves about the progress of the discussions,
and occasionally helped them work out internal disputes, but
the day-to-day business of communication was carried on by
the groups themselves.

The Environmental Alliance. The Environmental Alliance
included seventeen environmental organizations in the city
area. Some had been carrying on anti–water development campaigns for years as a part of broader environmental programs.
Others had been formed more recently for the single purpose of
opposing the city's plans for water development. Some groups
were extremely militant on the subject, while others were more
moderate in their approach. The challenge was to form a cohesive group that would support its representatives at the table. A
highly sensitive issue was the choice of the two persons who
would represent the alliance. As so often happens in long-standing disputes, the most intransigent spokespersons for the hardest line had assumed leadership in some of the groups. In fact,
representatives of other parties said that they would not sit in
the same room with one of the most prominent environmental
leaders.

The environmentalists agreed to participate in the negotiations and met to select their two representatives. This was a
critical point in establishing cohesion in the group. They found
that they could cooperate in solving what everyone knew was a
difficult problem. They chose two people who were knowledgeable about the subject matter, were leaders in their respective
organizations, and were known to be capable of getting along
with other parties.

During the entire eighteen months of the negotiation, the
representatives of the alliance faced the possibility that one or
more of the members would overreact to a setback in negotiations, break ranks, and attack the process in public, thus destroying the entire negotiation effort. Many were militant in
their mission to defeat the city's plans to construct a new water

facility. An additional hazard for the two negotiators was their members' lack of experience in cooperative problem solving. The alliance dealt with the danger of internal disruption by convening meetings between plenary negotiation sessions with representatives of all seventeen groups to review detailed reports from its representatives and to exchange views. Discussions were often heated, but throughout the long negotiation members were able to reach consensus on major policy strategies. Discussion *within* the alliance often took more time than reaching agreements at the table.

Perhaps the most compelling reason for their ability to reach consensus was the progress they were making toward some of their goals. Another was that for the first time they had equal standing with their adversaries in formal discussions. Finally, they knew that their next step outside negotiation would have to be litigation, with its enormous costs and uncertainties.

Western Water Advisory Council. Later in the negotiations, the roundtable members looked to the western slope for its ideas on an acceptable proposal for meeting the city's water needs and found no unanimity. As a result, the fifteen-member Western Water Advisory Council was formed, representing citizen groups and business organizations on the western side of the Continental Divide. Like other groups organized to support or oppose public policy decisions, they had little else in common. Many had never met before they gathered to represent western water interests. Some members, mostly middle-aged, were from the western water establishment and water management companies. Others, mostly young, were political liberals and citizen activists. They were united by their determination to keep western water on the western side of the mountains.

Recognizing the importance of communication in such a diverse group, they met frequently, at least twice a month, to receive technical presentations from their members and reports from their representatives. They decided on strategies for the negotiations by consensus of the group. Meeting attendance was high even though some members had to travel long distances at their own expense.

Although several of the members were well informed in water management matters, the group needed technical advice on many points. The services of an experienced water engineer were provided to the council at no charge by a western water management company. Most of the western organizations involved in the water roundtable were split into factions supporting and opposing negotiation with the city. The arguments were often acrimonious and strongly personal. Nevertheless, the Western Water Advisory Council was able to close ranks and endorse the actions of their representatives at critical moments.

Suggestions for Building Effective Constituencies

Following are some pointers for building effective constituencies.

Ensure That All Interests Are Effectively Represented. The manager should be certain that separate interests are adequately represented even if it means adding more participants at the table. It is important to resist the impulse to lump broadly similar interests into one umbrella party with one representative. "All those citizen activists are alike—why should they have more than one representative?" is a hazardous way of setting up a negotiation, because a party may break apart when negotiators try to synthesize an impossibly wide range of opinion. What pleases one end of the spectrum may infuriate the other end. Coalitions of interests should not be so diverse as to be unmanageable.

Help the Group Establish Regular, Predictable Methods of Communication. "You never told me you were going to do that" is a clear sign that constituents are being left out of discussions. It may be their fault for not coming to meetings or not reading their mail, but the danger is that they will block progress just to assert their resentment. They should not be given a chance to be resentful, and they should not be asked simply to trust their representative. They should be given useful, substantive information. The conveners of the Western Water

Advisory Council took great care to prepare in advance formal meeting agendas and interesting material for discussion, information that was worth driving 100 miles to hear.

Deal Promptly and Incisively with Disagreements. A dispute inside a party can be just as complicated and at least as heated as arguments among major parties. Rather than simple spats among pals, disputes may grow into permanent divisions and reduce the power of their representatives to carry out agreements made at the negotiating table. There may also be competition for leadership of the group. To deal with such disputes, the manager should use the conflict management techniques recommended for negotiation between parties: setting ground rules for discussion, agreeing on goals, identifying interests, developing options, and reaching agreements.

Make the Decision Process Clear. Everyone should understand how decisions will be made within a constituency group. If they decide to agree by consensus, the party's representative should make certain that everyone understands what that means. If the decision is to vote, the representative should get a commitment from the members to abide by the will of the majority.

Use Task Groups to Expand Participation. Much of the work of the water roundtable was accomplished in task groups made up of people with special knowledge of the group's assigned task. Some of the groups contained fifteen people or more, only a few of whom were roundtable negotiators. The rest were professionals and volunteers from interested organizations. Because several task groups worked on problems simultaneously, a substantial number of constituents became intimately familiar with the goals and methods of the roundtable.

Educate Constituents on Principles of Negotiation. Most people are unfamiliar with the concept of solving problems through a step-by-step process. People want to "get down to the nitty-gritty" in a hurry. They also fear the possibility of being overwhelmed by superior knowledge or majority rule. Members of the Environmental Alliance and the Western Water Advisory Council met periodically with boards of directors and members of organizations other than their own to explain the principles of negotiation. In addition, several roundtable members wrote articles about negotiation for organization newsletters.

Allow Adequate Time Between Meetings for Representatives to Meet with Their Constituents. The negotiation process must be designed to reinforce the representatives' need to communicate with their constituents. Negotiation sessions must not be scheduled so frequently—once a week, for example—that regular meetings with constituents are difficult. Sessions held once every three or four weeks permit negotiators to meet with their organizations to discuss and work out any differences. Adequate time for this process is essential, because parties frequently require more than one meeting to work out differences within their organizations.

Watch Out for the Last Stages of Negotiation. In the final moments of a negotiation, as major movements toward agreement occur, representatives run a serious risk of getting out ahead of their constituents. A negotiator can see and feel the push to solution, but constituents are back there outside the enthusiasm and still wary. This is the time when a negotiator must do everything possible to check with constituents as he or she adjusts to new developments. Representatives who keep their constituents informed throughout a negotiation will find it much easier to persuade them to support an agreement at the end.

Informing the Public

"I want to hear what is going on in that meeting. They are talking about my future!"

People want to know what decisions are being made for them and how those decisions will affect their welfare. They want decision makers to know what they think about the issues, and they want to know who makes decisions, who takes the risks, and what the costs may be. Especially in matters of health and safety, the public is ready to exercise its power by economic pressure or by legal challenge. Public officials are elected or appointed to serve the interests of all the people, which is a difficult enough task in itself, but they must also contend with a pervasive distrust of all powerful institutions, public or private, which results in sunshine laws and instant suspicion whenever public officials meet in secrecy.

Negotiators of public policy questions are faced with a dilemma: the public wants to be involved in decisions, yet negotiations do not go well in a crowd. The public's concern could be satisfied by holding discussions in a gymnasium for all to see, but it is hard to make difficult decisions in the glare of the public spotlight. On the other hand, negotiators of public disputes could act as private negotiators do when they bargain over wages: hold closed meetings and announce their findings afterward. But negotiators of public policy are not just responsible for making decisions. They must also do their best to conduct the process of negotiation in ways that will be acceptable to people outside the negotiations. If they do not, their conclusions may be set aside and their work will be fruitless.

"Public involvement" is unpredictable, because people are unpredictable. Some managers become adept in satisfying the requirements of the statutes without really permitting the public to have a say in decisions, but this can be a risky strategy because people know when they are going through a meaningless minuet and resent it. Sometimes they become angry enough to block a decision even if they do not seriously disagree with it.

This section of the chapter focuses on suggestions for informing the public about negotiations. Although it is difficult, if not impossible, to design a process that will satisfy the entire range of interests usually present in public controversies, trying to satisfy as many of them as possible is worthwhile and probably a lot safer than attempting to avoid them. The essential issue is that people outside a negotiation are asked to accept the results, but asking for support from an uninformed public is asking for a leap of faith that most people are unwilling to make.

In addition to achieving public understanding and support, another compelling reason for establishing dialogue with interested citizens during negotiations is the fact that people are likely to know a great deal about their own problems. Public disputes are often highly complex, and negotiators sometimes miss important factors as they assess their options. People directly affected by a problem are likely to know a lot about it.

The advantages of seeking advice from people most directly affected by a negotiated decision may seem quite obvious. Not long ago, however, a federal agency was organizing a review of potential effects of oil shale development on water resources in western Colorado. Agency officials invited federal and state officials, industry representatives, and urban environmentalists to participate. The plan was to discuss the issues, produce agreements, and then announce them to the world. No public meetings were held. The opinions of the agricultural and community water interests were not sought until after the discussions were completed. As a result, the agreements reached by the group omitted subtle but important long-term consequences to agriculture of diverting water to the oil shale industry. The report and the work that had gone into it were so flawed that it was never given serious consideration.

An uninformed public is likely to make up its own facts, and misunderstandings become new, separate conflicts that make the original problem more difficult to solve. Information does not guarantee public support, but it increases the chances that the public will come to the right conclusions. E. B. White said, "Democracy is the recurrent suspicion that more than half the people are right more than half the time." But how can the public be kept informed without destroying a negotiation process?

Methods for Keeping the Public Informed

The question of how and how much to inform the public is a difficult one for a manager trying to work out a sound solution, because the results of communicating with the public are unpredictable. Some people cannot be pleased no matter how much effort conveners make to keep them informed. They may be intent on disrupting cooperative discussions, or they may be beyond reach for other rational or irrational reasons. Everyone knows that "stirring up the natives" can have its drawbacks. It is tempting, therefore, to have private meetings in which a few key individuals make decisions and announce them afterward, but the orderliness of this approach may last only until the public is asked to accept decisions they do not understand. In matters of public policy, it is safer in the long run to develop and use effective methods for keeping the public informed (Bleiker and Bleiker, 1978; Creighton, 1980; Susskind, 1978).

Following are five ways to keep the public informed. The manager will need to determine which method or combination of methods is desirable for a particular problem.

Selecting Representatives of Interest Groups. Individuals from major constituency groups can participate directly in a negotiation as formally designated representatives. The representatives have the responsibility of keeping their constituents informed about the content of talks as they progress.

Designating Observers or Subcommittee Members. Members of the public can become official observers to the negotiation. Observers have the right to attend all sessions but are not allowed to participate in the discussion unless called upon. A second way to involve additional individuals is through subcommittee assignments. An individual may have a keen interest or expertise in one of the issues under consideration. Inviting people to observe and serve on subcommittees permits more people to participate without increasing the number of negotiators at the table.

Conducting Public Meetings. An effective way to keep interested individuals informed and to draw on their knowledge is to hold periodic public meetings. The purpose of such meetings may change as a negotiation progresses. Public meetings provide an opportunity to explain the purpose and structure of the negotiation and to inform the public of the progress of talks.

Participants in public meetings can help negotiators identify key issues that should be addressed in their sessions, and they can comment on options for resolving differences.

Holding Briefing Sessions. The organization responsible for convening the sessions, individual negotiators, or teams of negotiators who represent different constituencies can organize briefing sessions for individuals or organizations who want to be kept informed about the progress of the talks. Briefing sessions are also arranged to inform elected and appointed officials who may play a role in the implementation of an agreement.

Sending Written Material. The public can be kept informed through regular mailings. The negotiators must decide whether to make meeting minutes available or whether to issue general progress reports on the discussions. Technical studies and work group reports can also be distributed.

Two Case Examples

The Water Roundtable. The first meetings of the water roundtable were devoted to matters of organization and approach. The most controversial issue concerned the question of whether meetings should be open or closed to the public. About one-third of the thirty participants were elected officials, accustomed to open meetings. They were also under pressure from some of their constituents who wanted direct access to the discussions. At the same time, most of the negotiators thought that the sessions would be more frank and more productive if they were not public. They debated the question and finally agreed to proceed with closed meetings and to conduct an energetic public information program that included the following components:

- Press releases issued after each negotiating session to report on the discussions, and press conferences held after each session to allow reporters to question participants.

- Periodic mailings summarizing the issues under consideration sent to a mailing list of 400 people.
- Presentations about the negotiations made by participants at meetings of interested organizations.
- Public meetings held at several different locations in the state. They were announced well in advance by advertisements in local newspapers. Negotiators representing diverse points of view formed panels to listen to comments and answer questions.
- Task groups of agency managers and persons with technical knowledge formed to address technical issues. These groups included many more people than participated in the formal negotiations, people who had substantial responsibilities in the organizations in which they worked. As a result, information about the nature of the discussions was widely disseminated in organizations that had a stake in the outcome.

The Village. In the village case (see Chapter Two) the mayor and the manager of the real estate company holding the land designed a program of formal negotiations among designated representatives of the town government, several interested companies, local business interests, and citizen groups. They prepared for an expected uproar from those who preferred free-wheeling public arguments to formal negotiation by proposing a parallel program to inform the citizens and solicit their opinions. This program included:

- Public meetings to gather information from residents of the community about the issues they thought should be addressed and about specific suggestions for how the site should be developed.
- Questionnaires mailed to nonresident property owners (a substantial part of the community) seeking their comments and ideas.
- Questionnaires published in the local newspaper as an additional way to gather information.
- Regular presentations by participants in the negotiation to the town council in open session.

Some Guiding Principles

The three guiding principles that follow are fundamental to working successfully with the public. Although they seem to be expressions of basic courtesy and common sense, they are often ignored.

Acknowledge the Public's Right to Know. "We realize that this is a serious problem for you. You want to be sure that these meetings come up with reasonable answers. This is how we are going to keep you informed about the discussions..." Most people who exercise economic or political power are used to making decisions *for* people, whether the people like it or not. Members of the public know this and will not necessarily expect their concerns to be respected or regarded as legitimate. It is important that the manager make it clear to them that he or she will keep members of the public informed and will seek their advice.

Fit the Strategy to the Situation. "Our town newspaper comes out on Thursdays. If you could change your meeting schedule from Thursday to Wednesday, we could include an up-to-date report on the meetings each week."

"The commissioners meet on Monday afternoons. If we could get your meeting summaries first thing Monday morning, we could see that the commissioners have copies before they meet."

The symbolic value of answering "That is a good idea; I think we can make the change" is enormous. It gives positive evidence that the negotiators intend to work with the media and the public.

Expect Opposition. The group should expect suspicion, especially if the meeting is closed or limited to negotiation by representatives. The public should be expected to be skeptical of motives. Remember that they are being asked to break off from a pattern of confrontation and to suspend judgment about the alternative process being proposed. Credibility can be built by thorough and scrupulously accurate communication with people outside the discussions.

Working with the News Media

"Should we keep the press out of the meeting?"

"I don't trust that reporter. He writes only half the story."

"How do we get the media to report something positive for a change?"

Nearly everyone in public life has had an unpleasant experience with the news media. Journalists see themselves as the eyes and ears of the people, the heart of democracy's communication system, with rights and obligations protected by the First Amendment of the Constitution. Decision makers who have been bruised by inaccurate reporting, subjective editorials, and misleading headlines see reporters in a different light—more like vultures who can embarrass competent managers and even destroy careers. Managers know that the news media can make their jobs more difficult, and it is frustrating for them that fairness and accuracy of stories about their work are subject to the vagaries of the professional ethics, skill, and intelligence of whatever reporter covers the event. Because the quality of reporting is so unpredictable, even managers of soundly conceived projects commonly think of the news media as a threat and try to avoid reporters whenever possible.

Reporters, on the other hand, look on avoidance as a challenge and consider getting around it to be part of their job. It is their responsibility to uncover all aspects of the situation. Reporters are accustomed to hostility, and they expect their presence to make some people uncomfortable. Some enjoy their power; others accept it as a responsibility. But however they see their function in society and whatever their ethics and competence, they can be expected to do their best to get a story.

Dealing with Open and Closed Meetings

When people have a difficult problem to solve, the thought of trying to do it with the public watching is repugnant. There are enough uncertainties about the negotiation process without the additional worry about how the press is going to handle the proceedings. Parties considering entering into negotiation frequently hope that the meetings can be closed to the public and the news media. Sometimes they make the mistake of trying to separate the two, letting the public in but keeping reporters out, which is an impossible strategy unless one can distinguish precisely between a reporter and a citizen who is not a reporter. It is not a good idea to try, both because it is hard to do and because it makes the reporters very angry.

Very few meetings that involve public officials are actually closed, because the news media, among others, always object strenuously. Reporters talk about public officials "making deals behind closed doors," and newspapers publish indignant editorials. Public officials generally fear attacks of this kind, and they usually say that they want a meeting to be open. Those who favor excluding the press and the public from negotiating meetings use the following arguments:

- The parties will be reluctant to adjust their stated positions to accommodate new information if each step is criticized as it is made.
- The delicate business of testing for consensus is hard to do in public view.
- Building personal rapport with representatives of opposing views is important in negotiation yet difficult to do if constituents see overtures of courtesy or partial agreement as selling out to the enemy.
- Discussions become less candid when the press is present. Hard negotiating shifts from the formal sessions to informal meetings among participants between scheduled sessions.

In some circumstances, the public's right to know at once, which is strongly supported by news media people, must be balanced against the public's need for solutions to problems, and sometimes negotiations will not go forward if a meeting is open. Considerations that may require excluding the public and press include:

- Proprietary information will be exchanged.
- One or more of the parties has been injured by unfair or inaccurate reporting and will not negotiate with the press in attendance.
- Relationships between the parties are so bad that conciliation will be difficult in any case and impossible with the news media looking on.

When, in the judgment of the sponsors, a meeting must be closed, steps should be taken to reduce, as much as possible, the indignation of the news media and to prevent a party from using the act of closure for its own purposes. The group can proceed one meeting at a time. If one closed meeting is enough to put the discussions on track, the next meeting can be open to see how it works. The manager should hold a press conference after each closed meeting and have several of the negotiators at the conference. Written press releases approved by the group—describing the topics under discussion, who the negotiators are, and, if appropriate, any agreements that have been reached—can be given out. A press contact can be appointed to simplify and focus the efforts of reporters to obtain more information.

The negotiators must assume ownership of the decision to close meetings if the policy is going to work. Consensus of the group should be required to close meetings, and all parties should agree not to criticize the policy in public. Closed meetings should not be held without that agreement, because the reputations of participants may be harmed if they are attacked for favoring a proposal to keep the public out.

Ground rules should be established regarding the press. In one large negotiation, all parties agreed not to talk with the news media about what other people said and only to discuss what they thought or said themselves, a strategy that minimized miscommunications about the negotiation.

Making the Press an Asset

Public officials learn early in their careers to be wary of reporters, and reporters expect them to be cautious; but, all too often, managers go beyond mere wariness and treat the news media with such hostility that they turn neutrals into adversaries. A better approach is to handle reporters as part of the community with a legitimate, essential role to play. Following are basic steps in making the news media an asset rather than a liability.

Educate the Reporter. The manager should find out the names of reporters and editors who will be interested in the issue and, if at all possible, visit them and explain the project—why it is being done and what the approach will be. The manager should provide details and assume that the reporter wants to get the story right. One cannot be certain how a reporter will react to such efforts, but one can be quite sure that he or she will respond in kind if one is hostile or accusatory. The manager should be prepared for penetrating questions that go beyond his or her explanation. It is the reporter's job to find out all the facts. The reporter should be given a written description of the project. The manager should respond promptly to later requests for more information. One should not ask to "go off the record" unless absolutely necessary, because the request places the reporter in a difficult position. The manager should be as open as possible and should admit if he or she does not know the answer to a question. If an answer can be found, the manager should get back to the reporter as quickly as possible, because reporters are usually working under tight deadlines.

If a reporter is viewed as a nuisance or a threat, he or she will know it. The alternative is to remember that, however annoying they may be at times, reporters have a legitimate interest and an unusual function in society. The more carefully and thoroughly information is conveyed, the greater is the chance that the reporter will get it right.

Ask for Advice. The manager should interview the reporter, asking for his or her views about the situation, especially who the key actors are. Experienced reporters know a lot about their communities. They can be a valuable resource in preparing an analysis. As manager and reporter talk together, the reporter will learn the manager's approach to the issue and will respect his or her desire to collect different perspectives on the negotiations.

Be Explicit About the Media Strategy. A company was about to build a major facility near a small, rural community. Community leaders and company officials agreed that the project would have a substantial effect on the community, an effect that the community was unprepared to handle. They agreed that their most critical need was to inform the public about the issues and to keep the citizens informed as conditions changed. A lot of hard decisions about siting and funding would require citizen support. The organizers invited reporters and editors from the local newspapers to attend the planning meetings as regular members of the committees. They were told that public education was essential, and their advice was sought about methods to release factual information as it unfolded. For more than a year, the local newspapers carried regular reports of progress and problems. The tone of the articles was unsensational, even when the inevitable conflicts occurred. One newspaper designed a special logo and used it for quick identification of articles about the project. The news media played a crucial role in preparing voters for unfamiliar necessities such as school bond issues and hiring of planners. The press representatives were treated as interested members of the community, rather than as adversaries.

The press can encourage support of efforts to resolve a dispute. In one controversy between a mountain town and a construction company, a proponent of conflict management met with the local newspaper and explained a plan to use a third party to help the two sides develop a problem-solving strategy. The result was an editorial urging support of the use of a mediator and a series of articles describing the conflict management strategy.

Using a Third Party

Most conflicts are managed by the adversaries themselves. Only a comparatively small number of disputes are assisted by a third party, and of those, fewer still are managed by a professional mediator. However, as more trained mediators become available and as positive results of their efforts become more widely known, mediation will become more widely recognized as an acceptable option for managers to use in carrying out their responsibilities (Bacow and Wheeler, 1984; Bingham, 1984; Richman, White, and Wilkinson, 1986; Sullivan, 1984; Susskind and Ozawa, 1983).

Mediator or *third party* means any disinterested person brought in by agreement of the disputing parties to help them resolve their differences. This person has no direct stake in the outcome. He or she may come from another division of the same organization, from a different level of management, or from an academic institution, may be a respected member of the community, or may be a professional mediator. A mediator is never a judge or arbitrator with power to impose a decision. Instead, he or she has only the authority bestowed (or withdrawn) by the parties.

The parties should carefully consider three prerequisites in their selection of a mediator: impartiality, process skills, and ability to handle sensitive information. In proposing a person to be mediator, a manager may assume that everyone else thinks the individual is impartial. That assumption should be carefully tested, because anyone who is viewed with suspicion by any party cannot be successful as a third-party intervenor, even if the suspicions are unfounded. Any financial, professional, or personal ties with parties should be thoroughly aired and discussed by all parties before a mediator is selected. In tense situations, people quickly jump to erroneous conclusions about the motives of their adversaries, and it is essential that great care be taken to prevent accusations of bias later on.

The second essential qualification of a third party is skill in applying conflict management techniques. Quite often, disputing parties ask for the help of some respected individual whose standing as a university professor or congressperson seems to place him or her far above the fray. The individual is expected to bring order to the situation just because he or she is liked by all the parties. On the contrary, well-meaning but inexperienced third parties can create havoc by bringing the parties together and then letting normal conflict dynamics take over. Giving people an arena in which they can meet and carry on their arguments without the control and guidance of a care-fully worked out conflict management strategy can, and often does, make resolution of differences even more difficult.

In one controversy, a well-intentioned government agency and a private foundation paid a substantial sum of money for mediated negotiation of a statewide natural resource problem. The mediator was a public figure, well known and respected by all the parties, but, unfortunately, without experience in man-aging disputes. After six months of meetings the parties dead-locked. Antagonism produced by the hostile exchanges lasted years after the close of the program. Such basic conflict man-agement techniques as setting realistic time schedules, defining issues, agreeing on goals, and endorsing a negotiation process were never used. Without procedural constraints such as ground rules for behavior, the parties used the meetings to attack each other's positions and to make pronouncements to the news me-dia. The rough-and-tumble of public conflict is a hazardous place to try reasoning together without a repertoire of skills to assure that the discussions proceed in a productive direction.

Finally, the person selected to be mediator must be sen-sitive to the hazards of possessing confidential information and must be mature and wise enough to use such information with the utmost restraint. Mediators become the repository for pri-vate information, sometimes more than they can comfortably handle. This happens for several reasons. First, although medi-ators have no authority to enforce agreements and therefore have no official standing, they are sometimes endowed by one or more of the parties with the special status of "peacemaker" and are seen as a sympathetic and safe listener. The opportu-nity to talk to a person above the fray impels people to vent their pent-up anger and concern and to say things that could hurt them if used without discretion. Subordinates make critical comments about their superiors, allies condemn each other's policies, and friends say deprecating things about each other's competence. People in a dispute unload their fears and resent-ments and disclose or hint at their plans for future action.

Second, once a negotiation is under way, parties in a dis-pute may try to be as helpful as they can in the design of the process. They may feel that the person responsible must have all the relevant information even though it may be risky to disclose it. Interviews often begin with the person being interviewed saying, "Now that I have agreed to participate in this negotiation, I want to give you all the facts."

Third, there are the interviews themselves. A skilled interviewer designs the conversation so as to extract as much pertinent information as possible. Interviews are usually held in a person's home or office so that he or she will relax and be open to questions. The interviewer asks professionally designed questions, which the interviewee recognizes as intended to help solve a problem. Some people find the atmosphere irresistible and say a great deal.

When to Ask for Help

When Negotiation Is Deadlocked. If relationships have deteriorated into accusatory rhetoric or progress on substantive issues is blocked, a third party can help get discussions back on track. This book is designed to help decision makers avoid that moment of impasse if possible, but it does happen. The parties would do far better to recognize their lack of progress and their need for outside assistance before they reach deadlock and *before* the damage to their relationships has been done, because by that time the parties are looking toward litigation or some other adversarial proceeding and have all but abandoned hope of reaching cooperative settlement. They have no logical stopping place, and they see each other only as adversaries to be defeated (see "The Spiral of Unmanaged Conflict" in Chapter One). Nevertheless, mediators often enter at this stage in the conflict, since it is the most difficult for an involved party to manage.

When the Parties Need Help in Establishing Communication. At some point in a dispute, the parties may lose interest in talking about perspectives other than their own. Instead of exchanging information that might help solve the problem, they use information as a weapon to win a point. They no longer hear what their adversaries are saying.

A mediator was asked to assess a deepening controversy between an agency of the federal government and a small town. She asked the two sides whether they were having any difficulty talking with each other. The replies were as follows: "Communication is not a problem. We have told them what we want"; "Communication is not a problem. We have told them what we can do." In this case, the mediator initiated a tightly controlled discussion, not of what the parties had told each other but of what they wanted out of an agreement and why they needed it.

The conflict dynamics continuum in Chapter Four (see Exhibit 4) is a good reference tool for assessing such factors as attitudes about the problem, current relationships among the parties, tactics being used to deal with each other, and willingness to negotiate. If these elements cluster at the difficult or most difficult ends of the scales, the assistance of a third party may be called for.

When Sensitive Information Is Involved. A disinterested third party can sort out the issues and help the parties design a strategy for addressing them. It is sometimes difficult for an involved party to ask for and obtain candid comments about what the central problems really are, because such comments might reveal information that could be used by the other party in an adversarial proceeding. A skilled third party, on the other hand, enters accepted by both sides, handles confidential information discreetly, generalizing it if necessary, and produces a structure of issues for consideration by representatives of the parties. Fact finding is a productive service that a third party often provides, with or without going further into some other more comprehensive conflict management program. In collecting and assessing facts and reporting them to the parties, an experienced mediator may go one step further to describe or "name" what he or she identifies as the method the parties are using to negotiate with each other. Often a frank, straightforward, and impartial evaluation in open session will help the parties break off increasingly adversarial behavior and get them to focus on solving their problem.

When Negotiations Are Threatened by Disagreements Inside Groups. A third party can help the members of one group work out their internal differences. Participants in negotiations sometimes represent a loosely assembled group of people with widely differing opinions about the issues. Unless a great deal of care is taken to inform all members equally and to help the entire membership maintain a sense of ownership in the process, representatives may discover that they cannot bind the party they represent to agreements made in negotiation.

When a Process Is Not Working. Parties will convene with the best intentions only to find that they are talking about the same issues months later without having made any progress. A mediator can introduce and manage a process that will move parties through a sequence of steps toward their goal of agreement.

What a Mediator Does

Experienced third parties bring a kit of conflict management tools for helping people resolve their differences. They use them in different combinations and with a variety of emphases, but the techniques are well standardized. A skilled third party will perform some or all of the following functions (see Kolb, 1983; Maggiolo, 1971; Moore, 1986; Pruitt, 1981; Simkin, 1971):

1. *Analyze a Conflict.* One function of a mediator is to gather and assess information about a dispute to help parties sort out issues, identify stakeholders, determine what additional information is needed, and make decisions about how to proceed. A mediator can conduct interviews that would be impossible for one of the parties. A third party may be asked to analyze a conflict prior to convening representatives or after a negotiation has begun when parties find they are not making progress.
2. *Design a Strategy.* A second activity that can be performed by a mediator is to develop a constructive process for par-

ties to work out their differences. A mediator works with the parties to define the goals for a program and then identify a series of process steps that will guide the discussions. A mediator can suggest what type of meetings should be held and how they should be managed and can establish and get agreement on ground rules for behavior and process.

3. *Establish Productive Communication.* A third party can set up a system for communication that promotes the exchange of information and protects the parties from harm. A mediator may be necessary to ensure that proper safeguards have been established before the parties come together and to recommend procedures for communication between meetings, a time when direct control is difficult and the parties can unravel whatever has been accomplished in formal sessions.

4. *Manage a Process.* A mediator can conduct an entire negotiation program, guiding parties through each process step, naming problems as they arise, providing a reality check without bias, and offering process suggestions. A mediator's services may also be employed after the parties' own efforts to negotiate have failed.

5. *Deal with Data.* A mediator's services may be needed to help parties collect, organize, and assess relevant information. A mediator can work with parties to determine what baseline data are central to a discussion, what type of information should be collected, and how it should be assessed and by whom. When differences arise, the mediator finds ways for the parties to reach agreement on data. Mediators also work out ways to handle confidential information (see Chapter Eleven).

6. *Build and Maintain Teams Within Constituencies.* Many public disputes involve constituency groups that are neither well organized nor familiar with negotiation procedures. A mediator can help groups of like interests form coalitions, choose representatives, establish internal decision-making procedures, and learn more about the dynamics of negotiation. A mediator can continue to work with constituency groups to ensure that regular internal commu-

nication is taking place through the use of caucuses and reporting sessions and can help resolve disagreements between factions within groups. Finally, a mediator can assist
in building an understanding of and support for agreements
made by representatives.
7.   *Provide a Neutral Ground.* A third party can give the par-
     ties a place to meet that is not identified with one side and
     thus is less risky for the participants.

Why a Mediator Is Useful

A mediator performs functions and carries out tasks that
move people into negotiation, in circumstances that make it difficult for them to do so for themselves. However, third parties
introduce another element that is less tangible yet can be a major asset to people needing help in solving their problems. When
a third party enters a dispute, people *expect* things to change.
They expect the character of their negotiations to be different
after a mediator arrives. Because change and a new direction are
essential to interrupt the spiral of conflict, this expectation can
be a powerful aid to moving ahead and seeking new options.
Many books about mediation assert that a sense of crisis is
necessary to bring people to the negotiation table, and this is
true up to a point. But, while people must feel the pressure of
deadlines or accumulating losses to get down to hard negotiation, too much stress and fear can severely restrict their ability
to explore new ideas. The arrival of a mediator can reduce a
sense of crisis to manageable proportions and increase the willingness of the parties to be flexible (Deutsch, 1974).
A mediator places his or her expertise at the parties' disposal to help them solve their problem. Standing outside the
dispute, having seen other people going through similar experiences, a mediator can describe to people what they are doing,
where they are heading, and what the consequences are likely to
be (Buckle and Thomas-Buckle, 1986). With no stake in the
outcome, a third party can say things that no contending party
could say without instant retaliation. "You are bogging down
in details; let's return to the general problem" is a helpful de-

scription of what is happening when uttered by a third party. Delivered by a party in a dispute, however, the same statement might be taken as an attack.

Sometimes a third party must comment about what is happening between two people, a dangerous thing for an involved party to try. "You are demanding the same things from Bill that he has told you from the beginning he can't do. Let's see if we can't find a different way of getting at this." When delivered calmly, perhaps with a smile, direct statements from a third party are usually taken as efforts to move the problem-solving process along. Sometimes explicit warnings are necessary. Delivered adroitly, even very hard messages such as "It sounds to me like what you really want is revenge; we are not going to get anywhere if you insist on that goal" can be said by a third party without substantial risk to the negotiations.

Whatever the personal style of the mediator, the intervention must be completely open and fully understood by the parties. Trust in the process will come later if the parties believe the negotiations are serving their interests and are confident that they know everything that is going on. A third party explains and explains again what is happening, what he or she is doing, and why. Since the parties are under stress and suspicious of each other, the mediator must go to laborious lengths to assure the parties that all agreements are being scrupulously kept.

In one tense meeting, a mediator had worked with six representatives of disputing parties to draw up an agenda for a crucial meeting. Partway through the meeting, it became clear that all the parties' interests would be served if the order of the agenda was reversed. However, the mediator knew that if problems arose later on, any change in the agenda would become an issue and accusations of bad faith could result. The mediator called all six representatives to the front of the room where the entire audience could see them and asked whether everyone agreed to change the agenda. With general and publicly visible agreement, the mediator could safely proceed with the change. Caution of this kind is necessary when trust levels are low, as they often are when disputes have been going on for some time.

How to Select and Manage a Mediator

Before choosing a mediator it is useful to interview several candidates. They should be asked how they would handle the problem and their responses should be compared. The manager should find out whether they have handled similar cases and talk with people who have worked with them.

The group should consider using two mediators if a dispute involves many parties and a complex set of issues. They will work as a team during sessions and be available for assistance between meetings. Many of the most important activities conducted by a third party occur between formal sessions. The presence of two mediators provides additional assurance that help will be available when needed.

Here are some personal qualities to look for in a mediator and some questions to ask potential third parties in interviews:

- *Personal credibility.* What is the mediator's track record? Has the mediator handled cases in the same field in which he or she is being asked to work? Can former parties vouch for the mediator's past performance? Will the mediator agree to keep the proceedings of the session confidential if the parties choose to do so?
- *Institutional credibility.* Does the mediator work for a reputable institution known to be impartial in its interventions? Has the institution maintained confidentiality regarding the details of its cases? Does the institution have a conflict of interest that might affect the mediator's credibility with any party?
- *Procedural credibility.* Has the mediator adequately described the approach that he or she will take in managing the dispute? Will the parties have control over the process?
- *Cost.* Is the mediator's fee reasonable?
- *Availability.* Does the mediator have the time to attend sessions and work with the parties between meetings?

A mediator works *for* the parties. Mediators should be explicit about their role, what steps they are taking, and why. A mediator should check with the parties throughout a negotiation to see whether they are satisfied with the progress of discussions. If problems are raised, the mediator must explore the cause with the individual who raises them and with the entire group to determine whether an adjustment to the process is necessary.

Occasionally a mediator does not get along with the negotiators. The mediator may be highly qualified in handling some types of cases but inexperienced in handling others. For instance, a mediator who is accustomed to dealing with commercial disputes may not have the skills to work with angry citizens.

A mediator must encourage parties to express their concerns about the process and his or her performance: "If you feel that I am acting with a bias, it is your responsibility to tell me." A statement like this puts the responsibility on each participant to monitor the activities of the mediator. If a mediator appears to be biased or is not guiding the process effectively, he or she should be confronted and given an opportunity to explain his or her actions, in case there has been a misunderstanding. If the answer is not satisfactory, the group must decide whether to retain the individual. The dissatisfaction of one party is generally enough cause to remove a mediator.

If an organization is responsible for hiring a third party, it should also monitor the progress of the mediation program, determining whether the process seems appropriate and whether the mediator is acting with impartiality and integrity. If the organization perceives problems, it should check with the parties and ask them to decide whether or not to retain the mediator. If a mediator is asked to leave, parties must then decide whether to secure a new third party or proceed without one.

Mediators, like lawyers, systems analysts, and electrical engineers, are resources to be called upon when they are needed. When the parties find themselves in a situation similar to those described earlier in this section, calling in a third party for one or more stages of a conflict management process may save energy and peace of mind and probably will increase the chances of a successful outcome.

9

Paying Attention
to Underlying Dynamics:
Values, Trust, Power

The preceding chapter and the two following are concerned with process considerations, special tasks, and common problems. This chapter looks at three factors that permeate nearly every public encounter, sometimes subtly without being openly acknowledged but more often recognized as powerful influences on the course of discussions: values, trust, and power. All three have the potential for being or becoming the principal cause of conflict. Collisions over values are frequently an important element in disputes but are rarely made explicit in open discussion. Without trust, at least in the process itself, negotiations will almost certainly fail. Power, to harm or to bestow benefits or to carry out agreements, is always a question. These three factors are central underlying dynamics in public disputes. Their importance demands careful attention in the design and conduct of a conflict management program.

Values

Our values tell us how the world "ought to be." They are the standards by which we judge events and the behavior of other people and by which we decide what is worthy of our support and what deserves our condemnation. We learn our values through the influence of our families and friends, in our religious institutions, in school, and by reflection on what we see around us. Values are the composite record of our life experience and are therefore slow to change. Asking someone to adjust his values is like asking him to alter his sense of reality (Curle, 1972).

Value differences are always present in public controversies. Considering the infinitely variable sets of values that people bring into a room when they meet to talk about a problem, it would be surprising if they did not disagree, at least tacitly, about the relative importance of fundamental issues. But people normally disagree about all sorts of things, and differences in values do not have to cause conflict. People get along, grumbling a bit perhaps, but not fighting with each other, *except* when someone tries to force one set of values on another. Then disagreement escalates into conflict, not from the existence of differing world views but from the insistence that things must be either "this" or "that" and cannot be both. The bumpersticker declaration "America, love it or leave it" announces that no one can be a patriotic American and also question American policy. Conflict comes when such ideologies are acted out.

Differences in values affect issues in dispute and sometimes even determine them. Values also have a strong influence over the way people treat each other when they disagree. Values come from the heart and guts. If you believe that people are doing something morally indefensible, you address them with words that reflect your feelings. A proposal to tear down a historic building to make way for a parking lot is likely to produce words such as "greed" and "callousness" on the one hand and "elitism" and "selfishness" on the other, with both sides calling each other "special interests."

It is frustrating for managers trying to solve problems in a linear fashion, using what seem to them to be sound criteria, to bump into hostile responses to their decisions. The difficulty is that attitudes about public policy are strongly influenced by values, and values are distinctly nonlinear. An example of value-driven problems for managers is the conflict that planners run into when they try to develop county master plans. To the planners, planning and zoning are basic requirements for administering a county's business. They are therefore perplexed when they run head on into bitter opposition from citizens who believe that planning is an invasion of their property rights.

A basic premise in conflict management is: *Never negotiate on the basis of values.* Experienced conflict managers expect differences in values when they bring people together to resolve a public issue and know that efforts to negotiate values would be fruitless. A manager should detect the existence of divergent values and integrate them into a plan to carry out a successful negotiation.

Assessing the Influence of Values

Sometimes values are out in the open for everyone to see. Someone will say, "I believe in progress and I think a parking lot will bring in more money than that ugly old building," which may be horrifying to a person trying save a historic structure from demolition but at least says clearly what the other side is thinking. More often, the signals are more subtle, and careful listening is necessary to extract people's values from conversation. A manager knows he or she has a potential conflict when one person murmurs, "I sometimes wonder about these so-called public interest groups," and another person says, "I didn't talk with the company. Business people make me uncomfortable." The task of a conflict manager is to identify the part that values play in a controversy and to determine whether it is possible to work around the differences.

For purposes of discussion we review three conditions:

- Values are not a significant factor.
- Values are more important than they first appear to be.
- The battle is over ideologies.

Values Are Not a Significant Factor. In emotional situations, people tend to stereotype each other. Citizen activists are supposed to think and behave in a particular way, as are business people and government employees. People create dynamics that do not have to happen by assuming that individuals will act as people in their category of employment are supposed to act. The challenge for a conflict manager is to find ways of getting people to set aside their expectations of how other people will behave and focus on the problem they want to solve.

Conflicting values seemed to be the core issue in a conflict between a small Hawaiian community and the National Park Service (see "The Town and the Park" in Chapter Two). The residents of the town met with a park service official fully expecting him to meet their stereotype of the government official. He was expected to want greater power and more control over the piece of land in question, at the expense of local concerns. For his part, he expected unrelenting hostility from the community. As they began to talk with each other, the residents were amazed to find, instead of mainland, big-government values of power and control, the ideas of a well-informed person whose concern was the unique quality of the area and how to protect it. He found people beginning to let down their guard and willing to talk. If the meeting had not been designed to bring out the concerns of the parties and avoid dredging up old arguments, it might have followed the opposite scenario, confirming the stereotype. Each side had assumed for many months that differences in values precluded any common ground and that a confrontation was inevitable, but after learning that values were not an issue they focused on the land management problems they wanted to solve.

Values Are More Important Than They First Appear to Be. Failure to detect significant value differences early can be a serious trap for a convener. Values are not the dominant factor in many situations, but the danger is that values may be *more* important than is first apparent, and the issue may not be as simple as it appears. A city manager of a small town found himself in an unexpected pickle when he proposed to build a sewer system for an outlying community. Plans had come to a dead halt, a perplexing situation because the problem was obvious to anyone with a sense of smell. The local newspaper editor concluded that the community must be concerned about being annexed to the town when the sewer system was finished, but as

he conducted interviews with interested citizens, a simple matter of public health began to take on an entirely different character. The editor realized that the outlying community's leader
was vehemently opposed to all government "interference" with
the rights of individual citizens, in which she included the right
to have raw sewage flowing through her front yard. Her anti-
government convictions had been roused to a fever pitch when
the town manager announced that he was going to build a sewer
system, and none of her neighbors wanted to get involved in the
cross fire. When town officials realized that they were inadvertently involved in ideological warfare, they began a joint effort
with the residents to design a suitable system, but the process
took two years longer than necessary.

The Battle Is Over Ideologies. When the conflict is over
ideologies themselves, chances for constructive negotiation are
exceedingly dim, because two basic requirements of conflict
management are probably not present:

- It must be possible to reframe the issue into solvable incre-
  ments.
- There must be an effective core of moderate people on both
  sides of an argument.

Those who espouse a "right to life" are unlikely to find
common ground with people who believe in "freedom of
choice." And it is hard to imagine a way of reframing a conflict
between people who want to ban the use of handguns and those
who oppose restrictions on the use of armor-piercing bullets by
civilians. The value systems on which these positions are based
are so far apart that finding a mutually satisfactory compromise
seems inconceivable. If the moderates have departed, leaving the
field to the zealots on both sides, a conflict manager may lack
the necessary base of common sense among the parties on
which to build a constructive strategy. Trying to negotiate ideological battles between intransigent enemies is probably a waste
of resources and, worse, is likely to give adversaries a forum to
widen the conflict and make matters worse.

Integrating Values into a Conflict Management Strategy

Values are always a factor in public disputes, and sometimes they have a substantial influence on the outcome of negotiations. But most conflicts contain areas of common interest that can be expanded into bases for constructive negotiation, and there are usually enough reasonable people around to set aside differences in values for the moment to find a solution to a common problem. The manager needs to focus on what the parties need, not on their differences.

Listen for What Is Behind the Words. Strong words say a lot about how intensely people feel about an issue, but in themselves they are not a good measure of the influence of values. If people are stirred up enough to take part in a dispute and attend meetings, they are quite likely to use strong words in describing their feelings. The words flying about may be hostile and accusatory, but strong feelings are not necessarily insurmountable obstacles to constructive negotiation. The task of a manager is to look for clues to underlying values that may in fact be serious impediments. Argument over public issues eventually reaches a stage where adversaries talk about each other in clichés that have become so ritualized as to lose their original pungency. Being called a "power-hungry bureaucrat feeding at the public trough" might be devastating if one did not realize that the same trite phrase had been used a thousand times before. But when the words are accompanied by a tone of voice and facial expression that denotes hatred or fear, the underlying cause may be profound and insurmountable differences in values and therefore worthy of careful analysis by a conflict manager.

Pay Attention to Ideological Monuments. The manager should listen for the source of strong convictions. If, in making a particularly strident statement, a person refers to some reference point *outside* the context of the dispute, a conflict manager should be on guard for values that may be difficult to handle in a negotiation. When, for example, a militant preservationist says, as one did, "This is a battle to save the planet and it justifies some heavy tactics," he was asserting that his cause was so just that any means to his goal was warranted. When a public official said of a citizens' group opposed to his policies, "They are trying to bring America to its knees," he was saying that his position came from a higher patriotism and therefore was not subject to challenge.

Remember That Organizations Have Values. In assessing underlying values, the manager must remember that organizations have values just as individual people do. Representatives of agencies, companies, and citizen organizations sometimes speak as if their employers, being institutions and not persons, are value-free, thus infuriating people who disagree with them. "We have a staff of professional engineers. Our policies are based on their advice. You people are just being emotional about this" sounds as if decisions are made in some objective scientific laboratory when in fact everybody knows they came from the conference room down the hall where technicians are busily carrying out the organization's mission.

Concentrate on What They Need. The manager should focus on goals that are consistent with the parties' values. They may want to dredge up old wrongs and argue about their different views of how the world ought to be, but the manager should get them to talk about what they need out of a solution.

When a federal commission concerned with air quality convened representatives of industry, environmental advocacy organizations, and local government to develop alternative procedures for administering one controversial section of the Clean Air Act, the commission members knew that success depended on whether the three adversaries could set aside their clashing values and find areas of agreement. The letter of invitation acknowledged that the representatives had widely differing beliefs about major issues related to the Clean Air Act but asked them to address and solve one specific problem. The participants agreed that they should make the most of the exceptional skills that the group possessed collectively and work on options for solving a long-standing problem. Their values continued to be very different, but their discussions concentrated on satisfying goals that were not directly affected by their divergent values: clarity and timeliness of communication, effective public participation, and consistency in administration of regulations (Carpenter and Kennedy, 1980).

Acknowledge Difference in Values. "We are here tonight because we have a problem to solve. Some of us are from farms and some of us are from the city, and it is quite likely that we will look at things differently from time to time. But let's just accept that and get on with talking about solving our problem. Does that make sense to everybody?"

Saying that people have different values does not pass judgment on which values are correct, but acknowledging what everybody already knows reduces tension and the temptation to posture. People will be less likely to make a big point of differences in background that have been explicitly recognized.

Not making the differences explicit and trying to tiptoe around them encourages people to make speeches about their convictions and to assert the righteousness of their cause, which, in turn, provokes hostile answers and increases the difficulty of persuading participants to focus on their common problem.

Appeal to Their Sense of Fair Play. Fair play can be invoked on its own merits. Not everyone is able to act fairly toward others, and people often doubt that they themselves will be the beneficiary of fair play, but the idea is accepted nearly universally as a moral standard and can be a useful asset in building a constructive dialogue. Even when people disagree on practically everything else, they can agree that it is "right" to be fair. "In the interests of fair play, the speaker should have a chance to finish what she has to say before we comment. Do you agree?" "It is only fair that everyone have a chance to speak. Let's keep our comments short so we have enough time." These are impartial standards that nearly always produce order in a potentially disorderly meeting. They are almost never challenged, even in heated discussions. An appeal to fairness has another benefit; it says, "Look, we have something in common after all!"

Trust

Trust is an essential ingredient of negotiation, and the literature of conflict resolution devotes a great deal of attention to "building trust." But not enough thought is given to the nature and purpose of trust (Curle, 1971; Deutsch, 1974). When the word *trusting* is used to describe relationships that should be established among the parties, there is the implication that once established, trust should be unquestioning. In complex public disputes, however, representatives of conflicting parties should not trust each other automatically. The purpose of conflict management is to provide an open, explicit system for improving destructive relationships. The goal is to remove unnecessary obstacles to productive discussion, not to build lasting friendships. Individual negotiators may depend on their experience and instincts and accept the integrity of other individuals, but in complex disputes, where they represent the interests of others, they should always be watchful. A guiding principle, whether in buying a used lawn mower or in negotiating the construction of an international airport, is to watch out when someone says, "Trust me."

Trust is the expectation that people will deal honestly with each other. In this context trust means confidence that other people will act as they say they will act, not necessarily out of intrinsic goodness but because it is in their interest to keep promises made. Trust is a solid structure built brick by brick as people in a dispute understand the benefits of believing and being believed. The techniques described in this section help people build and test confidence in the convener, the negotiating process, and each other.

Causes of Mistrust

Past experience, incomplete information, differing values, stereotyping, misunderstandings, and many other factors all influence the way people in a dispute see and treat each other. Some public controversies do not expand into intense animosities and deep distrust. The parties know each other well and look at the cause of the problem in the same way even though they disagree over a solution. But even in these less stressful situations, where motives and goals are not an issue, as disagreement continues misunderstandings become more likely. "I don't understand why you said that" is a familiar indication of the first breach in an established trust relationship.

As a conflict grows, people become more interested in proving that they are right and less willing to accept positive initiatives from the other side at face value. Messages are dismissed as false or deliberately misleading just because they come from the other side. Real or perceived violations of trust become separate conflicts. Suspicion is extended to third parties or neutrals, and nothing is accepted on its merits, even genuine efforts to improve the situation.

Any experienced negotiator can draw up an extensive list of reasons why people distrust each other (see "Bringing People to the Table" in Chapter Ten). Some of the most common reasons for distrust, which nearly always appear in combinations, include:

- *The passage of time.* No matter how close and strong the ties are between individuals caught up in a conflict, their perceptions of each other are likely to become muddled if the controversy goes on long enough. They discriminate less between what they know about the other and what they fear the other will do.
- *Strangers.* If people can begin to distrust neighbors and friends, imagine how much easier it is for them to distrust people who come from different places, who are known to have different religious and cultural beliefs, or who represent different economic classes within a community.
- *Past experiences with each other.* When people have lobbied against each other and sued each other and opposed each other in the news media, they have good reason not to expect anything different in the future. They would be foolish to believe proposals for a truce without assurance that the offers are genuine.
- *Past experiences with people of similar views.* A "street wise" professional depends on practical knowledge and experience in planning a strategy for dealing with a dispute. If,

in the past, a manager has encountered people with views similar to those he or she is contending with now, the present adversaries will be expected to act as the others did. Often they do. But sometimes changes in economic conditions or in the political environment, new information, or new leadership change the character of opposing groups.

- *Past experiences with a similar process.* Conflict resolution has its own record of failures. Whether because of bad luck, poor design, or faulty execution, some cooperative problem-solving efforts do not solve problems. Some even make things worse. The victims of such unpleasant and costly experiences are understandably reluctant to try again.

- *Misleading information.* For people who are angry or fearful, every piece of information about their problem is important. One careless, inaccurate statement can severely damage trust. Any hint that a misstatement was deliberate can cause people under tension to suspect everything that is said from then on.

- *Incomplete information.* Rumors fly when factual information is lacking, and rumors usually carry disquieting messages. Decision makers too frequently wait until they are satisfied that they have all the relevant information before they disclose any of it, and in the meantime, people are thinking about the worst thing that could happen to them. An unfortunate consequence of insufficient information is that when the complete story is finally told, no one believes it.

Why Trust Is Important

Agreeing to negotiate, sharing responsibility for productive meetings, and cooperating with adversaries demand a shift, sometimes a wrenching shift, in the way disputing parties deal with each other. The purpose of building trust is to establish conditions in which people can exchange needed information and make and receive genuine offers.

Bringing People to the Table. People considering negotiation must believe that the potential benefits outweigh the risks. The ease with which prospective negotiators can be convinced to come to the table depends on many factors—personality, previous experience with the other parties, and the nature of the issues—but is likely to be most influenced by the intensity and duration of the dispute. In disputes of lower intensity, the parties may think that the risks are small and discussion is worth a try. If the conflict is severe, however, the risks may be significant, and parties must have adequate assurance that the convener and the process can produce the desired results.

Sharing Information. Negotiators must be willing to exchange substantive information necessary to analyze obstacles and develop options. A negotiator's willingness to disclose information to adversaries or even to give options to third parties will depend on his or her belief in the protection afforded by the negotiating process and its potential value in solving a problem. Communication, an essential ingredient of negotiation, can only be restored when people have confidence that the material they relinquish will not be used against them.

Generating Options. Moving from trying to gain advantage to seeking solutions demands a major change in attitude on the part of participants. Suddenly, they are expected to build on each other's ideas instead of breaking them down. This is an uncomfortable exercise at first for people who are accustomed to fighting with each other.

Making and Receiving Offers. Somewhere along the way, people in disputes stop believing what their adversaries are saying. Often they have good reason, because what people say is sometimes devised solely to win a point for their side. However, negotiators must be willing to make concessions and accept as genuine, concessions offered by the other side. This is not to say that trust is absolute or unquestioning, but only that the adversaries must be willing to offer a step forward and test the response. Again, among associates working out a disagreement the experiment will be less risky than an overture made to longtime adversaries with no other relationship than the conflict itself.

Dealing with Setbacks. When human beings negotiate, they bring to the table all the unpredictabilities of human nature. And negotiation, especially of public disputes, is subject to uncontrollable external events. The course of negotiation, like that of true love, is seldom smooth. Negotiators may be surprised by a newspaper quote or some official action taken in another part of the country that puts an unexpected twist on the discussions. All the parties must avoid leaping to conclusions about why and how the event happened. They must have sufficient confidence in their knowledge of the others' motives and integrity to know that the surprise was not deliberate.

Quite often, just as everything is going along swimmingly, someone will break a ground rule—stand up and attack the motives of the other side or bring up old injuries. At this point the parties can revive their earlier adversarial relationships and lose important ground in the negotiation, or they can rely on the process they have set up and deal with the violation as a temporary diversion instead of a permanent rupture of their progress.

Establishing Credibility and Building Trust

In Chapter Eight we discuss situations in which it may be advantageous to bring in a third party to initiate and perhaps manage efforts to solve complex problems. Writers on conflict resolution often suggest that the tasks of building trust and opening communication are so difficult that they demand third-party assistance. Certainly, if relationships among the parties are extremely hostile and suspicious, an outsider who is not a part of the confusion may be essential (see "Using a Third Party" in Chapter Eight). However, a great deal can be accomplished by the parties themselves.

Successful problem solving depends on three separate elements of trust: confidence in the convener's integrity and competence, belief in the process, and the expectation that the parties will deal honestly with each other. There should be a reasonable chance that all three elements can be achieved. If, for example, there is serious doubt that some individuals can ever be persuaded to deal fairly with others, the program should not go forward, because it may expose participants to harm if they act in good faith.

Trust in a negotiating process and confidence in the willingness of the parties to negotiate in good faith is constructed in small, incremental pieces. Especially where there is a history of distrust, there is always the possibility that parties in a dispute will see or think they see reasons for suspecting their adversaries of bad faith. Negotiations must therefore be carried on as if the connections between people are fragile, requiring careful protection and support at all times. The parties will trust each other as long as it is possible and acceptable for them to ask for assurance that the process is unbiased and offers hope of finding a mutually satisfactory solution to a problem. Following are suggestions for building trust.

Analyze Carefully. The manager should ask enough questions of people with diverse opinions to know what words and topics are sensitive. For example, it is possible to sidetrack discussions simply by using the word *zoning* in some conservative western communities. Zoning conjures up violation of private property rights, government interference, and other anathemas. One can avoid such sensitive points if one knows they exist. A careful analysis also helps the manager think through how a negotiation might best work and be prepared to suggest who could convene it, when it could be held, how often and where it should meet, and who some of the key parties might be. It is useful to ask the parties for advice.

Interviews gain valuable information and have an added benefit. Just the knowledge among the parties that everyone is talking about a need to solve the problem, and even considering talking together, can be an important signal that something new and perhaps hopeful is happening. The other side's willingness to talk may mean that dealing with them is not so impossible after all. The beginnings of trust are built on subtle signs and symbols.

Explain the Process. It is important to explain in precise terms why a different method for dealing with the problem is being proposed and why it could be in the interests of the parties to try a new approach. The manager will need to explain exactly what is in the plan and should expect people to have doubts about it. They may have spent time, money, and energy to pursue an opposite course, and they are being asked to change direction completely.

The manager should deal directly with people's natural concern that they may inadvertently hand over their decision-making authority to others. They must be confident that this will not happen. They should be told that the process is entirely voluntary and that participants can drop out at any time. The procedures for achieving productive discussion are open for everyone to observe. The parties know from the outset what the ground rules will be, how participants will be chosen, how the group will handle newcomers, how the group will deal with the news media, and other negotiating procedures. They need to know that they will be deciding as a group, by consensus if that is the agreement, how agreements will be implemented and how they will be monitored. Detailed explanation of the process is important at the beginning of negotiation, but it also must be repeated each time a newcomer joins the group, not only to inform the newcomer but to reinforce the commitment that the process will always be open to scrutiny. Openness builds confidence in the negotiation process. It also sets a standard for candor in discussions, which, in turn, encourages people to ask for proof, or evidence, that what has been promised will be delivered. What would otherwise appear to be questioning of someone's integrity becomes a nonconfrontational part of a larger framework of discussion. The most important point is that the parties control the process.

Keep Tight Control at First. Ground rules must be enforced to prevent clashes between parties. Rigid adherence to the agreed-upon standards of behavior is especially important at the beginning if there is tension and distrust between the parties.

Be Sure That Statements Are Clear and Accurate. The danger of misunderstandings to the negotiation process must be made explicit. If the parties come together with doubts about the accuracy of information, the manager should encourage them to press for accuracy and urge them to be especially careful about what they say.

Get Them to Talk About What Is Important. People should be encouraged to be explicit about their views on an issue and what is preventing them from reaching their goal. In talking about obstacles to solving a problem, they should express their feelings about the problem but not vent their feelings *at* their adversaries. If they see that they can talk about a problem without attacking each other, they will have evidence that negotiation without confrontation is possible. They will have seen their adversaries participate in discussion and follow the rules.

In the controversy involving the town, the land group, and the park service (Chapter Two), the three parties had never actually met and talked together before. As the discussion continued, the people in the room began to realize to their amazement that they had very similar goals for the land. Fears and suspicions began to disappear. Procedural problems remained, but the atmosphere changed dramatically as the representatives understood why the others had acted as they had. Everyone laughed as the land group representative told about his surprise at the government's condemnation action. What had seemed deceit emerged as confusion. Very often in complex disputes a simple, straightforward explanation of what really happened changes the feelings people have about their adversaries. Even more effective is a simple comment like "I was mistaken when I said that." Such candid statements are disarming.

Stop the Rhetoric. "The first thing to do is to shut up" is the comment attributed to diplomat George Ball when he was asked how the United States and the Soviet Union should control the accelerating ideological struggle. He went on to say that "rhetoric and vituperation" can only increase animosities between the two countries. The *Illustrated London News* calls it "megaphone diplomacy," but whatever you call it, accusations and derogatory remarks, in public or private, must stop completely if trust is to be built among parties in a dispute. The act of stopping becomes an asset in itself. The parties see that they are doing something rational to control the growing controversy.

Affirm Successes. The manager must make sure the parties know when they make a step forward. If one of the parties thinks that the group has made a breakthrough, he or she should be encouraged to say so. When one of the leaders of the town found that all three parties recognized the importance of preserving the religious and ecological qualities of the land tracts in dispute, he stood up and said, "Do you realize what we have just done? For the first time, we have agreed on the same goal!" In another dispute, the group reached agreement on one element of a larger problem. A representative declared, "Three months ago, we could never have talked this through and agreed on it!" Seeing how the small successes fit together gives people confidence in the process and in each other.

Give Them Time. The manager should watch for signs that someone is nervous because the process seems to be moving too fast. Substantial progress toward solutions is a heady feeling for people who have been frustrated and discouraged. It is convincing proof that the negotiation is producing what its sponsors had hoped it would. But rapid movement is also disconcerting. Sometimes people have good reason to be suspicious about the motives of others. Suddenly everything is moving smoothly, and people are agreeing and making commitments again. About this time, some person who has been the victim of earlier failures in performance will say, "Wait a minute. I want to think about this." Anxious hesitation should be treated as a normal, expected pause in the discussion. The manager must be careful to prevent suspicion that people are being pushed hard for some hidden reason. If someone says, "This is the way they used to force us into agreeing with them," or some other expression of lingering doubt, the manager should accept it and meticulously walk back through the process everyone has been following.

Propose Caucuses. The manager can suggest that people of similar views have a brief, informal caucus to talk over the progress they have made. In one meeting where the parties had made startling advances after months of wrangling, the facilitator could see pleasure changing to alarm on the faces of some of the participants. He said, "This seems to be a good time for everybody to catch their breath. Let's stand up and you can talk around the table if you like." The representatives gathered in little groups around the room. As they shared reactions about the discussions, they gained confidence in the soundness of their agreements. In effect, they consolidated their positions and prepared to move forward.

Double-Check Assumptions About Relationships. It is often unclear how people feel about relying on each other, and negotiators can trap themselves by assuming that all is well, only to find out in a meeting that all definitely is not well and the parties are going to have a hard time believing each other.

In the case of the village (see Chapter Two), where the town planner was looking into a growing disagreement between a land development company and a village council about the height of a proposed hotel, the issue seemed to be how to construct a building that would provide reasonable economic return for the company's investment and still not block the view of the mountains. The planner talked with a variety of people and realized that the problem was not so simple. To begin with, the key people knew each other socially. It was a small community and they were reluctant to say rude things about people they saw every day, but they had grave doubts about negotiating with each other. It seemed that the charming and urbane president of the land development company was extraordinarily skilled at making true but ambiguous statements that sounded convincing at the time, but when one got home, one wondered what he had really said. This unusual talent permitted the company to do as it pleased without being accused of making false statements. The members of the village council had learned from long experience not to believe what they heard. Subtle distrust of this kind is hard to detect unless one knows why it is there. What happens as a result is that discussions are carried on in a genteel manner but the parties never get to hard negotiating on the issues.

Name Any Doubts. Any doubts people have about the process or each other should be made explicit and dealt with openly. When one party expressed a suspicion that a mistake in the minutes of a previous meeting had been intentional, the group agreed that all minutes would be marked "Draft" until read and approved by the group and that the first item on every agenda would be a general review of the minutes. This procedure was important, because in an earlier series of meetings it was not followed. Minutes were written, sometimes inaccurately, and distributed to participants and outside officials simultaneously. By making their review of a draft an explicit commitment, the parties knew that they had control of that piece of the process and they also gained predictability, an important part of building trust.

In another negotiation, one representative had an annoying habit of reading a newspaper during discussions, showing little interest in the proceedings. The other parties would have seen his behavior as simple rudeness except that the same person also dropped unsettling remarks like, "Well, I am not sure whether I can sell that." The other representatives began to eye him with growing doubt about his commitment to good-faith negotiation. Finally, one of the representatives declared that he was becoming very uncomfortable with the person's behavior and wanted to know whether the person was there to work with the group or not. Doubts about the willingness of one person to negotiate in good faith had begun to affect the atmosphere of the discussions. The question was raised not to impugn the motives of the individual but to clarify his intentions.

Help Them Get to Know Each Other. Opportunities should be provided for individuals to talk with each other outside the meetings, at lunch, over drinks, or in the evening. It is often helpful to schedule informal lunches at which people can mingle and talk about matters other than the business at hand.

It is important to choose pleasant meeting places where people can go outside and walk around together, if possible far away from offices or other distractions. It might also be of value to take them on field trips. Sometimes they will learn to dislike each other, but more often they will find that they share some common interests. Most people are curious about the other people sharing the meeting room with them and want to know more about them. Small shared jokes and mutual interests such as football or travel can ease stressful negotiation.

One skillful negotiator found that others at the table were very concerned about the mercurial temperament of one of the representatives. They were afraid that when aroused he would take passionate exception to something that someone else might say and thus threaten negotiations. The negotiator had had lunch several times with the fiery individual, and they had established the beginnings of a friendship. At the feared moment when tension was high, the negotiator handed his friend a small beanbag with the word "Fit" written on it and said, "Here. Throw this." Everybody laughed and relaxed, and it was clear how important to future negotiations that little joke was going to be.

Power

"The company is a multinational corporation! They have unlimited money. We will never get a fair hearing," a citizen group complained.

"We are a victim of special interest groups. These delays are costing us so much we may have to drop the project," the company moaned.

"We are the agency that is supposed to make the final decision on this, but anyone who disagrees with our decision can block the whole process just by writing a letter," the government agency sighed.

The first question that usually comes to mind in assessing a dispute is, "Who has the power to coerce whom?" But public disputes are too untidy to take that approach with confidence. It is often difficult to determine just who has the power, how much power they really have, and how long it will remain where it is. In the initial stages of a dispute, it may not even be clear who the parties are. Questions about power are indeed essential in analyzing a conflict, and the situation is likely to be much more complicated than comparing balance sheets or counting numbers of lawyers. Attention solely to size of financial resources or legal staffs gives insufficient weight to such intangibles as ingenuity, obstinacy, moral indignation, and standing in court. Seemingly weak parties can achieve instant attention by suing. Anyone can sue.

The three statements opening this section were all made about one dispute over the issuance of a government permit. Each party complained that it was being treated unfairly because it had less power than other parties. In this case, the parties underestimated their own resources for influencing decisions. By contrast, decision makers often leap to conclusions about their ability to force a decision on their adversaries only to be confronted by unexpected difficulties that confound orderly plans and progressively increase costs.

The Many Forms of Power

The nature of power and its many forms other than coercive force has deservedly received a great deal of attention from writers and practitioners of conflict management (Curle, 1971; Fisher, 1983; Kriesberg, 1973). Our purpose here is not to explore the subject in depth but to remind people who are embarking on a conflict management program to take a hard look at their assumptions about the power possessed by the different parties. Rather than counting up available resources, a manager who is contemplating various strategies can look at power from the perspective of the capacities the parties have to benefit or harm each other and should ask questions such as "Do the parties understand their own power and that of their adversaries?" and "What abilities do the parties have to increase mutual gain by cooperation?"

In this context, power can be defined as:

- the ability to cause harm by withdrawing a benefit or increasing a cost.

- the ability to reward the other side for cooperation.
- the capacity to invoke authority.
- the efficacy of relationships among the parties and with others of power.
- knowledge possessed or available to promote an interest or solve a problem.
- the strength of official precedents.
- a sound alternative.

This list is not meant to be comprehensive—other sources of power would be evident in particular situations. But it makes the point that only one of the elements listed, the first, is exclusively negative in its effect. The other seven can be used positively or negatively, to promote one position over another or to encourage cooperation. A manager who assesses the possibilities of applying conflict management procedures in the settlement of a dispute is really considering the potential for combining the separate sources of power of the individual parties into a joint effort to find a solution.

The familiar theoretical argument that a "balance of power" must be achieved before meaningful negotiations can begin seems irrelevant. A manager with a problem to solve does not have the luxury of theorizing about balances, and furthermore, the resources of parties in public disputes are rarely if ever in balance. The issue is not one of "balance" but whether or not one party can influence the behavior of another. A manager takes the situation as it is and looks for an effective way of dealing with it.

The Negative Consequences of Using Force

Using raw power has its own costs—in damaged working relationships, in loss of public support, in dollars for legal fees, and in time and energy diverted from other activities. The use of force angers its victims, and if the force is excessive or vindictively applied, the goal of the victims can become an unrelenting desire for vengeance. Sooner or later, the chance may come to retaliate, through changes in the political environment or as the more powerful party runs into other problems. Using litigation as a weapon for the sole reason that one can afford the costs is an example of the excessive use of force. In one public dispute, a citizen's organization challenged the right of a public utility to construct a project. The utility's response was to select the officers of the group and sue them as individuals. Since they were people of modest means and were serving the interests of their organization, the utility earned the undying hatred of all of the members. People become particularly outraged when excessive force is used by a powerful organization.

A sportsmen's group leased a large tract of land in the foothills near a small city, fenced it, and put out "No Trespassing" signs. A local ski club had previously cleared a trail across one corner of the property and its members had used the trail for several years. They continued to use it after the signs were posted under the somewhat dubious theory that the sportsmen used the property for hunting and it wouldn't matter if people skied across it after the hunting season was over. The sportsmen's group responded by setting up teams of armed guards who patrolled the perimeter of the property. When a newspaper reporter asked the president of the organization whether his guards would shoot a trespasser, he replied that they would do whatever was necessary to protect their property rights, a statement that produced much outrage on the part of citizens, a stern warning from law enforcement officials that no one had better shoot anyone, and great loss of face for the sportsmen's group. People resent being bullied.

Like making threats, using coercive force begins a series of separate retaliatory actions that are expensive and tend to go further in commitment of resources than was originally intended. Once started, the thrust and counterthrust of coercive power are hard to stop.

Power to harm an adversary can be more potent unused than used. The costs that invariably accompany the use of force begin when the weapon is used. The threat of applying sanctions such as citizen protest, legal action, or regulatory restraint may fail if tried, but untried it has the effect suggested in Adam Curle's definition of power: "the capacity—moral, political, economic, or military, or any combination of these—to make the other fellow think twice" (Curle, 1971). An example of mutually destructive costs is the case of the rancher, the fishing lake, and a government agency. The public had fished in the rancher's lake for decades through an arrangement in which the agency paid the rancher an annual fee for access to his property. After some years, the rancher was told by another agency that the dam holding the lake was unsafe and had to be repaired. The rancher asked for financial help from the leasing agency, which refused all responsibility. The rancher pointed out that he was liable for any damage caused by a break in the dam and that he would have to drain the lake. He was stating a fact, not making a threat. The ensuing outcry from fishermen who feared the loss of their favorite lake got the attention of the agency, and it worked out a cost-sharing arrangement with the rancher to have the dam repaired. In this situation, the rancher had the power to withdraw a benefit—the pleasure of catching trout in his lake. If he had gone ahead and drained the lake, he would have lost the annual fees and water storage for his cattle. The agency would have been severely embarrassed and the trout would have been left flopping on a dry lake bed. The catalyst for action was the potential destruction of the dam and the realization of all the parties that the rancher *would do as he said.* Without cooperation he had no other choice.

The Importance of Making Power Relationships Clear

The manager should help the parties explain to each other the capacities they have to influence a final decision. One way of encouraging a positive discussion and avoiding confrontation is to set a ground rule that each person will explain without interruption his or her principal goal and how his or her group has tried to achieve it. The chairperson should remind the participants that the purpose of the discussion is to present to the group each person's perception of his or her part in the conflict. The manager might start out by noting the difference between describing a situation and the factors that may affect it and making a threat.

A threat says, "I am now preparing to do you harm unless you give in to my demand." As a tactic of communication, threat is the equivalent of slapping someone across the face. Anger is the predictable reaction. The other party raises the ante by making a counterthreat or by setting into motion whatever action will be necessary to prevent the threat from being carried out. A threat damages or destroys working relationships and initiates costs even if the threat is never carried out.

The difference between an explanation of the options available to each person and a threat can be seen in statements about a controversy common in the west—the closure of access to land historically open to public use for wood gathering, fishing, hiking, or skiing. The typical sequence goes like this: The landowner says, "Pay me more money or I will close the road" or "Clean up my property or I will lock the gate." The threats appear in the newspaper, counterthreats are issued, sometimes followed by vandalism, which in turn escalates the conflict and makes everybody angry. Everybody loses.

However, the exchange can have a different flavor. It begins with an explanation of the dilemma the landowner finds himself or herself in: "The road through my property is an unimproved track. In wet weather it is practically impassable, so people cut around the mud holes and make new tracks that wash out when it rains. I am having serious erosion problems and can't let it get any worse." Instead of issuing a threat that causes instant confrontation, the speaker describes a problem in terms that everyone can understand and sympathize with. In understanding why the situation cannot continue, the listeners assume part of the ownership of the problem. People do not like to be bludgeoned into submission, but most respond reasonably to a reasonable explanation of a problem.

The same principle holds true when parties explain the sanctions available to them. It is very different to say, "If you do that, I will sue you," than it is to say, "As you know, we oppose that action. We would like to talk with you about changes we think you can make in your plan. We both know that we have gone to court on this before, and this is still an option for us. We will go to court if we have to, but we would like to avoid

the cost and hassle if we can find a better way of doing this."
Rather than issuing an ultimatum, the speaker explains his or
her concern, makes explicit a willingness to apply sanctions if
forced to do so, and offers an alternative.

Using Power for Mutual Gain

The manager should ask for a cease-fire and explore with
the parties any possibilities for exchanging information. However tentative the process may be, it can be a safe first step in
sharing other resources. Suggesting that people in conflict hand
anything over to their adversaries may sound unrealistic. Yet
the strategy is used quite often by seasoned professionals who
definitely do not see themselves as Pollyannas. The following
example illustrates the practical value of using power for mutual
gain.

A state agency had the statutory power to decide some
highly controversial environmental issues that it usually handled
by making unilateral decisions without explanation. Its employees then stood back and tried to deal with the public outcry that always arrived soon after, a costly strategy for resource
managers who would have preferred to devote their energies to
practicing their professional skills. The agency director decided
to try negotiation. He made it clear to representatives of the
twelve organizations gathered around the table that he retained
authority to make final decisions, as he was required to do by
law, but he invited the participants to share with the agency
new information being gathered and the responsibility for choosing workable alternatives. The director offered to make the discussions and the group's conclusions public, thus placing himself under the pressure of public visibility to make decisions
that were consistent with the recommendations of the group.

In giving interested parties access to the decision-making
process, the director provided potential adversaries with information they could conceivably use against him later. But in
sharing information, he gained an informed constituency. They
began to understand the complexity of the problems he faced.
By empowering the parties to participate in making a decision,

he gained the knowledge of experienced people in a cooperative atmosphere instead of an adversarial setting. Their knowledge was applied to solving a problem and not to promoting one position against another. Most important perhaps, the director shared with a group of influential and conscientious people the responsibility for solving problems.

10

Handling
the Human Side
of the Process

Public disputes are negotiated by complex human beings who bring their own perceptions, feelings, and concerns into a process. A manager dealing with public disputes recognizes that people are as apt to create problems for a program as they are a poorly designed process or a tough substantive issue. Furthermore, it is not unusual to run into several difficult human problems at the same time. For example, the true intensity of feelings the participants have for each other may not emerge until the parties face each other across a negotiating table. Significant differences in comprehension of the issues and in negotiating skills among the parties may endanger the entire effort. Some of these difficulties can be anticipated and headed off by rigorous attempts to imagine what might go wrong, but not always. This chapter addresses questions of what to do when people are the source of the problem.

Bringing People to the Table

"They won't even sit down and talk with us."

The water commissioners of a large western city knew their plans for a new treatment plant were going to be challenged by public interest groups and other municipal governments. But they were accustomed to wielding enormous political and economic power, readily going to court when their lawyers decided to fight someone who disagreed with them. They were used to winning. Other members of the community assessed the strength of the opposition and predicted interminable delays in building the badly needed treatment plant. They tried, but failed, to persuade the commissioners to cooperate with their adversaries in finding a satisfactory solution.

Persuading powerful, angry, or suspicious people to negotiate with each other is the first and often the most difficult task in conflict management. Unlike labor-management bargaining, where power relationships are known and procedures for negotiating are well established, public disputes are commonly fought by people who are unfamiliar with negotiation and are not compelled to negotiate. On the contrary, if the dispute is hot and the parties are angry, talking with each other may be the last thing in the world they want to do, especially if they have attacked each other publicly. Differences in values may be so great as to make any kind of cooperation seem unthinkable. And the organizations themselves can present problems. Citizen groups contending with powerful government agencies or large corporations often must take the hardest possible line—total victory—to keep the support of their members and maintain their momentum. In government or business organizations accustomed to turning problems over to lawyers, it can be safer for a manager to litigate than to try something as unconventional as conflict management.

The most common reasons why people refuse to negotiate are:

1. Agreeing to cooperate may appear to adversaries and constituents to be an admission of failure or weakness.
2. The parties distrust each other so deeply that good-faith agreements seem impossible.
3. One of the parties thinks he or she can win without negotiating.
4. The process of negotiation is unfamiliar and seems too risky.
5. Other options may be available, such as informal communications, policy revisions, and legal decrees.
6. Meetings would increase the visibility of the dispute.

The first job is to review all of the methods by which the dispute might be resolved, assess the risks of harm to the parties

of embarking on an alternative course, and decide whether conflict management is appropriate in the situation. If the answer
is yes, the second job is to persuade the parties to come to the
negotiating table. An affirmative answer to the first question is
by no means a foregone conclusion. They may be right in their
reluctance to negotiate. They may know, for example, that one
of the other parties is agreeing to participate for the sole purpose of obtaining information and then intends to drop out. Or
someone may try to use the discussion as a forum to intimidate
opponents.

The manager can approach both tasks by using the conflict analysis summary (Exhibit 5, p. 91) and previewing the factors relevant to this situation. What, for example, are the tactics
the parties are using to compete with each other? How good or
bad are their relationships? How long has the fight been going
on? How public is it? If the negotiations should go forward, the
manager should look for ways to make the parties think twice
about prolonging the conflict. The challenge is to convince
them either that they have more to gain by negotiating than by
continuing the battle or that the risk of unbearable harm is too
great to continue. Following is a discussion of different methods for bringing people to the table.

Use the Power of Public Opinion. The adversaries should
be reminded of the importance of public opinion. It should be
pointed out that they may lose public support if they continue
to be recalcitrant. Because citizen groups are often accused of
opposing proposals but never offering positive solutions, they
may welcome a chance to be part of a solution. Large business
organizations and government agencies gain public approval
when they avoid confrontation and deal reasonably with less
powerful adversaries.

Sometimes, when deadlines are approaching or a situation is nearing crisis, it may be necessary to take a chance and
begin discussions, hoping that a recalcitrant party will see what
is happening and participate later on. The risk is that negotiations may have to be terminated later if the strategy is not successful, but circumstances may allow no choice. In a rural county
of a western state, a construction company was planning a ma-

jor new development that would bring in a large force of workers that the small, isolated community was unprepared to handle. Everyone, including company officials, citizen activists,
and local business leaders, agreed that they must begin to work
together to anticipate demands on local services—everyone, that
is, except the three very conservative county commissioners
who took a dim view of such unconventional goings-on. A series
of open planning meetings was organized, leading up to a workshop in which residents and officials would identify specific
needs and work out strategies for dealing with them. The commissioners were important because they would be responsible
for carrying out workshop recommendations. Before each planning meeting, the commissioners were invited to attend by one
of their local constituents. Gradually, one or another of the
commissioners would drop in on the meetings and listen to discussions. They began to realize that the project was not com-
munist inspired after all and that it made good sense to prepare
for major changes that were about to take place. By the time
the workshop was held, the three commissioners were participating actively. The commission chairman gave the welcoming
speech at the beginning of the workshop. Pressure on the commissioners to participate was at all times polite but persistent.
Most important, it was applied by local citizens (Carpenter and
Kennedy, 1980).

Explain the Advantages of Negotiation. The manager
should describe, step by step, how conflict management techniques offer a more effective way of getting at the problem. He
or she can point out that vital information that is not otherwise
available can be obtained by negotiating and that costs can be
reduced by stopping the fight. The manager can also emphasize
the advantages of having direct control over discussions with
adversaries, rather than doing it through lawyers or other intermediaries. Finally, it is useful to call their attention to the value
of establishing long-term working relationships for handling
other problems in the future.

*Make Explicit the Inevitable Costs of Continuing the Cur-
rent Course.* A new manager, taking over a project that had

been delayed by constant disagreement that frustrated both the company and the nearby community, suggested to the residents that they and the company try talking about their mutual problems in a more cooperative way. The residents responded, "We don't see why we should work with you. We have the right to tell you what we want."

The manager answered, "Are you satisfied with the results?" He pointed out that nobody on either side seemed to like the way decisions were being made, and he thought they could do a lot better if they tried another way of dealing with each other. He said they could continue the way they were going, and almost certainly get more angry with each other, or they could cooperate in holding some facilitated meetings in which the company and the community would jointly develop the agendas. He said emphatically that the choice was theirs—to incur the cost of frustration and lack of information or to share with him the responsibility for trying a different method of negotiating with each other. He made the costs of the current course explicit and offered to join them in an alternative approach.

Determine Who Has Political or Economic Power. Who listens to whom? If political decisions are involved, the highest possible public official should be convinced to take an interest. In the case of the village (see Chapter Two), for example, the mayor sponsored intervention in the dispute between town government and a land developer.

Occasionally, it is possible to find someone whose official position is powerful enough to compel parties to negotiate and who wants the parties to reach the best possible agreement. In one case snowmobile operators and cross-country skiers each wanted exclusive use of a part of a national forest. Faced with a bitter and nearly violent confrontation, the forest supervisor told the two sides that they must sit down and work out a solution or they would find that the road to the area would no longer be cleared of snow. The parties reached agreement.

In the water roundtable (Chapter Two), community leaders had to find a way to persuade city water commissioners to participate in discussions. The water commissioners were business people, so the proponents of negotiation went to bankers and business executives and explained to them the potential cost to the city of litigation over water issues. They convinced them that lawsuits were inevitable if the commissioners ignored growing opposition of suburbs and other interests to their policies, emphasizing the economic consequences of long delays and the unpredictability of court decisions. The proponents explained in great detail their strategy for using negotiation in place of litigation. Following these discussions, the business leaders, through the local chamber of commerce, persuaded the water commissioners to participate in the negotiations.

Later, the governor of the state was asked to be chairman of the water roundtable because proponents of the negotiation had been told by interested parties that an invitation from the chief executive officer of the state would bring diverse and highly suspicious political parties to the table.

Stress the Unpredictability of Adversarial Procedures. The manager should spell out the uncertainties, the risks of avoiding the issue, and the possibility (if it exists) that opponents are capable of actions that may seem irrational. He or she should be explicit about the unpredictability of what the judge will decide, what the politicians will do, or what the losers will try next.

It should be pointed out that once begun, disputes have a way of increasing in intensity. They rarely just go away. People who think they can win should be asked to consider what will happen if their victory is not total. They should be asked whether it is possible that the defeated will return another day to resume the fight in more favorable political or economic circumstances, and whether the losers will sue to delay a final decision. Experienced decision makers can usually assess their own capacity to carry on a fight, but they often underestimate their opponents' determination to continue, even at great cost to themselves. Technically trained people have trouble comprehending how others can sacrifice for a cause that technicians consider ridiculous. But what is ridiculous to one person may be a life's cause for another.

Try One Meeting. If the parties are too fearful of formal negotiation or too thoroughly locked in combat, perhaps they will agree to meet just once to talk things over. If necessary, a third party might be brought in to run the first meeting. Parties should be told about the protections of a facilitated meeting. The manager can offer to share the design of the agenda with them. After the first meeting, they can decide whether it was useful enough to try a second.

Fit the Plan to the Situation. A regulatory commissioner proposed to a division manager of a public utility and interested citizen groups that they hold a series of negotiating sessions to redraft a proposed regulatory procedure. He assumed that everyone would welcome the opportunity to improve the current draft. But in talking with the parties about his suggestion, he found that several of them were not interested in altering the wording. Some groups liked the proposal as it stood and took the view that any effort to change it would reduce the rule's effectiveness. Other groups were so opposed to the concept behind the regulation that they felt any discussion of wording would imply their support for the proposed rule.

The commissioner realized that the problem needed to be redefined. Rather than negotiating the wording of the draft rule, the parties first needed to see whether they could accept the concept behind the rule. Parties agreed to meet to discuss the concept, not to reach agreement on the wording.

Conflict management always demands flexibility from the manager. Quite often, the design of a problem-solving proposal must be altered substantially to address an issue that others define differently than the initiator. By fitting the program to the needs of others, a manager has a good chance of getting closer to what he or she wants to accomplish.

The purpose of explaining the advantages of negotiation and bringing to bear the power of influence and persuasion is to encourage the parties in a dispute to consider a new way of dealing with their problem (Fisher and Ury, 1981). The idea is to offer them a chance to improve the situation. But they must agree, however hesitantly, that conflict management is worth a try. If they do not, and enter a negotiation only as a means to manipulate or coerce their adversaries, or if they are forced by some higher authority to participate, the chances are slim that the negotiations will be successful. A manager must be careful to assess the potential benefits and risks before proposing negotiation in place of other decision-making procedures.

Educating Newcomers

A principal purpose of the preliminary conflict assessment is to make sure that the right parties are at the table. Conveners pay careful attention to selecting individuals who are capable of negotiating with adversaries and of keeping agreements made in good faith. But no matter how careful one is to design a sound conflict management program, a new party may emerge as the process unfolds. Sometimes, as parties begin their deliberations, issues that did not seem important at first become a significant part of the discussions, and the new subjects suggest new participants. In the case of the old railroad (see Chapter Two), wilderness advocates had been interested in the issue, but at first their concerns were peripheral to the focus on historic preservation. However, as the discussion continued, more topics of direct concern to the wilderness groups came up, and the parties and the wilderness advocates decided they should be involved. A representative of wilderness interests was added to the group of negotiators.

When new parties are identified as having interests not represented by parties at the table, it is reasonable to suppose that they should be included in a negotiation. Furthermore, if stakeholders are not included in discussions, they may sabotage the implementation of agreements later on. However, there are hazards in adding a new party to a negotiation, especially if it is well under way. Adding a person to an established negotiation should be done cautiously and with full concurrence of the parties.

Responsibilities of the Group

Decisions should be placed in the hands of the parties at the table. Their advice and agreement should be sought on both the desirability of adding a new party and the person selected to be a representative. This is an important step because, in effect, the conveners and the parties have a contract with each other to carry on a cooperative enterprise under the conditions agreed to at the beginning. Those conditions can be assumed to include the individuals who will meet at the table. When a new party is added, the contract is amended to include it, and all the participants should be asked for their agreement. Just as a decision to change an agenda should be cleared with the members, so should a change in the makeup of the group.

The manager should ask for the group's help in acclimatizing new members. This is not just a ceremonial duty. Their tolerance may be necessary. The newcomers may arrive with chips on their shoulders because they were not invited at the beginning. In any case, they will not have gone through the process of trust building among the representatives, and they may enter the situation with animosities that the others have discarded. They will not be familiar with the style of discussion and with the little but highly important conventions that individuals have worked out for disagreeing without confrontation. In the game damage dispute described in Chapter Two, the parties decided that they needed an additional member with expertise in a particular type of game management. They picked a person with the proper credentials, an individual whom many of the parties knew well and respected. In the first meeting after his arrival, the members listened with astonishment as they received a condescending lecture from their game management expert on the benefits of cooperation and the evils of conflict. Since they had been working hard for eight months in a cooperative effort to solve problems, the lecture was exceedingly unwelcome. Angry as they were, the representatives had to agree that they all were responsible for inviting the person and that they should find a way of bringing him along with the group. They asked a colleague of his to explain that they did not need any pep talks about conflict management.

Responsibilities of the Chairperson

The chairperson should educate newcomers about the process and the issues. When a negotiation is going well, it is very easy for everyone to assume that the new person will fit right in and that the process will carry him or her along. It is not surprising, however, that newcomers to a negotiation often arrive with the same prejudices and half-knowledge that other parties had when *they* entered the process. Someone, usually the chairperson or a facilitator if there is one, must bring the newcomer up to date on the interests the parties have agreed are important, the progress they have made toward agreement, and why. Any ground rules for behavior must be explained in detail.

It also behooves the chairperson to admit mistakes in the selection of participants if mistakes were made. If the new person comes to the table resenting his or her status as last-to-be asked, the chairperson should explain how the original selection was made. If the party should have been included earlier, the chairperson should say so matter-of-factly and go on with a description of the process. It is important that new people entering a negotiation feel that they are equal in status and have the same opportunities to make a contribution as all others present.

Coping with Differences in Negotiating Skills

It is the nature of public disputes that some of the participants have never before been involved in formal negotiation, and some are unlikely to be negotiators again after the principal issue is settled. They are parties in a dispute not because they have official positions that compel them to be there but because they have a direct personal stake in the outcome of that single controversy. Others, such as government engineers, are dropped into a controversy and expected to carry out negotiation with no idea of how to go about it. Unlike professional labor negotiators, who are trained by other more experienced bargainers in their organizations, representatives of citizen groups and public and private managers often arrive on the scene with a determination to protect the interests of their side but with little or no knowledge of the give-and-take of negotiation.

Some people at the table may represent established organizations, government agencies, business concerns, public commissions, and boards and expect to be back again, often facing the same parties in new disagreements. They have compelling reasons to maintain some sort of working relationships with the other parties. Members of ad hoc citizen groups, however, may not—they are there, often with intensely hostile feelings about their adversaries, to do their best. They come to win.

An imbalance of skill and experience among negotiators sometimes results in an unfair fight and victory for the more experienced side, a victory that may eventually be destructive for everyone concerned. But there are some less obvious consequences of wide differences in negotiating experience that also demand a manager's careful attention, because they can have a strong influence on the progress of negotiation.

First of all, dealing with inexperienced negotiators can be extremely frustrating for the other parties, and they may become so impatient with the discussion that they may think of dropping out. Second, and even more dangerous for a negotiation, inexperienced negotiators may, as Morton Deutsch points out, resort to tactics that other, more experienced parties will consider to be outside "norms for rational interaction" (Deutsch, 1974). They may, for example, issue threats or invoke ideological absolutes that the other parties cannot accept as negotiable. Sometimes people think that they will be so injured by a proposed action or that their values will be so violated that any means to the end of preventing the action are justified. Breaking agreements, betraying confidences, and indulging in public accusations about the other parties in violation of negotiation ground rules are tactics sometimes used by inexperienced negotiators to gain advantage over adversaries they consider to have overwhelming power. Public officials, on the other hand, occasionally indulge in activities that imply none too subtly that they can do as they choose and that they are just being nice to talk about options. Negotiating with inexperienced parties and trusting their commitments can be hazardous for other participants. It is up to the meeting manager to detect imbalances in negotiating skill and deal with them.

Use Ground Rules. Guidelines for behavior, established in advance and evoked when necessary, are particularly important when some of the negotiators are not familiar with the basic necessities of constructive dialogue. Blustering, posturing, threatening, and accusing are likely to put off the most patient adversary, and incisive enforcement of behavioral ground rules is absolutely necessary. Another tactic, one that is conventional for first-time participants in public arguments, is to hurry off to the newspapers immediately after a meeting and announce to the world how terrible the other side is. In describing a ground rule that precludes this kind of destructive behavior, a conflict manager makes it clear, perhaps for the first time, that the parties are involved in a new and different endeavor that operates on different principles than going-for-the-jugular combat.

Educate the Participants. It is vital that all parties have an accurate understanding of the issues under consideration, who the other parties are, and the specific steps that the negotiation process will follow. People in disputes often arrive at a negotiating table with a full bag of stereotypes about their adversaries—misperceptions about the character and motives of the parties that must be corrected because they can poison the atmosphere in which discussions take place.

The representatives need to be trained to negotiate with each other. Carefully tailored training sessions can greatly reduce the possibility that unskilled representatives will inadvertently upset a discussion. "Team building" or negotiator training by a professional third party is often used as a precursor to formal negotiation. In the case of the village, it was evident that dissension within the town government would severely limit its ability to negotiate with the company, and the company's internal management problems could limit its capacity to discuss options and keep agreements. Both sides agreed that they needed help in forming their negotiating teams. They each spent two months in conflict management training before discussions began.

The difficulty with initiating training of people to help reduce differences in negotiating experience is, of course, that those who need help the most will often be the least likely to recognize it. Some of the techniques described earlier in this chapter for persuading parties to come to the negotiating table may be effective in cajoling parties to accept coaching in their negotiating skills, but sometimes people do not appreciate the suggestion that they need help. An effective alternative is to hold training sessions to which *all* parties send representatives. Some organizations have invited parties with whom they negotiate regularly to participate in training workshops so that they will all proceed from the same set of expectations.

Beware of Moving Too Quickly. Time must be built into a conflict management strategy for bringing the parties along in the negotiating process. Especially when participants are aware that they are less experienced than others, they will and should be sensitive to any efforts to push them into accepting proposals they have not had ample time to consider.

Pay Attention to Constituents. If representatives are inexperienced, it is a safe assumption that the other people in their groups are at least as inexperienced as they are. There is a serious danger that participants will get too far ahead of their constituents as they gain knowledge about the process and begin to adjust their positions.

Wide variations in negotiating experience among constituents add an annoying uncertainty to an already unpredictable mixture of factors. Because constituents seem extraneous to the meat of the issue, a manager may be tempted to accept the situation as it is. The dangers of this strategy are considerable, as we have explained in this section. Sound conflict management strategy includes assessing the parties' negotiating experience and addressing deficiencies that exist (see "Involving Constituents" in Chapter Eight).

Keeping People at the Table

"I didn't come here to listen to their problems. We are not getting anywhere. I'm leaving."

Anyone who has been a part of bringing people together to resolve a dispute has heard these or similar words. One should be prepared for second thoughts. They are almost certain to come. If it has been difficult to get people to the table, it is likely to be difficult to keep them there until the value of a negotiating process is established. One can expect people unaccustomed to negotiation to have doubts about participating and fears that more experienced negotiators will gain the advantage.

Sometimes threats to break off discussions are a ploy to win concessions or to unsettle the other side, but more often, the concerns are genuine. Following are reasons people give for wanting to leave a program and some suggestions about solutions.

Progress Is Not Fast Enough

When people are angry or worried about a problem, they want a solution as quickly as possible. They want to "get down to brass tacks." And they expect a meeting with their adversaries to be an argument over opposing positions. It is not surprising then that the essential steps of discussing issues and defining what people need can be unbearably frustrating. The early stages of conflict management move slowly and carefully, building a base. This is the time in negotiation when representatives try to force confrontation over positions, either because of their own impatience and anxiety or because of pressure from constituents.

Tell Them to Expect Frustration. In explaining the separate tasks of a conflict management process—finding a common definition of the problem, describing issues and interests, determining what information is missing, and developing options—one should tell the participants that progress will seem slow at times.

Make Gains Explicit. If the parties are making headway, the manager should say so, or be sure that someone else says so. Unless gains are clearly understood by all members of the group, and often they are not, they should be spelled out in precise detail. If relationships among individuals have improved, that gain should be described: "Mr. Jones told me at a break that six months ago we could never have had a positive discussion like we had this morning. We have come a long way from trying to knock down everything each of us says." If people are acquiring new information, it should be pointed out that they could not have obtained the information if they were fighting each other. If communication has been established between individuals, one should be sure they understand the value of direct discussion: "I hear you and Margaret had a useful telephone conversation yesterday. What did you come up with?"

Use the Group. The manager can turn to the others and ask them what they think about a party dropping out: "George says we are not getting anywhere. Does anyone have a comment?" If the discussions have been constructive, some members of the group will know that progress has been made. They should be asked to spell out what they see as progress.

The entire group must realize its responsibility for keeping the negotiations alive. Chapter Three emphasizes the importance of building ownership in the design and implementation of the negotiation from the very beginning. Ownership and shared responsibility are particularly important in trying to persuade someone to stay on.

Try One More Meeting. If people are hesitant about committing themselves to a complete program, they should be asked to stay with it for just one more meeting—and for one more after that if possible. They may be willing to continue in small steps. One must be careful not to dismiss their concerns. It is helpful to say something like, "I understand what you are saying. But, since you have put so much time in this already, how about staying around for another meeting? I think we are going to make some progress now."

Look for Hidden Obstacles. The manager should ask for advice and seek help from the group. One person cannot possibly know everything that is going on among the participants, so they should be made responsible for finding the right direction to proceed. In the game damage project, negotiations were moving along, but some of the participants were becoming increasingly uncomfortable about the discussion. Something was bothering them but it was not clear what it was. The assessment of the conflict had indicated that the parties thought that they had been given inconsistent and inaccurate information by the Division of Wildlife, deliberately or not. However, the consequences of that perception did not become fully evident until a break in the discussion, when one of the participants said, "They will not budge until they get their pound of flesh. They want the Division people to admit they made a mistake." He meant that the parties would not cooperate until the agency admitted that its reports were misleading. In response, an agency executive was brave enough to stand up at the meeting and explain in detail how the reports had been written and why their findings were internally inconsistent. His careful and thorough explanation had two substantial benefits. He admitted that the Division had made a mistake, and, more important, the participants understood for the first time that the errors came from poor communication between geographically distant offices and not from deliberate attempts to mislead the public. This knowledge was extremely important to forging trust between the Division representatives and the other parties. This example also underscores an important point: People are pleasantly surprised when someone admits openly and explicitly to an error.

Discussions Are Moving Too Quickly

Sometimes, instead of moving too slowly, a negotiation goes forward too quickly. People who have battled each other for a long time without making progress are often surprised by the ease with which they can move into constructive discussion with their adversaries using conflict management techniques. They worry that they may have disregarded some piece of vital information, or they may become uneasy because progress toward agreement may be outpacing the growth of trust among the parties. They are confused to find that people who, at a distance, have seemed so irrational are turning out to be quite reasonable, which, in turn, requires an uncomfortable rearranging of stereotypes.

Another cause of concern can be the insistence of one or

more of the participants that the discussions skip the procedural steps they have agreed to follow and bargain over solutions. Whether it is "nitty-gritty" or "brass tacks" they want to get down to, unwise pressure to circumvent the process must be handled promptly and incisively.

To deal with this kind of anxiety, the manager should call a temporary break in the discussion, make sure everyone has had an opportunity to describe his or her case, and give people of like interests a chance to talk together about the progress they have made. They will need to check each other's reactions and build confidence in their agreements. The group can then review options on the table and decide whether they need additional resources to develop more options.

Behavior Is Offensive

"We don't like the way we're being treated. We think we ought to leave." This kind of message can be delivered in a general meeting or in a private conversation between meetings. Before responding, the manager should think through the reasons why they may be concerned. Most especially, the manager should not jump to the conclusion that they are making a threat for its effect. He or she should maintain an unruffled countenance and explore with them the reasons why they are dissatisfied.

Enforce the Ground Rules. Infractions of the ground rules can be headed off by explaining at the beginning why they are important and by emphasizing the participants' responsibility for following and enforcing them. Then a person who sets out to break a rule knows that he or she is confronting the entire group, not just the chairperson.

Let a Person Go. It may be better to let a destructive person leave a negotiation than to allow him or her to drag it down. In one situation, the negotiators thought so, after one person had repeated at every working session that he doubted that negotiation was a good idea and he probably should not be there. After a while, every time he raised his hand to speak everyone else in the room knew what he was about to say and resented it. When the chairperson finally said, "Well, if you really don't like being here, maybe you ought to leave," there were quiet sighs of relief. It is necessary to assess the consequences of one of the parties dropping out, and the group should be asked for opinions, but it is not a foregone conclusion that the departure of one individual will cause a major fracture in a negotiation.

Ask for a Replacement. Part or all of the problem may lie in the personality of the individual representative. Rather than assuming that the breach is permanent, one can ask the person's constituents whether they would like to appoint another representative. The door should be kept open unless the group is sure that they do not want participation from that constituency.

Parties Are Stuck in Old Relationships

Parties in conflict expect their adversaries to behave according to patterns established in previous encounters. They come to a meeting prepared for unpleasantness, and they react vigorously at the first hint that they may be right. "I *knew* he would act that way!" expresses a common self-fulfilling prophecy. The challenge for the chairperson is to keep people together until they can find by experience that they are in a new ball game. The participants in the water roundtable knew one another well. The argument had been going on for decades, and everyone knew his or her part and played it. People who were supposed to take rigid positions took them. People who were supposed to make self-righteous claims about the purity of their position made self-righteous pronouncements. In that negotiation, as in so many others, the parties had to realize that they were operating in a totally new context: mediated negotiation. They had to get over their expectations of how each would behave by working through the steps of the conflict management program. It took several months and several agreements on procedures before they relaxed enough to begin negotiation over substantive issues.

Personal Risks Are Increasing

Negotiation of public disputes is carried on with few accepted guidelines and without established traditions. Sadly, a negotiator sometimes pays a price, personally or professionally, for being a reasonable person among unreasonable people. Escalating conflict produces militants who do not take kindly anyone's efforts to communicate with the enemy. Some disputes can become so intense that participating in negotiation may become too costly, in lost personal or professional relationships, for a negotiator to continue. People leave negotiation, even when they believe in its purpose, when the danger becomes too great. It is important, therefore, that all members of a negotiation be aware of their responsibility to support and protect as much as possible their fellow participants, even if they disagree about the positions they take (refer to "Reducing Personal Risk" later in this chapter).

External Events Change the Context

A court decision, a change in personnel at the top of an organization, new policies, or new parties may change the conditions that existed when negotiations began. Changes for the better are welcome. New, more conciliatory attitudes on the part of management, resolution of other, similar issues, increasing support of powerful political figures, and other positive developments happen frequently in public issue negotiation, and the participants happily accept all the help they can get. On the other hand, changes may not be so constructive. Elections, changes in management, or economic problems may unexpectedly reduce or withdraw the support a participant receives from his or her organization. Public policy disputes are sensitive to outside influences.

Acknowledge the Change. If circumstances dictate that a party leave for his or her protection or for other reasons, the other participants and their constituents need to understand why. Misconceptions about the departure of a negotiating party can cause suspicion and apprehension among other parties at the table.

Enlist the Group's Help. There are times when it may be in the best interests of the parties to suspend or even terminate their discussions. The convener might say, for example, "Bill Smith's Washington office made a decision yesterday that makes him question whether he should continue to participate in these negotiations. He is not sure now that he could carry out his agreements. We have to decide whether we should continue without him or adjourn until the situation becomes clearer." This is certainly not a welcome development, but it does happen, and a chairperson is responsible for taking whatever action is necessary to avoid causing harm to any of the participants.

Handling Intense Emotions in Public Meetings

"I have just been warned that some of the people coming to the meeting tonight are so angry they might get out of hand." At these all-too-familiar words, the manager's anxiety level jumps to a new high. It is his or her job as facilitator or chairperson to make the meeting a success.

Sometimes angry, hostile people come to meetings to disrupt the discussions, challenge the speakers, and insult the sponsors. Because they attract news media, they divert attention from important issues. Emotional people are frustrating and sometimes a little scary (Bach and Goldberg, 1974; Bramson, 1981; Gordon, 1977; Keating, 1984).

It is important to know why people are angry because, so often, rage is closely connected to fear. Fear of change, fear of loss, fear of physical harm are expressed as outrage, *at* something or someone. Fear is also closely connected to perceptions of how much control people have over their lives. People react passionately when government or some other powerful force takes away their ability to choose how and where they live.

The fear may be unjustified and the anger unreasonable, but these emotions must be taken into account. Standing on one's professional credentials and announcing "I have the *facts*" ignores reality. Fear is as real as acre feet of water or miles of highway.

One must be particularly skeptical of simplistic statements like "Oh, she is just a troublemaker," because, while every community has a few souls who enjoy the excitement of controversy and public confrontation, most people dislike the wear and tear of strong emotions. One should assume, for safety's sake, that the distress is genuine and will affect the progress of the meeting.

One should never patronize people by telling them that they are being irrational. Maybe they know more about the issue. Perhaps they *should* be angry. The manager should be careful about describing the professional credentials of some people in terms that others may take as disparaging of their own knowledge. He or she should think about the worst thing that could happen and be prepared for it.

When a manager is confronted with the necessity of running a meeting without adequate time to prepare for it, he or she must depend on techniques for controlling behavior and handling problems as they come up. But, if there is time, much can be done to reduce tensions before the meetings start.

Before Meetings

Prior to a meeting the manager can review lists of people who have come to other meetings on the subject or who have acted as spokespeople. It is also useful to check newspaper articles, to collect as many perspectives as possible, and to telephone key people or, if at all possible, go see them. These key people should be told the purpose of the meeting in terms that would interest them. One can say, "We think we have new information that will be important to your plans and we want to tell you about it." One should avoid saying, "We are required by Public Law 378462, section 24F, subparagraph B-1-a to hold a public meeting." They should be told exactly how the meeting will be organized. The more detail they are given, the more they will realize that their understanding is important. They probably will express opinions about the meeting and the issues.

One should *listen* to but not comment on the substance of what they have to say. Many find the role of interviewer to be a strain because they often know that the speaker is wrong. Nevertheless, one must resist the impulse to set him or her straight. Above all, one should not argue. Their speaking out about their concerns can establish the beginnings of a working relationship, because in future meetings, they will know that their reasons for being angry have been heard. It is important to note that one does not endorse others' opinions by listening to them.

During Meetings

Set Boundaries. Participants should be told that arguments and accusations destroy any chance of having a productive meeting and that attacks on anyone's motives or integrity cannot be permitted. Most people think of themselves as fair and reasonable. One should appeal to their sense of fair play.

The group should be told how the meeting will be managed, including how comments will be recorded, how long people will have to speak, and what will be done with the record. The manager should emphasize the importance of everyone having a chance to speak. He or she should say, and repeat when necessary, that the group shares with the meeting chairperson the responsibility for making the meeting a success.

Acknowledge Feelings. Intense anger or fear threatens the conduct of a meeting. In the case of the airport (see Chapter Two), the federal agency was attempting to identify the specific concerns of nearby residents about the possible addition of an airport runway. A great many technical and political factors demanded attention, but it was also necessary to deal with the needs of elderly people on fixed incomes who were terrified that their mobile homes and small houses would be taken away from them. The meeting managers had investigated the situation and knew that, under the bitter rhetoric and accusations of official irresponsibility, there was a genuine fear that no one understood the predicament of the older citizens. The public meeting was designed to deal with the citizens' need to be heard and understood. The facilitators pressed people for detailed information about their fears—what might happen to their homes, decreased property values, and relocation problems. Comments from the audience were recorded on large paper wall sheets where everyone, citizens and officials, could see them. Care was taken to repeat exactly what had been said. The facilitators frequently asked, "Did we get that right?" and "Is that exactly what you said?" The elderly citizens could see the evidence that their concerns had been acknowledged.

   Identify Sensitive Words and Topics and Avoid Them. In the airport situation, the facilitators carefully avoided calling mobile homes "trailers," a term they had found was considered condescending. In another community dispute with a government agency, the residents of a small town were alarmed at the possibility that their municipal water supply had been contaminated by a nearby toxic waste dump. They wanted the responsible government agency to test their water. After some delay, the water was tested but the samples were mishandled in the laboratory and the entire effort was futile. The residents still did not know whether they were drinking contaminated water. In response to public outcry, a hearing was held, which the agency manager opened by saying that the community should relax because highly skilled technicians were there to help them. The residents, having recently observed the skills of the laboratory staff, let the manager know that he had made a major blunder, one that he could have avoided if he had done his homework. In his efforts to put the community at ease, he had chosen the one topic that he should not have touched.

   Ask the Entire Group for Help. When a small faction with extreme views attempts to dominate the meeting, the manager should describe what is happening and ask whether it serves the interests of the rest of the people in the meeting. Announcement of plans for the construction of a uranium mine produced expressions of concern from neighbors around the proposed site. A meeting was organized for the purpose of exchanging information about the project. The organizer learned that several individuals were planning to disrupt the meeting to express their opposition to nuclear war. The organizer announced that she could change the plan for the meeting and that the group could spend the evening talking about nuclear war if they wanted to. She suggested, however, that it was unlikely that the problem of nuclear warfare would be solved in one meeting, and she asked the group how it wanted to use the time available. Participants agreed not to talk about nuclear war, not because they were unconcerned about the problem but because they wanted information about the proposed mine.

Be Willing to Terminate the Meeting. If there is not enough support to continue in a productive manner, it may be best to close the meeting. It is better to stop the entire meeting than to lose control of it. A meeting manager is responsible for preventing harm to the parties, even if the parties themselves do not recognize the damage that can be done by personal attacks and accusatory rhetoric.

Explain the Process and Let the People Judge. People who are angry or frightened are likely to challenge a meeting manager's personal credibility and the meeting's approach to gathering information. People should be urged to speak out if they suspect bias in the process. If a meeting manager's neutrality is questioned, he or she should say something like, "Watch what I do. If you see any evidence of bias, tell me right away." The audience will be watching to see whether the manager becomes flustered or defensive.

The most effective way of dealing with a challenge is to act as if it is a reasonable concern, which it often is. A county official was facilitating a meeting between a county government and the residents of a community near a proposed new highway. About 400 people were crammed into a school gymnasium. Just as she was about to open the meeting, several people stood up in the front row, waved their fists in the air, and shouted that she had been hired by the county to hoodwink the community. She said that she thought the people had come to the meeting to hear about the county's plans and to tell county officials about their concerns. She told the audience that she was not asking them to trust her but, instead, to decide as the meeting went along whether it was serving their needs. She urged them to watch the recording of their statements and to speak out at once if the recording was not accurate. To her astonishment, the audience applauded at the end of the meeting. What she had said seemed reasonable to most of the people there. Negotiators should not be asked to trust an outsider. Why should they have to? Why should they stake their health and safety or economic well-being on a stranger? Instead, they should be told to watch the process and decide whether the meeting is serving their needs.

Quickly Interrupt Any Personal Attacks. If things start to get out of hand, the facilitator should stand up and, if necessary, stand between the individuals. He or she should point out to the entire group, not to the attacker, that the accusation is a violation of the ground rules. If the insult is directed at the facilitator, he or she should not respond in kind. The purpose of the attack may be to make the facilitator angry and thus provide an opportunity for the attacker to respond at a higher level of hostility. The entire group should be told that strong feelings are natural in the situation but that if such feelings are not kept under control, they will destroy the meeting. One should avoid raising the ante.

Act Incisively When the Boundaries of Decency and Fairness Are Breached. The manager should tell the entire group what has happened even though they can see it for themselves. He or she should then explain what will happen next. In a highly charged public meeting, a group of roughly dressed men marched to the stage and attached a long, scurrilous banner to the podium, attacking the integrity of the meeting conveners. The meeting facilitator immediately announced that the banner must be removed. He recessed the meeting and said that it would not continue as long as the banner was attached to the stage. He explained to the group that if the men who attached the banner forced termination of the meeting, the rights of some forty people who had come to testify would be violated. He knew that the governor of the state and a government official from another country were waiting to speak. He walked off the stage. The banner was removed.

The manager must keep control of the meeting. Symbolic gestures challenging the manager's control are likely·to be progressive. If he or she allows the first to stand, others will follow.

How to Handle a Tense Public Meeting—Odds and Ends

What about humor? Remember that these people are angry or fearful. One must be cautious about using humor to relieve tension, because it may seem to depreciate the seriousness of their concerns. One should never joke about what someone has said. Nor should humor be directed at an individual, because the group may take his or her side and interpret a joke as an attack.

Names should be used whenever possible. Saying "Sir" or "Madam" will create distance between the meeting manager and the group if everyone knows that a list of the names of the speakers is readily available. One must be cautious about using first names except for those of very young people, because it may sound patronizing. Using the person's name is especially important when discussion must be limited or a ground rule imposed. A reverse trap is for a manager to know the names of people from only one organization and by using them appear to be too familiar with one side.

Getting Even

In preparing for the first meeting to discuss the old railroad, the facilitator heard a new theme: the government agency had reversed a decision made years before, and the change in policy caused the preservation group expense and considerable concern that the tunnel and trestle would not be preserved after all. Representatives of this group wanted to preserve the historic structures, but they also wanted to hear the agency supervisor admit publicly that he had acted in bad faith. This situation illustrates a common condition when opening negotiations: the parties are carrying some excess baggage that must be handled before getting down to business.

A second example involves a small community that had tried for six years to persuade a company to clean up an abandoned factory. Residents were afraid that children would hurt themselves in the tangle of steel and glass, and they were also deeply concerned about the contents of leaky old storage drums. The state health department could not find evidence of hazardous materials, but the residents were not convinced. The company had ignored requests for action except to issue occasional patronizing assurances that folks could trust the company and that there was nothing to fear. They would get around to cleaning up the site sometime. Finally, through the influence of a congressman, local newspapers, and other businesspeople, the company agreed to meet with the citizens in an attempt to resolve their differences. An impartial third party was asked to facilitate the meeting. Although the residents were genuinely fearful of the hazards present on the site and had wanted for years to clean it up, they had come to hate the company so much that they focused all of their preparations for the meeting on thinking up ways of getting revenge.

Why People Want to Get Even

Betrayal. People react strongly and sometimes vindictively when they have been injured by a violation of trust. And betrayal is deeply felt when it is perpetrated by someone who has the responsibility of being a protector. This explains why government, the protector of people, comes in for its own special brand of vengeance when it causes harm by some action or by failure to take appropriate action. People feel betrayed—their own government has let them down.

Threats. Threats express a willingness to do harm. If people believe a threat, they accept it as a form of violence done to them. They feel injured and humiliated. Threats produce instant escalation in a conflict because they violate commonly accepted standards of decent behavior and produce a sense of outrage. Experienced negotiators, therefore, rarely issue threats, but inexperienced negotiators may issue threats without being aware of the danger or without caring about it. Threats create a desire for reprisal more than any other negotiating tactic except, perhaps, direct action.

Rhetoric. What people say to each other and about each other often becomes a separate cause for retribution. Hostility among parties grows worse as parties exchange accusatory statements. If the attacks are made in public, so much face is lost by the victim of accusatory rhetoric that simple apologies may not be enough. Getting even can become the injured person's primary goal. Like threats, accusatory rhetoric sets up an expanding system of attack and counterattack that must be broken off if negotiations are to begin.

Economic Harm. When it is measurable and the responsible party can be discovered, compensation for property damage is customarily sought through the courts. But some economic injuries cannot be redressed through the legal system. When uranium tailings were found in the foundations of houses in a subdivision, property values plummeted, but it was not clear just who was responsible. The innocent victims suffered economic loss but had no hope of compensation from a responsible party. When people are hurt and cannot recover their financial losses, they often look for relief in the form of retaliation. Finding someone to blame becomes an absorbing mission.

Fear. Managers who enter a situation where economic loss is combined with fear are sometimes astounded by the ferocity of the attacks made on anyone even remotely associated with the cause. People who have lived for years in fear of hidden health effects of a nuclear accident or toxic waste spill feel they have suffered an unforgivable intrusion into their lives. They feel violated by another human being. Through no fault of theirs, their lives are changed, sometimes permanently, and they want someone to pay for the pain.

Dealing with the Desire to Get Even

It is important to watch for signs that getting even may be one of the goals of the parties. Often a desire to redress a grievance is not expressed overtly, because nice people do not talk about getting revenge (except, of course, when the injury is so severe that others would be likely to applaud a demand for vengeance—after a brutal murder, for example). Unless a conflict is at the top of the conflict spiral, people choose other ways of saying they want to get even. They talk about "setting things straight" or "making them admit that." What they are really saying is that they want redress of a grievance. Unlike a much less common demand—revenge—the parties do not necessarily want to harm their adversaries. They just want to "set things straight."

Fit the Procedure to the Case. In the old railroad meetings, the facilitator anticipated a demand from the preservation group that the agency manager admit to double-dealing. The facilitator also knew that the agency manager thought that his behavior had been entirely honest and responsible. The facilitator realized that the discussion would end abruptly if the parties began to exchange accusations, in spite of the genuine commitment of the parties to solve the problem of the tunnel and trestle. At the first session a hand went up and the representative of the preservation group said, "I would like to know why the agency went back on its word." The facilitator said, with a smile and in a relaxed tone, "I don't think we ought to pursue this. Remember, we all agreed that we wouldn't attack each other, and that last remark sounds pretty close to an attack." He did *not* confront the speaker. He did *not* say, "You are making an attack." He relied on the common sense of the group and their interest in solving the problem to head off a destructive confrontation that no one really wanted. Satisfaction of the grudge was far down their list of goals, but in this case, as in so many others, the parties might have pursued the discussion and quite probably broken off negotiation. Instead, the speaker simply nodded and dropped the subject. She understood the value of proceeding with the negotiation, and because the facilitator made a process observation—"that last remark sounds"—and not a personal reproach, the speaker did not have to save face by insisting on pursuing the point and thus raising the ante.

Affirm the Importance of the Grievance. In the old railroad case, the facilitator knew that the old grievance was relatively unimportant and used a simple ground rule to guide the discussion back on track. But what if the complaint is more important to one or more of the parties and they are not so willing to drop the subject? What if the parties want very much to solve a larger problem but an old injustice, real or only perceived, stands squarely in the way? Other cases may require more than invoking a ground rule and moving on. In these situations a manager should acknowledge the importance of the grievance and, if appropriate, offer an explanation. Only then will parties be able to focus on solving their problems.

Maintain Control by Establishing and Enforcing Ground Rules. In the uranium tailings case, the community wanted to retaliate for the anxiety it had suffered for years at the hands of the company. A decline in property values was also a cause of bitterness, but it was the callous disregard for the health and safety of the citizens that infuriated them the most. A manager acting as intervener in a case such as this will follow rigid procedures in running a meeting where the parties face each other in the same room. The first task is to decide whether it is in the interests of the parties to meet—whether it is possible to control the participants and prevent destructive attacks. If the circumstances suggest that a productive meeting is not possible, the responsible person should refuse to convene such a meeting—recognizing, however, that separate discussions with parties might be possible.

In this case, a third party was asked to convene and facilitate a meeting. He decided that both parties had a large enough stake in finding answers to the central problem that there was a reasonable chance that they could participate in a constructive session. He knew, however, that the meeting would have to be very tightly managed and that he must be prepared to stop the entire process if it threatened to get out of hand. He set ground rules and announced them to the parties in writing.

Name What Is Going On. The discussion over cleanup of the abandoned factory proceeded in conformance to the rules, but the tone of the comments was so strident and hostile that, midway through the morning, the facilitator called a halt and said, "There are some very strong feelings here. But no matter how justified you are in feeling the way you do, if you concentrate your energies on getting revenge against each other, you are all going to lose." The tone of the meeting changed. The participants did not like each other any better, but they recognized their need to find a solution, and for the first time someone had called their attention to how much effort they had been devoting to seeking vengeance. The explicit naming of what they were doing gave them a reference point for the rest of the day.

Reducing Personal Risk

Ironically, even agreeing to participate in negotiation may damage one's professional standing or personal relationships. This is because people in escalating conflict progressively lose their tolerance of other points of view. They begin to see people who disagree with them as adversaries and then as enemies who must be defeated (see "The Spiral of Unmanaged Conflict" in Chapter One). As a conflict expands, moderates become militants or drop out of the argument. New militants come in, people who tend to think that they are entirely right and their adversaries totally wrong, and they assume that anyone who deals with the enemy at all must have "sold out." This is true for citizen interest groups, and also for companies and government agencies that are accustomed to using adversarial methods for achieving their goals.

An additional hazard for a participant in a highly polarized dispute is the possibility that an unscrupulous adversary will try to exploit the participant's vulnerability within his organization. This happened to the agency manager in the game damage project when he decided to use negotiation in place of long-established adversarial proceedings. By doing so, he stepped outside the agency's traditional hard-line approach to dealing with the public. It was common knowledge outside the agency that some of his associates were outraged by his willingness to negotiate, but he persevered and made progress. This was not what another participant in the negotiation wanted to happen. His group had been formed to oppose the agency's policies, and progress toward agency goals would be inimical to the purpose of his group. When he realized that the agency manager was vulnerable within his own organization, he went directly to the manager's superior, berated him for allowing the agency to participate in the negotiation, and tried to persuade him to withdraw.

While negotiators must always be careful to maintain the confidence of constituents, risk of the kind discussed here occurs primarily in situations at the extreme end of the conflict dynamics continuum (see Exhibit 4, p. 88). Attitudes must have hardened, relationships must have become hostile, and, as a general rule, the parties must have committed substantial resources to winning a victory. The majority of public disputes are less intense, and a person trying to deal responsibly with the issues is usually recognized by the community as a public-spirited citizen. Personal risk is not a common problem, but it is a serious one, and the consequences of not recognizing and dealing with the possibility of damage to a negotiator's personal interests can be severe. It is a guiding principle in conflict management that negotiation should do no harm to anyone.

Avoiding Risk

Choose Representatives Who Are Secure in Their Positions. Representatives should be chosen from as far up the organizational ladder as possible. Vice-presidents or presidents are less likely to be subjected to open criticism than are their subordinates. It is inviting trouble to pick as a representative someone who associates believe is at the fringe of the organization, without support or influence. That person is already too far out on a limb (Perritt, 1985).

Change the Role. If one of the representatives is particularly at risk, he or she may want to attend as an observer until the program is accepted more securely by all the parties. Even if the meetings are ostensibly closed to anyone except negotiators, exceptions can be made by agreement of the parties. It is our experience that exceptions of this kind can be explained to the other parties and are not difficult to make. They will know that it is highly desirable that a person who may later be a representative participate in the conflict management program from the beginning.

Keep Constituents Informed. The manager should announce a plan to inform constituents in advance of negotiations. If constituents are sure they will have a regular and predictable method for learning about the progress of negotiations, they will be less anxious about their representative "giving away the store." Representatives will then be able to explain in a cohesive way the context in which adjustments in position and agreements are made (see "Involving Constituents" in Chapter Eight).

Ask for Support in Advance. Whenever possible, negotiators should anticipate and deal with the possibility of outside interference in the internal affairs of a negotiating party. The facilitators in the game damage project knew that there were animosities between the parties. However, they underestimated the vindictiveness of one of the representatives and did not anticipate his attempt to discredit the work of the agency manager. If they had, they would have asked the manager's superior to agree to support the negotiation, at least through the initial sessions.

Reducing the Potential Harm

Look for the Help of Influential People. In the section on "Bringing People to the Table" at the beginning of this chapter, we described methods for building support for a conflict management effort. Some of the same techniques, such as keeping the public informed and explaining the advantages of negotiation to people with political or economic power, also serve to enlist the understanding of influential people when their support is needed to protect a representative from personal harm. Their understanding of the purpose of a negotiation and their willingness to endorse it can be a determining factor. "Well, I don't think much of this business myself, but if Mr. Jones is for it, I won't interfere" is a common sort of reaction when influential people express their opinion about a negotiation. The representative of the oil and gas industry in the oil and gas exploration project (see Chapter Two) came under sharp personal attack from the militants of his group, who said that he was being too accommodating with their traditional enemies. However, one of the group's officers who had taken a substantial part in organizing the negotiation insisted that the group continue to support its representative.

Use Representatives of Both Sides to Affirm the Importance of a Negotiation. In the case of the game damage project, the other participants, including those of opposing views, condemned the attempts of the one representative to undercut the agency manager. They told the offending representative that they resented such unscrupulous behavior. Several went to the agency director and urged him to support the efforts of his manager. The manager's participation remained vulnerable to criticism, but the overt attempt to exploit the vulnerability of his situation failed.

Negotiation of public disputes is carried on with few accepted guidelines and without established traditions. People who agree to represent a point of view may do so with some personal or professional risk, especially if the dispute is polarized. All members of a negotiation should be aware that it may be necessary to support and protect their fellow participants, even if they disagree on the issue at hand.

11

Removing Roadblocks

Well-planned and skillfully executed conflict management programs are less susceptible to stalemate than more haphazardly organized discussions, but they are not immune to them. Information is an essential ingredient in successful negotiation. Its accuracy, availability, and application may well determine the course and effectiveness of problem-solving discussions, yet negotiators sometimes find that they disagree over basic data. Deadlocks can occur at any stage of a negotiation for an infinite variety of other reasons as well, such as destructive relationships, offensive personal behavior, and need for changes in the program design. This chapter reviews obstacles to progress that have the potential for destroying an entire conflict management program and suggests methods for overcoming them.

Negotiating Differences in Data

One often hears statements like "If we could only forget the emotions and get down to the facts, we could solve this problem in a hurry." But public disputes are not that simple. Disagreements over data cause otherwise successful negotiations to break down, because the "facts" in a case are not always true. Public officials and private managers make decisions about the future as best they can, using the information available to them. But if an adversary can persuade the public or a court that the information is flawed or obsolete, the decision and the data behind it become the center of a dispute. Information is also used selectively as a weapon to persuade the public of the validity of one point of view or to intimidate a rival. A person who urges replacing "emotion" with "facts" is likely to have a set of figures that support his or her own position. An effort to

258

get to the facts must also recognize that sound statistics are subject to widely differing interpretations. Finally, it is often difficult to distinguish fact from long-held assumptions that have taken on the same reality as fact. People sometimes take for granted that everyone else is working from the same set of assumptions, only to find to their surprise and anger that their "facts" are open to challenge. Arguments over securely held beliefs can produce new disputes, accompanied by accusations of dishonesty and bad faith. Separating emotions from fact is a lot harder than it sounds (Bacow and Wheeler, 1984).

Problems with Data

Inaccurate or Incomplete Information. Quite often in negotiation of public issues, the parties find they do not have all the information they need to get on with solving their problem. The next step is crucial. If they can focus their efforts on obtaining the necessary material, they will continue to make progress. But if they are distracted by bad relationships and distrust and their search for data is disrupted, their negotiations may be seriously threatened.

In the case of the old railroad, the participants in the first meeting focused on obstacles that had blocked progress in the past and on assessment of possible options. In talking about the type of road that they should build and maintain, they realized that the counties and the state and federal agencies involved might have different standards for road classifications. The question was twofold: "What kind of road do we want—a road for heavy-duty four-wheel-drive vehicles or for Winnebagos?" and "What do each of our agencies require for these road standards?" They acknowledged that they needed a common definition of standards before they could negotiate the type of road they would build. Questions of this kind can either remain noncontroversial building blocks in efforts to resolve a larger issue or can become new separate disputes. In the case of the old railroad, the parties readily agreed they needed the information and appointed a small task group to find the information and recommend a standard to the entire group.

In contrast to the constructive approach taken by the parties in the case of the old railroad, the proponents of the city's plans for water development *assumed* that the city would grow indefinitely at the same rate as it had in the past (the water roundtable case, Chapter Two). Their belief in the manifest destiny of the city became an ideology for some of the business leaders and city officials, who believed after a while that what they hoped would be true *was* true. They were outraged and reacted in harshly adversarial terms when their assumptions were challenged by others who used more modest projections of population growth to support a counterview. The intensity of the city's reaction and the acrimony with which it was expressed produced a new dispute, separate from the issue of incomplete information.

Differing Interpretations of the Same Set of Data. An impasse over a highly complex set of statistics occurred when members of the water roundtable disagreed about a projection of maximum yield of the city's water system. The quantity and size of the reservoirs, conduits, and treatment facilities were known, but the participants of the roundtable held widely differing views about the potential effects that drought, variations of snowpack, and other external climatic and management variables would have on the amount of water the system could produce. This was a topic of critical importance in estimating the city's need for new facilities. The roundtable had to find a way around the statistical obstacle of annual yield before negotiations could proceed.

Parties' Insistence on Using Their Own Data. "I am willing to talk about this, but only if we use my figures." Such a pronouncement causes instant impasse, even before negotiations have begun. It is frustrating to hear someone throw down a gauntlet that is likely to create more controversy. The convener is faced with a roadblock and must remove it before negotiations can proceed.

Fear of Opening the Door Too Wide. "If I agree that my figures are a little inaccurate and should be changed, what will the changes look like? Will I be able to integrate them into my description of the situation, or will the changes demolish my entire plan?"

One of the most pervasive fears of weaker parties in a dispute is exposing their data to volumes of self-serving information produced by larger, more powerful institutions. A federal agency, for example, can bring to bear large research and public relations resources to overwhelm the technical positions of their adversaries. If weaker parties are so much less able to produce convincing statistics than their powerful adversaries, they may decide that it is safer to refuse to discuss the data.

More powerful groups can be reluctant to have their figures examined, too. They know that behind their glossy documents may be questionable assumptions or errors in calculations that, if revealed, could seriously undermine their positions. Just as in bringing people to the table, persuading people to negotiate their data and accept adjustments requires trust in the negotiating process. The parties must be confident that more can be gained by using the best possible information than by holding fast to their own data.

Invested Resources. "This study cost us $150,000. It *must* be good." Whether the investment in a set of data is in dollars or in time and energy, it can be terribly difficult to admit that the data are flawed or inadequate, especially if doing so is a concession that resources could have been better spent in other ways.

Clash of Values. In the section on values in Chapter Nine, we suggest that everyone, even large organizations, operates by a set of values. Values tell us how the world "ought to be." Since challenging the validity of someone's data may be close to challenging that person's sense of reality, persuading someone to accept contrary information can be very difficult. If a group has mounted a campaign to bring about substantial changes in public policy on the basis of information its members accept as true, they may have a hard time giving it up, even in the face of powerful evidence that their statistics are wrong.

Numbers may be neutral, but the conclusions people draw

from them can be determined by their values. Take, for example, a report that "45 percent of black employable teenagers do not have jobs." Depending on the values of the listener, two entirely different conclusions may be drawn for this statistic:

- Black teenagers do not have a fair chance at available jobs.
- Black teenagers do not want to work.

The challenge for the manager is to help the parties set aside their values, reach a common definition of a problem, and focus on finding a solution.

Biased Information. Sometimes the data the parties are using to define a problem and assess options are intentionally biased. As a conflict expands, people begin to use information as a weapon to prove a point or to injure an adversary. Information becomes a means to prevail over other positions instead of a resource for solving problems. Data may or may not be deliberately inaccurate, but they are used selectively to prove a point. Instead of sharing information to solve a problem, parties release it to the public through the news media to gain public support and to promote their victory. In all-out warfare of this kind, data are not just *perceived* to be biased. They are biased and are known to be. One of the consequences of using biased information is that later attempts to exchange valid information are rejected.

In less contentious circumstances, bias may be more apparent than real. The figures may be inaccurate or incomplete because of careless or inept work rather than deliberate attempts to mislead. Stalemates over deliberately biased data are more difficult to handle than those caused by mistakes. The latter can often be resolved by going back into the material and finding and correcting the errors. The former, on the other hand, may require hard negotiation to produce valid data and assurance that there will be no more attempts to be deceptive.

Proprietary Data. When parties get together in a cooperative effort to resolve their differences, they quite naturally find

holes in the material they are using in their deliberations. Filling
the holes is not a serious problem unless the information needed
is held by one party as proprietary. The question then is how to
share it without doing harm to the owner. One side in the water
roundtable, led by the Environmental Alliance, challenged the
city's assertion that it needed a new water storage facility. The
water department and city officials, on the other hand, declared
that the evidence was irrefutable: new people were going to arrive in droves and they would run out of water unless water department plans were carried out immediately. When the opposition said, "Prove it," the water department replied "Oh, no!
Our data are proprietary." The Alliance then announced that it
could not talk about options unless it had some way of assessing the validity of the data on which the options were based.
This position seemed reasonable to the other parties, all of
whom recognized that the Alliance could delay decisions indefinitely by going to court if discussions did not achieve a more
satisfactory answer. It was quite likely, too, that the material
could be obtained by discovery in legal proceedings if it came
to that.

The problem was to protect the confidentiality of the information, which would have been valuable to competing water
interests, and still allow engineers of the Environmental Alliance to see the material. The parties worked out a memoran-
dum of agreement that specified in detail the obligation of two
Alliance engineers, who would be permitted to see the information, not to disclose the data and the length of time they would
be held to the agreement. In this case, the parties realized the
importance to the water roundtable negotiations of finding a
solution to the issue.

Managing Confrontation over Data

Go Back to Reasons for Addressing the Problem. The parties can be asked to return to the reasons why they want to
solve the problem and what they need in a solution. They can
then work from a detailed review of those interests to a workable proposal. The water roundtable participants, for example,

used a range of figures for conservation potential, agreeing that they wanted to move forward and that they had to use some basis for further discussions. Going back to their original reasons for participating dislodges the parties from frozen positions about a set of figures they demand be accepted. It also saves face for those who know they must adjust their positions but do not want to admit they are wrong. Going back to interests avoids forcing anyone into a corner.

Dissect the Data. The parties can peel back the layers of information and assess the validity of the basic information, its accuracy, and its relevance. It should be worked over until the parties are comfortable with using the information as a base for extrapolating other conclusions. The parties should have the chance to challenge statements of fact until they are proven.

In plenary sessions or in small groups, whichever will most effectively involve all the parties, participants can go back to the calculations on which the controversial information is based and walk through them step by step, *with the full participation* of everyone. (See Straus and Clark, 1980, for a discussion of ways to use a computer to build consensus around and resolve differences over data.)

The practical value of an open process of review was demonstrated dramatically in the water roundtable when the federal agency responsible for developing the environmental impact statement discovered what it called a "fatal flaw" in its study. For many years, a major focus of dispute had been the contention of the parties who opposed the city's water development plans that the basic data were incorrect. In working over data with other roundtable members, engineers in the Environmental Alliance found serious methodological errors in the study and advised the responsible federal agency. Water use data had been recorded in many different ways. For example, multifamily dwellings were sometimes treated as commercial and sometimes as residential. The agency acknowledged the mistake and embarked on an improved system for reporting water use. The agency's prompt and positive response substantially reduced suspicions that data were deliberately biased.

Form a Task Group. Water roundtable participants formed a small group of their members representing both sides, with the single assignment of understanding how the city had calculated its annual yield figures. Because most of the roundtable members were policy-level people, they requested additional technical expertise on the task group. They added several individuals who were specialists on the subject.

Agree on an Acceptable Range of Figures. When parties find it impossible to agree on a common figure, they may be able to agree on a workable *range* of numbers. This way, they can narrow their differences without agonizing over reaching an agreement on one number. Parties can also use high, medium, and low figures for projections such as population growth of an area and then consider the implication of a proposal for each figure.

Use an Outside Expert. Information given in confidence can be used to enhance the process of negotiation, and the interests of the person disclosing the information can still be protected. If the party agrees that the information can be shared but only in outline and without attribution, it can be generalized into material useful to the negotiators. Detailed technical data essential to the progress of a negotiation can be delivered by the parties to an acceptable, technically qualified third party for review. The third party can then report the information, disclosing only the parts that are significant to the discussions.

When county commissioners and companies were negotiating a policy for sand and gravel extraction, they agreed that they had to know how much gravel was being produced in the county. The problem was that it was a highly competitive business and local companies and companies outside the area would love to know what each of their competitors was producing. They solved the problem by agreeing to give their production figures to a trusted third party for aggregation by a computer. They selected as recipient the local college, which was held in high esteem by all of the parties.

Be Sure the Parties Have the Resources to Analyze the Data. The parties must be capable of analyzing data, or they will not trust the data later on and may use their inability to validate information to block progress. Because equipping people to acquire and analyze data is equivalent to giving them power, it is not an easy thing to do among adversaries. Yet this is exactly what must be done.

The homebuilders realized the value of having "worthy adversaries" when the water roundtable grappled with the issue of forecasting water supply. All the members knew that sooner or later they would have to deal with long-standing, widely diverging views of the assumptions the city was using to predict future water use. The Environmental Alliance, among others, had accused the city of issuing false estimates in order to justify its plans for transmountain water diversion. The homebuilders decided to make sure that the Environmental Alliance had the resources to develop its own capabilities to assess data. The homebuilders joined with the Environmental Alliance in soliciting financial support of philanthropic foundations for hiring a consulting engineer and to build their own computer model of the city's water system. The homebuilders did not expect to like all the conclusions the engineer would produce, but for them, the value of enabling the Environmental Alliance to build and test options outweighed the risks. If analyzing data is expected to be an important part of a conflict management program, a manager can designate a portion of the program's budget as a resource pool to be drawn on by one or more parties, always with the full group's approval.

Treat It as a Routine Problem. Efforts to resolve disagreements about data are more likely to be successful if they are undertaken as routine problems to be solved than if there is an atmosphere of suspicion that the whole problem is someone's conspiracy. Most problems associated with basic assumptions and background information are the result of inadvertent error or ignorance rather than being deliberate attempts to mislead. However, it is also quite common for the parties to wonder about the causes, and a matter-of-fact attitude about resolving disagreements will help to defuse a conspiracy theory.

Breaking Deadlocks

The possibility of deadlock hangs over every negotiation. Even in the highly structured setting of labor-management negotiation, bargaining over wages sometimes reaches an impasse, at great cost to both parties. In the free-form, unpredictable arena of public disputes, which often involve many parties with complicated relationships and an assortment of reasons for being there, a roadblock in discussions can come from any direction at any time.

A substantial part of this book is devoted to suggesting methods for designing and managing a sound conflict management program, thus reducing the possibility of a deadlock. A well-conceived strategy carries negotiators through a series of planned steps, built one on another in logical order to a resolution of the dispute. An important principle is that the disputing parties be involved in designing the plan in order to build a sense of ownership in its performance. The parties themselves should share in crafting a plan that fits their own special needs. These measures are critical in moving negotiators through a successful process. But however well conceived the plan is and however cooperative the parties are in carrying it out, discussions can come to a startling halt, to the surprise and dismay of everyone who wants them to continue. When this happens, the chairperson and the parties suddenly find themselves under additional pressure they did not expect. Now, in addition to trying to negotiate as skillfully as they can, they have to find a way to remove the deadlock and rescue the discussions.

The Importance of Moving Quickly

It is tempting to back away from a deadlock and see whether things will straighten themselves out. After all their efforts in defining the problem and working cooperatively on a strategy, it is reasonable for the parties to want time to assess where they are, even for them to say, "Let's take a few months off and think about it." But breaking stride may be fatal to a negotiation unless a definite date is set for the next meeting, because negotiations tend to unravel when the participants are not pressing forward. The parties came together in the first place to solve a problem, and if they have reached an impasse, the problem remains unsolved. Their anxiety about it returns, and they begin to move in other directions to find a solution and to say and do things that damage the good-faith relationships they have built up over weeks or months of working together. Without direct personal contact, they return quite soon to suspecting each other of devious purposes, and their rhetoric changes to charges of evil deeds. The exchanges may even be sharper than before, because expectations were raised and then dashed. When one party unilaterally obstructs progress, the others can consider the action a violation of good faith and may deal more harshly with the offending party than they would have before the negotiation began.

The participants in the game damage project (Chapter Two) learned how quickly the dynamics of negotiation can change. When the parties could not agree on a common definition of a key word in proposed legislation, they decided to suspend further meetings until an agreement could be reached on the term. Even though preliminary plans were made for solving the problem, the participants left the meeting unsure as to whether the issue would be resolved. The momentum they had established came to a halt. They did not set a time for their next meeting. Within a week, the facilitators received a call from one of the parties complaining that he had heard that another participant had made a critical comment about his competence as a negotiator. In a few days, another party was quoted in the newspapers as saying that his group would have to draw up its own suggestion for legislation if the negotiators could not find a solution soon, a statement that other negotiators naturally took as a threat. The trust that had been built up so carefully over the months began to unravel. Although the facilitators had made the mistake of allowing the parties to break off discussion without agreeing to meet again, they did keep up active communication with all parties, and they learned promptly when relationships between the parties began to deteriorate. The first move was to call key representatives and ask them to meet to talk about next steps and an agenda for a next plenary meeting.

An impasse in negotiation will result from a mixture of factors and must be managed by a combination of techniques. In the following section we examine causes of deadlocks and suggest ways to overcome them.

Unacceptable Personal Behavior

People sometimes break off discussions when one of them behaves so badly, so arrogantly, or so rudely that no one wants to be in the same room with him or her. Some methods for dealing with an offensive person are described in "Keeping People at the Table" (in Chapter Ten), such as enforcing ground rules of behavior more stringently. A representative may define for the entire group what kinds of behavior are unacceptable to him or her personally, thus preparing everyone to recognize an infraction of the ground rules. Often, a warning of this kind comes as such as surprise to the person who is accustomed to acting willfully that peer pressure is enough to correct his or her behavior. Sometimes, however, when a person comes to a meeting *intending* to disrupt it, it may be necessary for the other parties or for the convener or facilitator to ask the person to leave. Theoretically, of course, it is important to have all the parties at the table, but the other parties may decide it is better to continue with one party absent than to stop entirely.

Old Patterns of Relationships

To some extent, deadlock happens when people expect it to happen. They come to a negotiating table with their old animosities intact. If they still believe their adversaries are unreasonable and irresponsible, any setback confirms their fears. They are in the midst of a self-fulfilling prophecy, stuck in old relationships and ready to return to confrontation at the least sign of trouble.

Whatever the reason for a stalemate, relationships will have a strong influence on the way the parties handle it. The break in discussion may be accompanied by acrimony and divisiveness, or it may be a simple, more or less amicable agreement that they have to get more information before they can proceed. The atmosphere in which a break in discussions takes place will be as likely to depend on past relationships as on what is happening at the time. And relationships may be influenced by or be the cause of the methods used to address their common problem. A manager responsible for getting discussions back on track will take a careful look at his or her analysis of the situation and avoid leaping to conclusions about the real cause of the impasse.

Show Them They Are in a "New Ball Game." One way to deal with relationship problems is to use process techniques such as breaking the negotiation session into tightly facilitated small groups where people can let off steam without venting emotions *at* each other. The facilitator should make the ground rules explicit and call the slightest infraction until the parties understand that they are engaged in a process that will protect everyone in the room equally. The manager should focus on interests and name adversarial comments as soon as they occur.

Try One More Meeting. After they have had a chance to understand that they are dealing with each other in new and different ways, the parties should be asked to try one more meeting. They will be able to accept a tentative resumption of negotiations and, at the same time, save face because they are not agreeing to back off entirely. A cardinal rule in conflict management is to avoid forcing people into a corner in which they must give a big "yes" or "no" answer. A smaller "yes" can lead to a larger, more permanent one later, but a big "no" is hard to undo.

Review Past Procedures. The manager should take a second look at the way parties have dealt with each other in the past and consider whether the past patterns are affecting current efforts to find a solution. If individuals with the power of government or large organizations behind them have dealt with other parties arbitrarily or arrogantly in the past, the parties may be reluctant to yield their positions.

The Wrong People at the Table

The problem may lie in the group itself or in the way it operates. The parties may have reached an impasse because there are too many people trying to discuss issues and reach agreements. If people feel overwhelmed by the size of the group and are reluctant to speak up, they may quietly block progress by refusing to go along with a consensus or to cooperate in efforts to find an approach that is satisfactory to them. Or the wrong people may be trying to negotiate. They may be too far down the administrative ladder to commit their organizations to an agreement. At the other extreme, they may be at the policy level and not have the technical knowledge to assess and agree on solutions to technical issues. Despite the best efforts of conveners to influence the selection of effective participants, they often will not have final say over who appears at the table.

If negotiations have reached a standstill and the problem seems to be in the group, the manager can get agreement from the participants to change the mix. "Keeping People at the Table" in Chapter Ten suggests methods for sharing with the group the responsibility for reshaping the membership so they can get on with the job. It may be necessary to ask one or more of the participants to leave or to ask their organizations for different representatives. The group might also consider expanding the number of participants. New faces signal a new game, too.

Problems of Content

What if the process is sound and the parties are working together satisfactorily, but they just cannot find a solution that satisfies everyone at the table? What if they are doing everything right, but they still cannot solve the problem? This is where flexibility is critical. Parties who have arrived at the negotiations with a suitcase full of preconceptions about the issues and their adversaries may be asked to take another look at their problem and define it in terms that will break the deadlock and allow negotiations to move ahead. This can be quite a challenge.

Many negotiations of public issues operate through consensus, a system that works well most of the time. The procedure has one drawback, however: it can be blocked by a single party who wants to bring the discussions to a halt. That person's motives may be reasonable and responsible, or they may be destructive and malicious. It does not really matter, because the process is vulnerable regardless of the merits of the individual's position.

Break the Problem into Smaller Pieces. Smaller problems may be easier to understand and may be addressed without the politics of larger issues. Success in finding solutions to smaller parts of a larger problem will encourage the parties to continue negotiation and take on larger pieces of the issue when they can handle them (Fisher with Ury, 1978).

Everyone wanted to find a way to save the old railroad (see Chapter Two). *No one* wanted to destroy the tunnel and trestles, but representatives of each of the federal and local agencies with jurisdiction over their part of the problem had declared exactly what they would be willing to do. They had also said publicly what they would *not* do unless other agencies cooperated. For their part, citizen organizations, a historical preservation group, wilderness advocates, and railroad buffs had made their positions clear, and facing them all was the harsh reality of cost. The price of repairs and renovation would be enormous, well beyond the funding capacity of any single agency. They had to get together, but the situation had become so complicated that one agency manager said privately that he was about ready to throw some dynamite into the tunnel and "blow the damn thing up."

At their first meeting the parties were feeling so much frustration and concern that there were some sharp exchanges but some laughter as well. They all knew that they had the same goal if only they could pull it off. Each representative described in turn what he or she thought would be required to accomplish the main task. These statements, several dozen in number, were listed on wall sheets without comment from the other participants. With the list of components on the wall for reference, they proceeded through a piece-by-piece analysis of what would be required to *solve* each separate problem. Problems that had seemed overwhelmingly complicated became manageable when they were separated into simpler segments. The problem of money was one of the most serious. It would cost more than $100,000 for the engineering design, construction, and materials to do the work if they were able to find answers to the political issues and differences of opinion about how the work ought to be done. An additional concern was that the entire problem had gone on so long that the county with the largest amount of money in reserve might lose it in the next fiscal year, which was coming up shortly.

A spark of hope came with the comment of a county commissioner that she thought it would be possible to carry the money over into the next year. It was unclear whether she had not given the possibility serious thought before or whether she had been holding out until she saw what others would do, but she was willing to make the offer when the separate elements had been analyzed and everyone had acknowledged that money was a serious obstacle.

Brainstorm New Options. Brainstorming is a process for rapidly generating new ideas without pausing to consider how realistic or workable they are (see Chapter Six). The negotiators of the old railroad case were asked to brainstorm a list of tasks that should be done. They agreed not to criticize what each speaker proposed. People were encouraged to suggest ideas even though some thought the situation was so bad that their ideas might never be considered. After they began to identify solutions to small problems, they realized that the larger ones were solvable as well.

Look Behind the Content. An absolute stalemate declared in substantive terms may actually have little or nothing to do with the issue on the table. When the negotiators of the game damage issue reconvened after a month's absence, they were startled when one of the representatives declared at the beginning of the meeting that he would not participate in the negotiations unless reports of the meetings were couched in *statu-*

tory language. Everyone in the room knew that freezing free and wide-ranging discussion into formal legalistic idiom would be an enormous task, one beyond the capability of the Division of Wildlife staff. Worse, it would so constrain the discussion that creating new options to solve the problem would be impossible.

To everyone's surprise, they were suddenly in a deadlock. The statement was strangely contrary to the constructive role the representative had played in negotiations up to that time. Other participants began to ask what the measure would accomplish and why it was demanded in such proscriptive terms. As the discussion continued, a new subject that had not even been mentioned before began to emerge. When the negotiators had given their report of eight months' work to the Wildlife Commission, the commissioners had allowed themselves to become distracted by trivial details and had failed to acknowledge the substantial value of the report and the contribution the negotiators had made to the formulation of state policy. The response of the commissioners was so foolish that it infuriated the negotiators, who had to ask themselves why they were going to all the trouble of discussing the issues if the decision makers were unable to comprehend the final results of their efforts. Clearly, what the representatives wanted was not *statutory language* but some tangible evidence that their work in the future would have a positive effect. As soon as the participants understood why the individual was making his demand, they were able to devise a way around the deadlock. They asked two commissioners to join the negotiators as observers, and the misgivings of the representative, feelings shared by the rest of the group, were clearly and forcefully described to the commissioners. Next, the group agreed on a procedure for joint authorship of the next report in place of reporting through Division of Wildlife staff, a strategy that would compel the commissioners to pay attention, since the authors were well-known and respected citizens. The demand for statutory language evaporated.

Ask for an Alternative Proposal. The responsibility for finding an acceptable option can be shifted to the dissenting person. If the person wants to find a way out of the impasse, he or she can suggest an approach that would be satisfactory to everyone.

Ask the Person to Stand Aside. A dissenter can be asked to stand aside so the consensus can proceed without involving the individual in direct responsibility for the outcome. The difficulty with this option is that the person may not feel committed to implementing the agreements of the rest of the group.

Record the Disagreement. The group can proceed toward consensus after giving assurance that disagreement will be included as a minority statement. Parties may be willing to proceed if they know their objections are recorded.

Form a Separate Consensus. In the rare instance when a person agrees to abide by consensus agreements and then clearly uses the good-faith nature of the consensus process to block agreements, it may be necessary to take the risky step of overriding the objection. This action should be taken only as a last resort and must be endorsed by the rest of the group. The procedure must not be allowed to set a precedent in which the group decides who is rational and who is not.

Adjust the Procedures. Discussions may move too quickly, and some participants may feel that decisions are being made that they do not fully understand. They may block progress to catch up. Or one side may think that another is receiving more attention than it should and fear that one party will dominate the process. The chairperson should be aware of procedural problems that may deadlock discussions and be prepared to suggest alternatives.

Sometimes a simple shift in the procedure will change the dynamics and enable parties to approach a problem differently. When parties in a large negotiation found themselves stuck on a particularly sensitive issue, the chairperson suggested that they break into small groups to discuss the problem, and several new suggestions emerged.

Go Back to Interests. The manager can suggest that it is time to make sure that everyone's interests have been fully described and that everyone in the room understands them. This procedure will give tangible evidence that all interests have equal standing and will be given due consideration.

Ask Parties to Be More Specific. People may be reluctant to accept a proposal when it is subject to widely different interpretations. Asking for greater detail will sharpen the parties' understanding of the alternative and make it easier to assess its merits.

Keep Trying. Frequently, a group will not reach consensus the first time it tries. Repeated testing and asking for suggestions may produce a shift in approach leading to a consensus decision.

Use a Mediator. On occasion, an impasse becomes so rigid and so antagonistic that the parties themselves find it impossible to step out of their roles as adversaries, break off an escalating spiral of conflict, and work together on removing a roadblock. This is a good time to bring in a mediator (see "Using a Third Party" in Chapter Eight). It is important to remember, though, that mediators are not magicians and that the final responsibility for removing a deadlock rests with the parties.

A Final Word

Facing disagreement and dealing with it effectively are part of a manager's job. The possibilities for a dispute to escalate into destructive conflict increase substantially when the public, with its diversity of interests and personalities, becomes involved. The question for the manager is not how to reduce the part the public has to play but what measures to employ in making the interchange productive.

A manager must determine the strategy that best serves the interests of his or her organization. An array of problem-solving techniques is available for the manager who chooses to work with the public to solve a problem. Many of these techniques can be performed by people within an organization. They include analyzing conflict, designing a management strategy, facilitating meetings, improving communication, finding needed data, and working with others to reach agreements. One individual can assume all these responsibilities, or they can be distributed among several people. A separate question is whether to use a third party for part or all of the program.

Conflict management is neither an art nor a science. It is a skill that can be learned like any other skill through study and practice. The principles of conflict management provide mental discipline and a framework for making sound decisions.

References

Aggerholm, D. "Can Environmental Mediation Make Things Happen?" In R. Platt and G. Macinko (eds.), *Beyond the Urban Fringe: Land Use Issues of Nonmetropolitan America.* Minneapolis: University of Minnesota Press, 1983.

Alinsky, S. *Rules for Radicals.* New York: Random House, 1971.

Bach, G., and Goldberg, H. *Creative Aggression: The Art of Assertive Living.* New York: Avon Books, 1974.

Bacow, L., and Wheeler, M. *Environmental Dispute Resolution.* New York: Plenum Press, 1984.

Berger, W. "Let's Stop Building Major Cases Out of Minor Disputes." *Bar Leader,* 1977, *3* (2), 2.

Bingham, G. *Resolving Environmental Disputes: A Decade of Experience.* Washington, D.C.: The Conservation Foundation, 1984.

Blake, R., and Mouton, J. S. *Solving Costly Organizational Conflicts: Achieving Intergroup Trust, Cooperation, and Teamwork.* San Francisco: Jossey-Bass, 1984.

Bleiker, A., and Bleiker, H. *Citizen Participation Handbook for Public Officials and Other Professionals Serving the Public.* Laramie, Wyo.: Institute for Participatory Planning, 1978.

Bok, D. "A Flawed System." *Harvard Magazine,* May–June 1983, pp. 38–45.

Boulding, K. *Conflict and Defense: A General Theory.* New York: Harper & Row, 1962.

Bradley, R. *Managing Major Metropolitan Areas: The Application of Collaborative Planning and Negotiation Techniques.* Washington, D.C.: International Downtown Association, 1985.

Bramson, R. *Coping with Difficult People.* New York: Ballantine, 1981.

Buckle, L., and Thomas-Buckle, S. "Placing Environmental Mediation in Context: Lessons from 'Failed' Mediations." *Environmental Impact Assessment Review 21,* 1986, *6* (1), 55–70.

Carlson, C. "Negotiated Investment Strategy." In N. Huelsberg and W. Lincoln (eds.), *Successful Negotiating in Local Government.* Washington, D.C.: International City Management Association, 1985.

Carpenter, S., and Kennedy, W.J.D. "Information Sharing and Conciliation: Tools for Environmental Conflict Management." *Environmental Comment,* May 1977, pp. 22–23.

Carpenter, S., and Kennedy, W.J.D. "Environmental Conflict Management." *Environmental Professional,* 1980, *2* (1), 67–74.

Carpenter, S., and Kennedy, W.J.D. "Environmental Conflicts in Mineral Development, or the Art of Creating Unnecessary Conflict." *Minerals and the Environment,* 1981, *2,* 159–164.

Carpenter, S., and Kennedy, W.J.D. "The Metropolitan Water Roundtable: A Case Study in Reaching Agreements." *Natural Resources Journal,* forthcoming.

Clark-McGlennon Associates. *Patuxent-River Cleanup Agreement.* Boston: Clark-McGlennon Associates, 1982.

Coser, L. *The Functions of Social Conflict.* New York: Free Press, 1956.

Creighton, J. *Public Involvement Manual: Involving the Public in Water and Power Resources Discussions.* Washington, D.C.: U.S. Department of the Interior, 1980.

Curle, A. *Making Peace.* London: Tavistock, 1971.

Curle, A. *Mystics and Militants.* London: Tavistock, 1972.

Delbecq, A., Vandeven, A., and Gustafson, D. *Group Techniques for Program Planning.* Glenview, Ill.: Scott, Foresman, 1975.

Deutsch, M. *Resolution of Conflict.* New Haven, Conn.: Yale University Press, 1974.

Dinell, T., and others. *Land Use Dispute Resolution in Hawaii: Expanding the Options.* Honolulu: University of Hawaii, Department of Urban and Regional Planning, 1985.

Doyle, M., and Straus, D. *How to Make Meetings Work.* Chicago: Playboy Press, 1976.

Filley, A. *Interpersonal Conflict Resolution.* Glenview, Ill.: Scott, Foresman, 1975.

Fisher, R. *International Conflict for Beginners.* New York: Harper & Row, 1969.

Fisher, R. "Negotiating Power: Getting and Using Influence." *American Behavioral Scientist,* Nov.-Dec. 1983, *27* (2), 149–166.

Fisher, R., with Ury, W. *International Mediation: A Working Guide.* New York: International Peace Academy, 1978.

Fisher, R., and Ury, W. *Getting to Yes: Negotiating Agreement Without Giving In.* Boston: Houghton Mifflin, 1981.

Forester, J. *Planning in the Face of Conflict: Mediated Negotiation in Local Land Use Permitting Processes.* Cambridge, Mass.: Lincoln Institute for Land Policy, 1986.

Fox, J. "Breaking the Regulatory Deadlock." *Harvard Business Review,* Sept.-Oct. 1981, pp. 97–105.

Gordon, T. *Leadership Effectiveness Training.* New York: Bantam Books, 1977.

Harter, P. "Negotiating Regulations: A Cure for Malaise." *Georgetown Law Journal,* 1982, *71* (1), 11–118.

Himes, J. *Conflict and Conflict Management.* Athens: University of Georgia Press, 1980.

Huelsberg, N., and Lincoln, W. *Successful Negotiating in Local Government.* Washington, D.C.: International City Management Association, 1985.

Karass, C. *The Negotiating Game.* New York: Thomas Y. Crowell, 1970.

Keating, C. *Dealing with Difficult People.* New York: Paulist Press, 1984.

Kolb, D. *The Mediators.* Cambridge, Mass.: MIT Press, 1983.

Kriesberg, L. *The Sociology of Social Conflicts.* Englewood Cliffs, N.J.: Prentice-Hall, 1973.

Lake, R. (ed.). *Resolving Locational Conflict.* New Brunswick, N.J.: Center for Urban Policy Research, Rutgers University, 1987.

Lax, D., and Sebenius, J. *The Manager as Negotiator.* New York: Free Press, 1986.

Levitt, R., and Kirlin, J. (eds.). *Managing Development Through*

Public/Private Negotiations. Washington, D.C.: Urban Land Institute, 1985.

McCarthy, J., with Shorett, A. *Negotiating Settlements: A Guide to Environmental Mediation.* New York: American Arbitration Association, 1984.

Maggiolo, W. *Techniques of Mediation in Labor Disputes.* Dobbs Ferry, N.Y.: Oceana Publications, 1971.

Maier, N. *Problem-Solving Discussions and Conferences: Leadership Methods and Skills.* New York: McGraw-Hill, 1963.

Marcus, P., and Emrich, W. (eds.). *Working Papers in Environmental Conflict Management.* New York: American Arbitration Association, 1981.

Meeks, G. *Managing Environmental and Public Policy Conflicts: A Legislator's Guide.* Denver, Colo.: National Conference of State Legislatures, 1985.

Moore, C. *The Mediation Process: Practical Strategies for Resolving Conflict.* San Francisco: Jossey-Bass, 1986.

Murray, F. (ed.). *Where We Agree: Report of the National Coal Policy Project.* Boulder, Colo.: Westview Press, 1978.

Nagler, M. *America Without Violence.* Covelo, Calif.: Island Press, 1982.

Perritt, H. "Analysis of Four Negotiated Rulemaking Efforts." Report to the Administrative Conference of the United States, Washington, D.C., 1985.

President's Commission for a National Agenda for the Eighties. *A National Agenda for the Eighties.* Washington, D.C.: U.S. Government Printing Office, 1980.

Pruitt, D. *Negotiation Behavior.* New York: Academic Press, 1981.

Raiffa, H. *The Art and Science of Negotiation.* Cambridge, Mass.: Harvard University Press, 1982.

Richman, R., White, O., and Wilkinson, M. *Intergovernmental Mediation: Negotiations in Local Government Disputes.* Boulder, Colo.: Westview Press, 1986.

Sebenius, J. *Negotiating the Law of the Sea.* Cambridge, Mass.: Harvard University Press, 1984.

Simkin, W. *Mediation and the Dynamics of Collective Bargaining.* Washington, D.C.: The Bureau of National Affairs, 1971.

Straus, D., and Clark, P. "Computer-Assisted Negotiation: Bigger Problems Need Bigger Tools." *Environmental Professional*, 1980, *2* (1), 75-87.

Sullivan, T. *Resolving Developmental Disputes Through Negotiation*. New York: Plenum Press, 1984.

Susskind, L. *The Importance of Citizen Participation and Consensus-Building in the Land Use Planning Process*. Cambridge: Massachusetts Institute of Technology, Laboratory of Architecture and Planning, 1978.

Susskind, L., and Ozawa, C. "Mediated Negotiation in the Public Sector." *American Behavioral Scientist*, Nov.-Dec. 1983, *27*, 2.

Susskind, L., and Persico, S. *Guide to Consensus Development and Dispute Resolution Techniques*. Cambridge, Mass.: Harvard Negotiation Project, 1983.

Talbot, A. *Settling Things*. Washington, D.C.: The Conservation Foundation, 1983.

Thomas, K. W. "Conflict and Conflict Management." In M. Dunnette (ed.), *Handbook of Industrial and Organizational Psychology*. Chicago: Rand McNally, 1976.

Walton, R., and McKersie, R. *A Behavioral Theory of Labor Negotiations*. New York: McGraw-Hill, 1965.

Wehr, P. *Conflict Regulation*. Boulder, Colo.: Westview Press, 1982.

Wessel, M. *The Rule of Reason: A New Approach to Corporate Litigation*. Reading, Mass.: Addison-Wesley, 1976.

Wondolleck, J. *An Evaluation of the U.S. Forest Service Natural Resource Conflict Management Training Program*. Ann Arbor: University of Michigan, 1986.

Zartman, W., and Berman, M. *The Practical Negotiator*. New Haven, Conn.: Yale University Press, 1982.

Index

A

Accountability, of interested parties, 8
Adversarial approach: in conflict management, 19-22; outcome of, 21; unpredictability of, 229
Advisory committees, meetings of, 98
Agenda: establishing, 158; focus on, 158-159
Aggerholm, D., 149
Agreements: analysis of reaching, 137-148; building block approach to, 139-141; carrying out, 148-154; comprehensive proposals for, 140-142; constituency group review and approval of, 146-147; draft of, 145-146; enforcing, 148, 153-154; final, 147-148; general approaches to, 137-141; objective criteria for, 142-143; in principle, 138-139; procedures for reaching, 102; process for carrying out, 67, 69, 148-154; reaching, as goal, 97; renegotiation of, 153; signing, 148; steps in reaching, 141-148; test for, 164; violations of, 153-154; written, 150-151
Agricultural land use dispute, external constraints in, 95. See also Game damage dispute
Air quality dispute: interests, not positions, in, 62; and values, 203-204
Airport scoping meetings dispute: case example of, 36-38; feelings acknowledged in, 245-246; identifying issues and interests in, 96, 130

Alinsky, S., 79

B

Bach, G., 243
Background materials, assembling, 114
Bacow, L., 150, 187, 259
Ball, G., 212
Berger, W., 21
Berman, M., 101
Betrayal, and revenge, 250
Bingham, G., 29, 149, 187
Blake, R., 26
Bleiker, A., 178
Bleiker, H., 178
Bok, D., 21
Boulding, K., 17
Bradley, R., 26
Brainstorming, for options production, 134, 135, 273
Bramson, R., 243
Briefing sessions, for informing the public, 179
Buckle, L., 193

C

Carlson, C., 26
Carpenter, S., 19, 47, 95, 204, 227
Caucuses, and trust, 214
Chairperson: responsibilities of, 232-233; role of, 107
Clark, P., 264
Clark-McGlennon Associates, 150
Clean Air Act, 203
Clean up dispute, revenge in, 250, 254

Coal mine dispute, relationships conflict in, 53-54

Colorado, oil shale development in, 177

Communication: clarify statements for, 159-160; in conflict spiral, 13; and constituent support, 170, 173-174; and mediation, 189-190, 192; of new information, 166-167

Community development dispute: media strategy for, 186; and power of public opinion, 227

Community relations dispute, interview subjects for, 77-78

Compound 1080, and constructive definition of problem, 59

Conflict: communication stops in, 13; cost of, 16-17, 227-228; crisis sense in, 15; dynamics continuum for, 86, 88-90, 190, 255; outcomes vary in, 15-16; outside community, 14; perceptions distorted in, 14-15; positions harden in, 13; problem emerges in, 11; as procedures, relationships, and substance, 52-54; as productive, 3-4; resources committed in, 14; ripening of, 16-17; sides form in, 13; spiral or unmanaged, 11-17

Conflict analysis: chart for, 86-87; information assessment in, 85-91; information collecting for, 74-85; and issue identification, 128; by mediator, 191; preliminary review for, 71-74; process of, 71-91; purpose of, 231; summary for, 90-91, 226; and trust, 210

Conflict management: adversarial approach in, 19-22; alternative approaches to, 26-29; analysis of, 18-51; avoiding harm in, 64-65; avoiding issue in, 19; case examples of, 29-51; conclusion on, 276-277; consensus in, 29; conventional approaches to, 18-26; and deadlocks, 267-276; direct involvement in, 27; dynamics

underlying, 197-223; facilitation in, 26-28; flexible process for, 62-63, 230; goals of, 95-97, 205; guidelines for, 157-196; human side of, 224-257; interests, not positions, in, 60-62; leaping into battle in, 19-22; and negotiating differences in data, 258-266; overview of, 1-65; planning for problems in, 63-64; positive working relationships for, 57-58; and power, 216-223; principles of, 52-65; problem solution in, 27; problem understood for, 54-56; process for, 67-154; process shaped by parties in, 27, 29, 59-60; purpose of, 16, 205; quick fix in, 22-23, 27; removing roadblocks to, 258-277; Solomon trap in, 22, 24-26, 27; steps of, 100-102; strategy planning and following in, 56-57; successful, 155-277; and trust, 205-216; and values, 197-204

Consensus: to close meetings, 184; and data handled by computer, 264; and deadlock, 275; for decision making, 29; and number of participants, 104; on options, 144-145

Constituents: agreements review and approval by, 146-147; concept of, 169; education of, 124-132, 174-175; informing, and risk, 256; involving, 168-175; meeting with, 175; and negotiating skills, 236; negotiation support from, 169-170; team building for, 173-175, 192-193. See also Interested parties

Constraints, identifying external, 94-95

Convener, role of, 106

Convention center dispute, issues in, 127-128

Coser, L., 3

Creighton, J., 178

Criteria: applied to options, 143-144; for mediators, 187-189; objective, for agreements, 142-143

Curle, A., 3, 73, 125, 198, 205, 217, 219-220

D

Data: acceptable range of, 265; agreeeing on, 131-132; biased, 262; differing interpretations of, 260; dissecting, 264; fear of revealing, 260-261; inaccurate or incomplete, 259-260; managing confrontation over, 263-266; and mediators, 192; negotiating differences in, 258-266; parties' own, 260; problems with, 259-263; proprietary, 262-263; resources invested in, 261; resources to analyze, 266; routine problems with, 266; task group for, 265; and technical expert, 265; and values clash, 261-262. *See also* Information

Deadlock: and alternative proposals, 274-275; breaking, 267-276; and consensus, 275; and content problems, 271-276; hidden reasons for, 273-274; and old relationships, 269-270; and persistence, 276; quick moves away from, 267-269

Decision making: by consensus, 29; and constituent support, 170, 174; among network of interests, 7-8

Delbecq, A., 134

Deutsch, M., 17, 193, 205, 234

Division of Wildlife, 43-46, 97, 239, 294

Downtown development dispute: interview questions for, 81-82; strategy in, 56

Doyle, M., 134, 144, 158, 163

E

Economic harm, and revenge, 251

Education: and agreeing on data, 131-132; of constituents, 174-175; and discussing interests, 129-131; function of, 125-126; and identifying issues, 127-129; of interested parties, 124-132; of new participants, 231-233; of news media on negotiations, 185; of participants, 235-236; on procedures, 101-102; and reviewing history and context of problem, 126-127

Electric utility dispute, perception clarification in, 166

Emotions: acknowledging, 245-246; and process observation, 247-248; in public meetings, 243-249

Emrich, W., 82

Environmental Alliance, 49, 50, 51, 171-172, 175, 263, 264, 266

Environmental dispute, power in, 222-223

Expertise, levels of, 5-6

Experts. *See* Technical resource expert

F

Facilitators: in case examples, 31-32, 33-34, 37-38, 42-43; role of, 107; and workshops, 99

Fair play, and values, 204

Fear: and public meetings, 243-244; of revealing data, 260-261; and revenge, 251

Federal agency dispute, and mediation, 190

Filley, A., 90, 101

Fisher, R., 9, 101, 133, 145, 146, 150, 217, 230, 272

Flexibility: in conflict management, 62-63, 230; and deadlock, 271; as process issue, 111

Forest Service, 72

Forest service dispute, ground rules in, 120

Forester, J., 106

Fox, J., 9

Funding: as process issue, 110; securing, 112

G

Game damage dispute: case example of, 43-46; and constructive definition of problem, 59; and deadlock, 268, 273-274; developing recommendations in, 97; ground rules for, 120; group responsibilities in, 232; hidden obstacles in, 238-239; information collecting for, 74; reducing risk in, 255, 256, 257

Goals: of conflict management, 95-97, 205; and values, 203-204

Goldberg, H., 243

Gordon, T., 243

Grazing rights dispute, designing process in, 60

Ground rules: agreeing on, 118-120; applying, 121; approving, 120-121; changing, 122; concept of, 118; and deadlock, 269, 270; designing and applying, 120-124; developing, 112; and emotions in meetings, 245, 248-249; enforcing, 121-122, 124, 161; forms of, 119-120; initiating, 120; and negotiating skills, 234-235; and news media, 184; and offensive behavior, 240; and revenge, 253-254; sample set of, 123-124; and trust, 211; types of, 119

Group memory, 163-164

Gustafson, D., 134

H

Harter, P., 26

Hawaii, values in, 200

Health facility dispute, interests in, 129

Highway dispute, and emotions at meeting, 247-248

Himes, J., 3

Huelsberg, N., 26

I

Ideology, and values, 201, 202-203

Implementation: of agreements, 148-154; components of, 151-154; defining procedures for, 149-151; and details, 152-153; monitoring system for, 151-152, 154; and renegotiation, 153; and violations, 153-154

Information: assessing, 85-91; collecting, 74-85; communicating new, 166-167; for constituents, 256; from direct observation, 75-76; exchange of, 95-96; ground rules on, 123; interpreting, 90-91; interviewing for, 77-82; need for, 75; organizing, 85-90; from personal interviews, 76; recording, 83-84; secondary sources of, 76; sensitive, and mediators, 188-189, 190; sources of, 75-76; and trust, 207, 208; verifying, 90. *See also* Data

Informing the public: case examples of, 179-180; guidelines for, 181-182; methods for, 177-179; reasons for, 175-177

Initiator, role of, 106

Interested parties: accountability of, 8; data of, 260; decision making by, 7-8; direct involvement of, 27; education of, 101-102, 124-132; expertise levels among, 5-6; forms of power among, 6, 217-218; individual talks with, 165; informal meetings of, 215-216; network of, in public disputes, 5-8; new, 5; notifying, 113; in old relationships, 241, 269-270; perception clarification for, 165-166; process shaped by, 27, 29, 59-60; relationships between, not continuing, 6-7; representatives of, 178. *See also* Constituents; Participants

Interests: concept of, 129; discussion of, and education, 129-131; identifying, as goal, 96; review of, and data, 263-264; review of, and deadlock, 276; solutions based on, 60-62

Interviews: by appropriate person,

78-79; conducting, 77-82; format for, 80-82; information sheet for, 84; listening in, 82; location of, 85; and mediators, 189; personal, 76; questions for, 79-80; sequence of, 79; subject selection for, 77-78; tape recording, 83; telephone or in-person, 84-85; timing of, 85; written notes of, 83

Issues: avoiding, 19; broad range of, 9-11; concept of, 127; identifying, 96, 127-129; negotiating separate, 139-141; newly emerging, 9; and technical information, 9-10; and values, 10-11

K

Karass, C., 101
Keating, C., 243
Kennedy, W.J.D., 19, 47, 95, 204, 227
Kirlin, J., 26
Kolb, D., 191
Kriesberg, L., 17, 217

L

Lake, R., 26
Land access disputes, and power, 219, 220, 221, 228
Lax, D., 17, 106
League of Women Voters, 106
Legal system, and conflict management, 21-22
Levitt, R., 26
Lincoln, W., 26
Listening: and emotions before meetings, 245; in interviews, 82; and values, 202
Location: of interviews, 85; as process issue, 109-110
Logistical support person, role of, 107-108

M

McCarthy, J., 17, 149
McKersie, R., 133

Maggiolo, W., 191
Maier, N., 158
Marcus, P., 82
Media. *See* News media
Mediators: analysis of using, 186-196; concept of, 187; criteria for, 187-189; and deadlock, 276; for draft agreement, 145-146; for first meeting, 230; functions of, 191-193; and ground rules, 253-254; need for, 189-191; role of, 108; selecting and managing, 195-196; and sensitive information, 188-189, 190; team building by, 235; and trust, 194; usefulness of, 193-194
Meeks, G., 26
Meetings: activities between, 164-168; agenda for, 158-159; arranging first, 114-115; avoiding sensitive words and topics in, 246; clarifying statements in, 159-160; closed, consensus for, 184; with constituents, 175; emotions before, 244-245; emotions during, 245-249; and formal negotiation sessions, 99-100; ground rules enforced for, 161; idea exploration in, 160; idea testing between, 167; open and closed, and news media, 182-184; participation encouraged in, 160-161; planning for, 168; positive tone for, 161, 213; of problem-solving workshops, 98-99; process observations for, 162; process suggestions for, 162-163; productive, 157-164; public, 97-98, 178-179, 243-249; record keeping for, 163-164; strategy of selecting structure for, 97-100; summarize statements in, 160; of task groups and advisory committees, 98; tense, 249; test for agreements in, 164; terminating, 247, 249; trial, 230, 238, 270
Megaphone diplomacy, 212
Mine development, and information exchange, 95-96
Moore, C., 101, 144, 150, 191

Mouton, J. S., 26
Murray, F., 118

N

Nagler, M., 16
National Park Service, 200
National Register of Historic Places, 41
Natural resource dispute, mediator for, 188
Negotiation: adopting procedures for, 117-124; advantages of, 227; background on, 116-117; barriers to, 225; constituent support for, 169-170; and constructive definition of problem, 58-59; of data differences, 258-266; deadlock of, 189, 267-276; and developing options, 132-136; differing skills in, 233-236; education on, 124-132, 174-175, 185; formal sessions for, 99-100; hidden obstacles to, 238-239; last stages of, 175; between meetings, 164-168; one-text, 146; persistence in, 236-243; process of, 67, 68-69, 116-148; quick progress in, 239-240; and reaching agreements, 137-148; readiness for, 207-208, 224-231; situational fit of, 230-231; slow progress in, 237-239; and values, 199
News media: advice from, 185-186; as asset, 184-186; dealing with, 113-114; educating, 185; ground rules on, 124; and open and closed meetings, 182-184; as process issue, 111; strategy explicit for, 186; working with, 182-186
Nuclear facility dispute, levels of expertise in, 6

O

Observers: ground rules on, 122, 123; and informing the public, 178; role of, 108

Offers, making and receiving, 208
Office building dispute, understanding problem in, 55
Oil and gas exploration in Wilderness Study Areas dispute: and avoiding harm, 65; case example of, 38-41; risk in, 257; written agreement for, 151
Oil shale development dispute, and informing the public, 177
Options: advantages and disadvantages listed for, 144; brainstorming for, 134, 135, 273; consensus on, 144-145; criteria applied to, 143-144; developing, 96, 132-136; forms of, 136; generating, 102; intermediary for gathering, 135-136; organizing to produce, 133-136; and trust, 208
Organizations, values of, 203
Ozawa, C., 187

P

Participants: categories of, 103; disagreements among, 191; educating, 235-236; emotions of, in public meetings, 243-249; and external events, 242-243; group responsibilities of, 231-232, 238, 243, 246-247; and handling human side of process, 224-257; identifying, 104-105; interests discussed by, 130; inviting, 112-113; issue identification by, 128-129; negotiating skill differences among, 233-236; new, educating, 231-233; number of, 103-104; and offensive behavior, 240-241, 269; options produced by, 133-134; persistence of, 236-243; personal risks for, 242; proposals by, 135; and readiness to negotiate, 207-208, 224-231; reducing risk for, 254-257; replacements for, 241; revenge by, 249-254; security of, 255-256; specificity by, 276; substitutes for, 123; wrong, and deadlock, 271. See also Interested parties

Participation in meetings: encouraged, 160-161; expanded, by task groups, 174; forms of, 103; strategy for determining, 102-105

Perritt, H., 256

Planning: conflict analysis for, 71-91; for meetings, 168; process of, 67, 68, 71-115; and setting up program, 111-115; strategy design for, 92-111

Power: attention to, 216-223; clarifying, 220-222; concepts of, 217-218, 219-220; forms of, 6, 217-218; holders of, 228-229; and mutual gain, 222-223; negative results of using, 218-220; of public opinion, 226-227

President's Commission for a National Agenda for the Eighties, 8, 19

Press. *See* News media

Problem: conflict management for solution of, 27; constructive definition of, 58-59; defining, for strategy, 93-94; dividing, to break deadlock, 272-273; emergence of, 11; history and context of, 126-127; understanding of, 54-56; workshops for solving, 98-99

Procedures: for activities between meetings, 164-168; adjusting, 275; adopting, 101; for agreements, reaching, 102; in conflict, 52-54; description for, 111-112; educating parties on, 101-102; explaining, and trust, 210-211; and generating options, 102; ground rules for, 118-124; and guidelines, 8, 157-196; identifying, for strategy, 100-102; for implementation, 149-151; for informing public, 175-182; for involving constituents, 168-175; issues of, 108-111; for mediators, 186-196; for negotiation, 117-124; for news media, 182-186; for productive meetings, 157-164; for public disputes, not standardized, 8-9; and revenge,

252-253; review of past, 270; reviewing general, 117-118

Process: flexibility of, 62-63, 230; and mediators, 192, 193-194; shaped by parties to, 27, 29, 59-60; suggestions for, 162-163

Process observation: and emotions, 247-248; for meetings, 162; and revenge, 252-253, 254

Proposals: alternative, and deadlock, 274-275; comprehensive, 140-142; by participants, 135

Pruitt, D., 191

Public: informing the, 175-182; opinion of, and power, 226-227

Public disputes: analysis of, 3-17; background on, 3-4; characteristics of, 4-11; concept of, 4; conclusion on, 276-277; human side of, 224-257; issues in, 9-11; network of interests in, 5-8; nonstandardized procedures for, 8-9; overview of, 1-65; power in, 216-223; process for managing, 67-154; sequence in, 11; and spiral of unmanaged conflict, 11-17

Public utilities dispute, relationships in, 7

Q

Quick fix: in conflict management, 22-23, 27; and strategy planning, 56

R

Raiffa, H., 146

Railroad dispute: case example of, 41-43; and data problems, 259; deadlock in, 272-273; educating newcomers to, 231; ground rules for, 119-120; network of interests in, 5; preliminary review for, 72-74; revenge in, 249-250, 252-253; written agreement for, 151

Ranger station dispute, interests, not positions, in, 61

Recommendations, developing, as goal, 96-97

Record keeping, for meetings, 163-164

Recorder, role of, 107

Relationships: in conflict, 52-54; human side of, 224-257; old, 241, 269-270; positive working, 57-58; process techniques for, 270; and trust, 214-215

Revenge: dealing with desire for, 252-254; and importance of grievance, 253; and procedures, 252-253; reasons for, 250-251

Rhetoric: and revenge, 251; and trust, 212-213

Richman, R., 26, 187

Risk: avoiding, 255-256; personal, 242; reducing, 254-257

Role: changing, and risk, 256; confirming, 113; defining, 105-108

Rules. See Ground rules

S

Sand and gravel dispute, data problem in, 265

Scrap metal processing plant dispute, categories of participants in, 103

Sebenius, J., 17, 106, 146

Sewer system dispute, values in, 200-201

Simkin, W., 191

Solomon trap: in conflict management, 22, 24-26, 27; and designing process, 60

Sponsor, role of, 106

Strategy: analysis of designing, 92-111; and external constraints, 94-95; goal establishment for, 95-97; for informing the public, 181; management components in, 56-57; mediator design of, 191-192; for meeting structure, 97-100; for news media, 186; for participation, 102-105; planning and following, 56-57; and problem definition, 93-94; and process issues, 108-111; and process steps, 100-102; and role functioning, 105-108; values integrated into, 202-204

Straus, D., 134, 144, 158, 163, 264

Subcommittees, for informing the public, 178

Sullivan, T., 187

Susskind, L., 178, 187

T

Talbot, A., 29

Task groups: for constituent participation, 174; for data problems, 265; meetings of, 98; for options production, 134

Technical resource expert: access to, 167-168; and data problems, 265; and history and context of problem, 126-127; and issues, 9-10; for options production, 134-135; role of, 107

Third parties. See Mediators

Thomas, K. W., 26

Thomas-Buckle, S., 193

Threats: and power, 221; and revenge, 250-251

Timing: of interviews, 85; and negotiating skills, 236; as process issue, 108-109; and trust, 213-214

Town and park dispute: case example of, 30-33; defining problem in, 93-94; history and context of, 126; problem-solving workshop for, 99; and trust, 212, 213; and values, 200

Toxic waste storage dispute, range of issues in, 9

Trust: and affirmation of successes, 213; attention to, 205-216; barriers to, 205-207; building, 209-216; and caucuses, 214; clarity and accuracy for, 211-212; concept of, 205; and conflict analysis, 210; and doubts, 215; and expression of views, 212; importance of, 207-209; and information, 207, 208; and mediators, 194; and options, 208; and readiness to negotiate, 207-208; and relationships, 214-215; and rhetoric, 212-213; and setbacks, 209; and timing, 213-214

U

Uranium mine dispute, emotions at meetings on, 246-247
Uranium tailings dispute, and revenge, 251, 253-254
Urban park dispute, objective criteria for, 142-143
Ury, W., 101, 133, 145, 146, 230
Utility disputes: perception clarification in, 166; power in, 219; relationships in, 7; situational fit in, 230

V

Values: acknowledged differences in, 204; attention to, 197-204; clash of, and data, 261-262; concept of, 197-198; and fair play, 204; and goals, 203-204; greater importance of, 200-201; and ideology, 201, 202-203; influence of, 199-202; integrated into strategy, 202-204; and issues, 10-11; and negotiation, 199; significance of, 199-200
Vandeven, A., 134
Village dispute: case example of, 33-35; and constructive definition of problem, 58; informing the public in, 180; power in, 228; and team building, 235; and trust, 214
Violence, as outcome of conflict, 16

W

Walton, R., 133
Water contamination dispute, sensitive topics in, 246

Water management dispute, new parties to, 5
Water quality dispute, and positive working relationships, 57-58
Water roundtable dispute: agreements in principle for, 138-139; case example of, 46-51; and constituent involvement, 170-173; and data problems, 260, 263, 264, 265, 266; defining problem in, 94; final agreement for, 141; flexible process in, 62-63; ground rules for, 122-124; history and context of, 126-127; informing the public in, 179-180; interests discussed in, 130-131; monitoring system for, 152; old relationships in, 241; power in, 228-229; preparation phase of, 115; and public meetings, 98; and reaching agreements, 97
Water treatment dispute, and readiness to negotiate, 224-225
Wehr, P., 82
Wessel, M., 118
Western Water Advisory Council, 50, 172-174, 175
Wheeler, M., 150, 187, 259
White, E. B., 177
White, O., 26, 187
Wilderness Study Areas dispute. See Oil and gas exploration . . .
Wilkinson, M., 26, 187
Wondolleck, J., 29, 74
Workshops, problem-solving, 98-99
Written material, for informing the public, 179
Wyoming, coal mine dispute in, 53-54

Z

Zartman, W., 101
Zoning dispute, flexible process in, 63

CPSIA information can be obtained at www.ICGtesting.com
Printed in the USA
LVOW060643190413

329706LV00001B/2/P